COLLABORATIVE ANTHROPOLOGY TODAY

COLLABORATIVE ANTHROPOLOGY TODAY

A Collection of Exceptions

**Edited by Dominic Boyer
and George E. Marcus**

CORNELL UNIVERSITY PRESS   ITHACA AND LONDON

First published 2020 by Cornell University Press

Library of Congress Cataloging-in-Publication Data

Names: Boyer, Dominic, editor. | Marcus, George E., editor.
Title: Collaborative anthropology today : a collection of exceptions / edited by Dominic Boyer and George E. Marcus.
Description: Ithaca [New York] : Cornell University Press, 2020. | Includes bibliographical references and index.
Identifiers: LCCN 2020015520 (print) | LCCN 2020015521 (ebook) | ISBN 9781501753343 (hardcover) | ISBN 9781501753350 (paperback) | ISBN 9781501753374 (pdf) | ISBN 9781501753367 (epub)
Subjects: LCSH: Anthropology—Methodology. | Group work in research. | Interdisciplinary research.
Classification: LCC GN33 .C63 2020 (print) | LCC GN33 (ebook) | DDC 301.01—dc23
LC record available at https://lccn.loc.gov/2020015520
LC ebook record available at https://lccn.loc.gov/2020015521

Contents

COLLABORATIVE
ANTHROPOLOGY TODAY

INTRODUCTION

Collaborative Anthropology Today: A Collection of Exceptions

Dominic Boyer and George E. Marcus

This collection assembles several notable ventures in collaborative anthropology and puts them in dialogue with one another as a way of capturing something of the diversity and energy surrounding collaborative experiments in anthropology at this moment. Although all the projects featured here seem similarly motivated to push beyond the norms of solo research and writing that have predominated in anthropology since the 1960s, each one develops its own distinctive approach to doing so.

While collaboration has been an important dimension of anthropological inquiry since its earliest days, there has been a recent surge of interest in creating new kinds of ethnographic and theoretical partnerships that have expanded the boundaries of anthropological practice in stimulating ways. The range of partnerships and forms of collaborative engagement has been quite broad: some explore new modes of ethnographic representation, some build new kinds of research and information infrastructures, some seek new kinds of public outreach and community engagement, some pursue new conceptual interventions through collaborative analytic work.

Although all these kinds of partnerships are represented to a greater or lesser extent in this volume, we particularly highlight projects in which collaboration has generated new possibilities of expression and conceptualization of anthropological research and also, in many cases, prototypes that may be of use to others contemplating their own collaborative ventures.

This volume emerged from a workshop hosted by the Center for Ethnography at the University of California, Irvine, in May 2017 and follows two companion projects, *Fieldwork Is Not What It Used to Be* (Faubion and Marcus 2009) and *Theory Can Be More Than It Used to Be* (Boyer, Faubion, and Marcus 2015), which have reflected on the transformation of anthropological field research and concept work in the wake of the reorganization of disciplinary identity and practice since the 1980s. As with its two predecessors, there is a pedagogical subtext to this volume as well. We wish not only to sound the vibrant field of collaborative experimentation today but also to ask what place collaboration should have in the process of graduate training and in first project design.

In the previous two volumes, collaboration was a thematic largely in peripheral vision, but in retrospect it is telling that both projects were fundamentally collaborative in character. The insight that prompted this volume is that, as multisited research has mainstreamed in anthropology, collaboration appears to have gained new relevance and traction as a critical infrastructure for both fieldwork and theory, enabling more ambitious multisited research designs as well as forms of communication and analytic inquiry that are frequently multimodal and dialogical in character. Some collaborative partnerships have emerged from the juxtaposition of one or more solo research projects with the aim of exploring a specific thematic or phenomenon; others have formed ateliers to pursue multiple projects collectively; still others have coalesced around infrastructural projects oriented toward communication or information management.

Without pretending to be able to map out the landscape of collaboration in anthropology in its totality, we engaged several sets of collaborative partners, some intersecting, with the aim of discussing collaboration's place in anthropology's evolving culture of method. As our initial prompt for the workshop, we asked participants to reflect on the proposition that "collaboration seems an important object of self-reflection for anthropology today in that, (a) it has the potential to re-scale and re-frame the anthropological endeavor, (b) that its process can generate new terms of mutual worth among participants that would not have occurred without it and (c) that its incorporation of participants as more than informants highlights the potential for new, intermediate forms of knowledge-making."

Our conversations during the workshop were wide-ranging and made abundantly clear that the stakes in collaboration differed from project to project and partnership to partnership. Still, certain centers of gravity and areas of overlapping interest and attentiveness emerged. Many participants engaged other analytic and expressive traditions, ranging from art and design to informatics and science and technology studies, and so disciplinary authority, hierarchy, and policing—particularly as foils for interdisciplinary collaborative experimentation—became frequent touchstones of reflection. Late liberal subjects that we were, we talked much about freedom and constraint and debated the need for prompts, rules, protocols, and institutions to facilitate the most effective kinds of collaborative partnerships. We also found ourselves less compelled by considering collaboration as a problem of method and more as a catalyst for conceptualization; we called "collaborative analytics" those kinds of insights that could only, or best, be realized in the context of juxtaposing or cocreating concepts that could be ported across different fieldwork contexts. This prompted us also to reflect on the optimal timing of collaborative engagements during an anthropological career. Could and should graduate training more robustly incorporate collaborative methodology? Or was collaboration something better left for a later career stage for both pragmatic and intellectual reasons?

We talked at length about the deep histories of collaboration in anthropology and the human sciences, how and why the "lone ranger" model of field research and writing developed in the twentieth century and later became reinforced by neoliberal audit procedures in higher education. We also talked about collaboration as a reaction to the perceived failure of conventional forms of ethnography and publicity to reach wider audiences. The affective dimension of collaboration—whether pleasure, frustration, anxiety, or hope—was never far from us; we agreed that collaborative anthropology was usually aspirational, it sought something beyond whatever was construed as conventional anthropology. Yet we also recognized that the collaborative partnerships gathered at Irvine—even though many actively worked to encourage decolonizing and feminist ethics in the human sciences—did not forefront the kinds of overtly activist and political collaborations that have become so salient to anthropology over the past decade, orbiting flashpoints and social movements like Occupy, Black Lives Matter, and Standing Rock.

As we moved from workshop to volume, we (editors) wanted to take seriously the consensus that we (collaborators) arrived at in Irvine that this group of projects represents a "collection of exceptions" in two senses. Despite growing receptivity to collaborative research and writing, we still interpret the projects themselves as departures from the norms and forms of conventional anthropological research practice. Yet they are also relatively singular in their forms of departure. There was little programmatic spirit in our collective; we agreed, though, that all the projects resisted efforts to unify them under a common concept, sign, or thematic. Thus, despite many forms of family resemblance among the projects presented here, they also for the most part are exceptional with respect to one another. Respecting that sense of exceptionality means that this volume cannot put itself forward as a handbook of best practices for anthropological collaboration; it is also not, as we will discuss at greater length later on, a "call for more collaboration" among anthropologists, between anthropologists and other scholars, or between anthropologists and their research partners. What we believe the volume offers instead is a series of snapshots of the complex field of collaborative anthropology today, a gallery that will hopefully offer many resources of inspiration and reflection for those engaged in, or wishing to engage in, collaborative ventures of their own.

Legacies of Anthropological Collaboration

Before discussing the projects collected here in more detail, it seems important to comment briefly on antecedents to the kinds of collaborative inquiries we highlight in the volume. Collaboration, as noted, is not new to anthropology. In the early decades of North American and European ethnology, the discipline's close ties to fields like geography and natural history meant that the scientific expedition was an important apparatus of anthropological research practice. In the late nineteenth and early twentieth centuries, projects of linguistic and cultural salvage and analysis remained closely allied with archaeology and museology, which explains how some of the most ambitious and important collaborative anthropological enterprises of the era—Boas's Jesup North Pacific Expedition (1897–1902), for example—were organized principally around building natural history collections (Stocking 1974). As the twentieth century wore on, an individualistic model of field research came to predominate in American and European anthropology, at least normatively, and was celebrated for the transformative qualities of participant-observational immersion. One scarcely needed to scratch beneath the surface of any ethnographer-informant dyad to illuminate the complex webs of social enablement—involving research assistants, translators, laborers, middlemen, government agents—that made anthropological research in classic Malinowskian mode possible (Boyer 2015; Middleton and Cons 2014). Still, anthropology, perhaps especially in the Boasian vein, incorporated no small degree of romanticism surrounding the fieldwork encounter between the anthropological Self and the cultural Other.

We might note in passing, here, that the underlying rationale of earlier collaboration projects in anthropology was deeply tied to the comparativist orientation of the discipline and both small- and large-scale ethnographic engagements were frequently constructed to service the needs of comparative data acquisition. This rationale for large-scale collaborative endeavors continued well into the twentieth century. Today, comparison retains some aspirational significance in anthropology but it is no longer the raison d'être of the discipline; and, pragmatically, the rich comparative frameworks and projects are gone. Comparison remains, nonetheless, an ideological stalking horse of a variety of collaborative projects that arise today even though there are often no clear channels or prospects by which they find their way to institutionally supported comparativist programs as in the post–World War II heyday of area studies. The latter's common successor, globalization studies of one form or another, encourages much ethnography of a collaborative nature in the found and exceptional ways we document here. But these collaborative projects are not as tied to case comparison formats as in earlier years. They grow their own contexts out of collaboration itself (see Yanagisako and Rofel, this volume). The void of systematic comparative work is precisely the space of exception for ethnographic projects today in their found relationships and innovative strategies of collaboration. They gain scale which only later suggests lines of systematic comparison that are sometimes surprising. With or without literal comparative strategies, the field from which research is constructed today beckons collaborations in order to fully develop cases of ethnography and to give them context. How they reconnect with older ideas of systematic comparison is a matter worthy of further investigation (see, for example, Schnegg 2014), but beyond the scope of this volume.

After the Second World War, a new emphasis on interdisciplinary area studies research in the social sciences expanded and intensified anthropology's range of collaborative engagements around the world. Much as expedition-era anthropology was absorbed into colonial and imperial knowledge making, the area studies–era was imbricated with the national and international political dynamics of the Cold War. Governments sought to enroll anthropologists in military and intelligence operations across the world—Project Camelot being one of the most well known. However, anthropology was also broadening its epistemic ambitions and moving from cultural salvage projects toward grappling with modernity and the complex cultural and social dynamics of cities, nations, and world systems. This brought anthropologists into close and sometimes generative exchanges with other social scientists in the context of interdisciplinary area studies projects in the 1950s and 1960s. Although these projects continued to coexist with projects in the Malinowskian mode, enterprises like Cornell University's Vicos project in Peru (creating a "laboratory for social change") or the MIT Modjokuto project studying modernization in Indonesia (which gave the Geertzes their first fieldwork opportunity) cultivated long-term interdisciplinary research networks that also strongly influenced graduate training and pedagogy in anthropology (Lynch 1982; Price 2016; see also Afterword, this volume).

The postwar period also saw an efflorescence of anthropological collaboration mediated through marriage and other life partnerships. Mead and Bateson is a classic example; Mead and Benedict a more elusive but possibly more substantial one. Then came the Geertzes, the Nashes, the Stratherns, the Turners, and the Wolfs, followed later by the Tedlocks, the Prices, and the Comaroffs, to name only a few of those couples who shared credit for research and writing jointly undertaken. There were, of course, still more cases in which the labor and research contributions of wives were subsumed and rendered invisible by the dominant masculinist heteronorms of the discipline and the university in the second half of the twentieth century. In the twenty-first century, anthropology has seen couples continue to practice the crafts of research, teaching, and writing under at least a partly shared sense of identity, each navigating their own relational and epistemic dynamics. Several projects gathered here—Boyer/Howe, the Fortuns and Hegel/Cantarella—participate in this ongoing anthropological tradition.

By the late 1960s, the funding resources for large-scale collaborative research endeavors in the postcolonial world had largely dried up, as had scholarly enthusiasm for Cold War empiricism and realism. The 1970s and 1980s were a transitional period for anthropology in many respects. Feminist and Marxian paradigms ascended in some departments, interpretive, poststructuralist, and reflexive approaches in others. Two developments were crucial for collaborative anthropology. The first was that relational ethics and an attention to the situatedness of all knowledge claims, academic and otherwise, came to displace (or at least profoundly challenge) the cult of scientific objectivity with which anthropology had aligned itself for much of the twentieth century. This opened up the possibility for new modes of collaborative engagement of the kind that were realized in agenda-setting collective interventions such as *Woman, Culture and Society* (Lamphere and Rosaldo 1974) and *Writing Culture* (Clifford and Marcus 1986). At the same time, opportunities for collaborative anthropology were dampened to some extent by a second development: the amplification of norms of individual research practice and productivity across the human sciences as a matter of the evaporation of funding for team-based research intersecting with the rise of neoliberal "audit culture" (Strathern 2000). Although audit mechanisms have been more or less impactful depending on country and institution, the emphasis on individualized accountability measurement reinforced, through technocratic evaluation procedures, the romantic individualism that was already central to the Malinowskian imagination of fieldwork, theory, and writing. By the 1980s, graduate training in anthropology almost wholly abjured collaborative models of research practice. The dissertational norm became the solo-authored account of an individual scholar's fieldwork with an emphasis on scholarly entrepreneurship and innovation rather than the performance of dutiful mentor-clientage. Although many forms of labor and care (teaching, editing, peer review) are obviously occluded by this norm as well, it continues to be the case that dual (or more) research and authorship remain basically unthinkable from the point of view of establishing the requisite scholarly credentials to begin a professional career in anthropology.

At the same time, the ambitions and methods of anthropological research practice continued to evolve in the 1990s, the decade that we modestly propose helped pave the way for the recent resurgence of interest in collaborative anthropology. The end of the Cold War between 1989 and 1992 helped to unlock anthropological interest in studying nascent processes of cultural, economic, and political globalization, both those organized under the banner of market (neo)liberalism and those "flows" and "scapes" (Appadurai 1990) that emerged from the informatic, mediatic, and transportational deterritorialization of Cold War empires and nation-states. The new frontier of anthropological ethnography was the challenge of articulating the interface between local situations encountered through fieldwork and increasingly visible global or translocal processes that were typically interpreted as overdetermining local lifeworlds or catalyzing projects of cultural resistance. This situation also breathed new life into the aspirations of public anthropology, including modes of action research oriented toward collaborative engagement with communities. Luke Eric Lassiter (2005a, 2005b) and his colleagues (see the journal *Collaborative Anthropologies*) have made a strong case for centering collaborative ethnography on action-research norms.

Multisited ethnography (Marcus 1995) meanwhile consolidated in the 1990s and 2000s as a new norm of anthropological fieldwork and writing that represented a partial but also highly flexible response to the deterritorialization of traditional anthropological research sites and subjects. Analytic practices optimized for use in the village-, culture-, and system-centered studies of the mid-twentieth century were displaced by new modes of ethnographic construction like "follow the thing" or "follow the people." However, at the same time, anthropology retained a heavy emphasis not only on the virtues of Malinowskian individualism in fieldwork but also on the literary and hermeneutic "thickness" of ethnography in the Geertzian mode. The divergent trajectories of multisited research and romanticist ethnography created new kinds of tensions and occasional incommensurabilities in the discipline. With research funding even for individual fieldwork diminishing in the 1990s and 2000s, it seemed increasingly difficult for individuals to design and undertake ambitious multisited research programs while at the same time delivering the depth of situational intimacy and characterization expected in anthropological writing. The maturation and normalization of multisited research over the past two decades have not fundamentally changed the core dilemma that it is difficult for an individual field researcher to maintain both depth and multiplicity of research attachments.

One response to this situation, we suggest, is the exploration of collaborative modes of inquiry and writing. Where collaborative partners work together on project design to elicit complementarity from individual research objectives, new qualities of multisitedness can be derived from parallel research inquiry and conversation. Even where solo projects are brought into alignment post facto, a transient kind of multisited inquiry can be staged that allows for different field knowledges and "portable analytics" (Boyer and Howe 2015) to interilluminate one another. In both cases, the old anthropological virtue of comparativism is reactivated and given new purpose even after the decline of culture theory as the conceptual glue of anthropological inquiry.

Still, what is most striking about the projects in collaborative anthropology we feature in this volume is that, while some projects (Yanagisako-Rofel, Yurchak-Boyer) focus principally on collaborative partnerships among anthropologists, others are pushing the boundaries still further. Some are forming interdisciplinary ateliers committed to generating new epistemic and communicative infrastructures. Others are generating not only new ethnographic modalities but also new multimodal approaches through which to capture and convey anthropological craft and knowledge. The intersection between the arts and anthropology has perhaps never been such a creative, experimental space in the discipline's history. We cannot predict how collaborative anthropology will continue to evolve and unfold in the future (Konrad 2012; Estalella and Sánchez Criado 2018). We will simply say that this abundance of generative outreach to and engagement of other disciplines and arts seems to us to bode well for the liveliness of anthropological fieldwork, theory, and ethnography going forward.

Seven Modes of Collaboration

There is nothing like a common ideology of or approach to collaboration shared by the groups featured in this volume. Nonetheless, we have identified seven modes of collaboration that inform one or more partnerships and that also connect projects featured here to other influential ventures in collaborative anthropology, which we will touch on briefly.

1. Collaboration emerges as a generative dialogue between ethnographic projects that were conceived and executed according to normal conventions of solo anthropological research. The dialogue evolves into new joint field research endeavors or toward projects of collaborative analysis.

In this volume, the most ambitious example of this mode is surely Lisa Rofel and Sylvia Yanagisako's collaborative ethnography of Italian-Chinese fashion. Rofel and Yanagisako each had completed a great deal of field research at different ends (Como, Hangzhou) of the "silk road" before they decided to work together, leveraging the potentiality of collaborative multinational fieldwork to gain more substantial and nuanced analytic traction on "transnational capital-ism" which, as the authors rightly argue, "is often portrayed as a monolithic and purely economic force that acts on local communities that are characterized as the sites of culture." They note that their own collaboration built upon collab-orations that had developed since the 1990s between Chinese and Italian silk firms and textile producers. And they share their experience that a collaborative ethnographic approach to transnational business collaboration permitted them to bridge the scalar breadth of transnational anthropology to a more intimate understanding of all partners involved: "Most research on transnationalism has had access to only one of the parties in these encounters, which too often results in analyses that overlook the intentions, meanings and interpretations of other parties. Listening to both sides of the conversation placed us in a better position to forge a more comprehensive, interactional analysis of the actions and reac-tions, interpretations and misinterpretations, understandings and misunder-standings through which the Italians and Chinese in these transnational business collaborations reformulate their goals, strategies, values and identities." Rofel and Yanagisako's project culminated in a coauthored book, *Fabricating Transna-tional Capitalism: A Collaborative Ethnography of Italian-Chinese Global Fashion*, which has created further opportunities for staging long-form multiperspectival ethnography. Their question "Should a collaborative ethnography produce an account that not only incorporates multiple perspectives but also analytically resolves them?" resonates also with Dominic Boyer and Cymene Howe's project to produce two single-authored ethnographies drawn from the same fieldwork (a "duograph").

Similarly, Alexei Yurchak and Dominic Boyer's work on the genre of ironic performance known in Russia as "stiob" also emerged in the dialogue between their individual (dissertation) research projects on late socialism and postsocial-ist transitions. Insights gleaned from Yurchak's work on the hypernormalization of authoritative discourse in post-Stalinist Soviet socialism and Boyer's work on East German media and intellectual culture were ported over to the context of the late neoliberal United States and used there to reveal a kindred overformal-ization and monopolization of political discourse and performance that helped license similar kinds of parody and ironic performance to those which flour-ished in the waning years of socialism. Although the collaboration did not lead to new field research per se, it did lead to an extensive project of cultural analy-sis as Yurchak and Boyer sought "to capture the kinds of performative occupa-tion of U.S. authoritative political discourse that were taking place in 2004, 2005 and 2006," including *The Colbert Report* and the work of the activist duo the Yes Men. They comment that the concept of hypernormalization was transformed through the collaborative process, becoming "more autonomous from concrete contexts and more flexible, without losing its original meaning and analytical power." Its emergence as a portable analytic thus owed much to a collaborative analytic process that helped reshape it for use in different contexts of anthropological engagement.

Douglas Holmes and George Marcus's contribution also represents collaboration in this mode in that it describes a situation in which the dialogical encounter between two different research projects—Holmes's on European Far Right integralist movements (2000) and Marcus's on Portuguese aristocracy (2005)—prompted a "joint reimagining of the scene of fieldwork," giving rise to their influential analysis of "para-ethnography" (Holmes and Marcus 2005, 2006, 2008) and "epistemic partnership" in anthropological research with experts and elites (see mode 4 for a fuller discussion of this partnership). Another example is the overlapping fieldwork (and experiments in collaborative writing, 2009) undertaken by the Matsutake Worlds Research Group (Anna Tsing, Shiho Satsuka, Miyako Inoue, Michael Hathaway, Lieba Faier, and Timothy Choy), a project that has inspired many contributors to this volume.

2. Collaboration centers on a collective effort to develop new communicative platforms, channels, and media in order to expand or reorient the audience or public for anthropological knowledge.

Sherine Hamdy and Coleman Nye's project, *Lissa* (2017), is an excellent multifaceted example of this collaborative mode. The project involved the creation of a graphic novel thematizing difficult medical decisions (concerning kidney failure and cancer) in the context of the political violence of the Egyptian Revolution, a "making of" documentary film about the project, and a website. Although previous research experience informed the collaborative work, as mentioned in mode 1, the *Lissa* project concentrated on the "possibilities of collaborative scholarship to unsettle conventional ideas of authorship, expertise, voice, text, theory, and study" and involved several kinds of collaborative partnerships: between Hamdy and Nye; between the authors and artists and letterers in the making of the novel; and between the authors and Egyptian scholars, artists, and doctors who helped refine the story to better reflect life before, during, and after the revolution. The graphic novel seemed to Hamdy and Nye an apt medium for broadening the audience for insights drawn from anthropological fieldwork and analysis: "We were both finding that the visual genre opens up exciting possibilities for engaging with unfamiliar contexts, the politics of representation, and the complexities of embodied experience in more tangible ways than text alone." The comic medium also allowed them to visualize "the social and political embeddedness of the patient's body in the world" in a way that was informed not only by oral dialogues in Egypt but also by dialogue with the rich graphic tradition of the revolution itself, epitomized by figures like the muralist Ganzeer who also became a collaborator in *Lissa* along the way.

The work of the *Limn* editorial collective (Stephen J. Collier, Christopher Kelty, and Andrew Lakoff) was also animated by a sense of the communicational, aesthetic, and epistemic limitations of conventional forms and temporalities of scholarly publishing in anthropology. The collaboration emerged from the Anthropology of the Contemporary Collaboratory at the University of California, Berkeley, and centered on the making of a magazine, a "small-scale, outsider experiment in publishing short, timely, and conceptually engaged work." The *Limn* group is clear that the magazine was never meant to be an end in itself but rather to serve as a vehicle for conversation and concept work around well-defined public problems. In this respect, like the work of the *Ethnographic Terminalia* Collective (see mode 6), the medium is not the mission let alone the message of their collective work. However, the *Limn* collective's interest in questions of publicity and their presentation of concept work as a way of "doing theory in the absence of a critical, disciplinary or jargon-laden vocabulary" suggests that experimentation with making new kinds of communicational and epistemic infrastructures is a nontrivial dimension of the work of the group. Among the catalysts for their collaborative intervention, they name "the rise and spread of open access, the increasing standardization and normalization of journals and article forms, a renewed sense of disciplinary gatekeeping in the publishing world, and the rapid change in the availability and suitability of technical tools suitable for the job." The circulatory and reputational success of the magazine has created a very compelling prototype for further collaborative ventures of this kind.

Finally, Dominic Boyer and Cymene Howe's podcast, "Cultures of Energy," produced by the Center for Energy and Environmental Research in the Human Sciences (CENHS) at Rice University, offers an example of the transduction of anthropological (and other human-scientific) insight and expertise into a serialized, popular forum. They comment on the "opportunity in this podcast medium to expose folks to academic scholarship so long as you could keep it lively and engaging," making use of the charismatic pull of natural speech "in its more extemporaneous forms" to overcome the exclusionary qualities of academic writing to create proximity and intimacy among hosts, interviewees, and audiences. Much as with Hamdy and Nye's use of the graphic genre to create a different ethnographic sensorium, Boyer and Howe explore the epistemic and affective possibilities of aurality, oscillating between ruminating on the anecdota and news of everyday life, serious often-technical conversation, joking, and storytelling. In terms of content, like other CENHS projects, "Cultures of Energy" focuses on bringing scholars, artists, and activists into conversation around

Anthropocene phenomena such as climate change and species extinction. The seemingly intrinsically heavy and serious character of the podcast's thematics makes weaving ludic moments in both challenging and important. Boyer and Howe share a sense that any genuine effort at unmaking the Anthropocene requires a more complex affective engagement than simply earnest concern.

3. Collaboration focuses on building experimental research, and ethnographic and analytic infrastructures, using the affordances of digital media, platforms, and tools. The collaborative process is optimized to maintaining projects such as long-term data acquisition, management, and visualization.

In their contribution to the volume, Mike and Kim Fortun (representing many other collaborators) discuss a series of projects they have helped define and lead that exemplifies this collaborative mode. They describe this series—including The Asthma Files (TAF), the Platform for Comparative Experimental Ethnography (PECE), and the 6+ Cities Research project—as pursuing an "archival (infrastructural) style" of collaboration, which is oriented less toward specific project outcomes and more toward keeping "an archive becoming, keep[ing] it troubled and feverishly excited and excitable." The projects themselves substantively engage problems of environmental health data and governance and the platforms they have created allow for researchers across the world to share data and facilitate comparative ethnographic studies. The platforms also create opportunities for "collaborative analytics" at a much broader scale than in mode 1. At the same time, what seems critical to the Fortuns' work is that the mode of collaboration remains fundamentally iterative, "less directed at or by a defined collective end product, tangible result, culminating exhibition, or project, and more attentive to organizing the work of a collective towards continually reiterating itself." The infrastructural style of collaboration requires both trust and care to maintain itself; it reinvests labor in its own maintenance of the type that is crucial for its large-scale infrastructures to be preserved and updated. It thus involves both a patient attitude toward the "interminable work of building collaborative infrastructure for future collaborations that might and might not be there" and a sense of "impatient deferral," a willingness to remain open to "un-planned futures." The Fortuns conclude that "each of our projects builds from and enacts this collaborative, experimental form: structural and infrastructural work (technical, organizational, interpersonal) laying the grounds for both reliable and useful results, while remaining open and supple enough to allow unknown futures through."

A second example of this mode worth mentioning is the Environmental Data and Governance Initiative (EDGI), which self-organized as a research and analytic collective in the wake of the 2016 US presidential election with the prospect of new science-hostile leadership taking over the administration of the Environmental Protection Agency. The EDGI network (https://envirodatagov.org) has been active and successful in resilient infrastructure, data rescue/archiving, and digital watchdogging efforts. They seek to make environmental data both more visible and charismatic as a means of attracting public attention and political action. Although EDGI operated, by their own admission, very much in an emergency mode at the outset, they also view their work as informed by a longer-term commitment to advancing the ethics of feminist and decolonizing science and technology studies, to principles of environmental and data justice, and to "collaborative, horizontal, transparent, and participatory knowledge-making and governance."

4. Collaboration decenters the conventional ethnographer-informant relation through para-ethnographic epistemic partnership with expert interlocutors or by involving audiences in projects of media and knowledge making.

Douglas Holmes and George Marcus have long worked to unravel the challenges of anthropological research in an era in which ethnographic practices "have been assimilated as key intellectual modalities of our time." Against the sense of (naive) disciplinary exceptionalism that considers fieldwork and ethnography as some intellectual property reserved to anthropologists, Holmes and Marcus begin with the all-too-familiar problem of field research in the context of "cultures of expertise" that one's research methods are already anticipated and to some extent absorbed in advance. They are particularly mindful of those epistemic communities and "reflexive subjects" whose "para-ethnographic tendencies and desires" are sharply defined enough to be "fully capable of doing superb ethnography in their own idioms." The research context becomes meta-ethnographic and, rather than denying or deflecting this condition of anthropological research, Holmes and Marcus seek to embrace it as a generative opportunity. They see a route forward through "*aligning* our work with the analytical endeavors of our subjects." "Ethnography advances today by deferring to, absorbing, and being altered by found reflexive subjects—by risking collaborative encounters of uncertain outcomes for the production of ethnographic knowledge in the forms that have been regulated by the disciplinary communities that propel anthropologists into fieldwork." Their key proposition is that ethnographers need to refunction fieldwork designs to allow them to "operate with their own research agendas inside the pervasive collaboratories that define social spaces today." Refunctioning ethnography is not a Trojan horse meant to smuggle anthropological analytics past the gatekeepers of other expert communities; rather, it is an effort to share analytic labor and stakes with one's epistemic partners. "We have no interest in collaboration as a 'division of labor' among the investigators who control the design of a project or as the basis for blending of academic expertise or as gestures to a canonical inter-disciplinarity. The corrective is, again, to integrate fully our subjects' analytical acumen and insights to define the issues at stake in our project as well as the means by which we explore them."

The spirit of refiguring the conventional ethnographer-informant relation also animates several other projects in the volume, whether in Hamdy and Nye's work with artists who also witnessed the events portrayed in *Lissa*, in the *Ethnographic Terminalia* Collective's many curatorial projects and creative workshops, or in Boyer and Howe's effort to blend conventional interviewer, interviewee, and audience roles in their podcasting.

5. Collaboration aims to augment collaborative practices and potentials within conventional anthropological research and ethnography by engaging insights and practices drawn from other arts and disciplines.

Christine Hegel and Luke Cantarella offer a rich example of this mode of collaboration in their documentation of their work with the Anthropology of the World Trade Organization group (including Marc Abélès, Máximo Badaró, Jae Aileen Chung, Linda Dematteo, Paul Dima Ehongo, Cai Hua, George Marcus, Mariella Pandolfi, and Phillip Rousseau) to produce the film *Trade Is Sublime*. The film followed the primary fieldwork of the WTO collaboration and Hegel and Cantarella (working together with Chung and Marcus) imagined it as "a return to the site of fieldwork to deepen and reignite questions that arose in the initial project by drawing on and thinking through ethnographic material collected through work in a performance drama." The target audience for the film was the WTO community so the collaborators sought to create an intervention "that would speak to or unlock something latent or unarticulated in their daily discourse, though perhaps complexly registered and reflexively grasped by them in earlier responses to ethnographers." Hegel and Cantarella note that anthropology lacks "standard collaborative arrangements and norms," which produces collaborative commitments that are always "evolving and unstable." However, one advantage of this instability is an openness to creative experiments between anthropology and the arts. Given that the film was "neither *for* the WTO, as if they commissioned it, nor *against* the WTO, as a piece of oppositional art," they decided that contact improvisation would be a generative performance tradition to draw upon, given how it eschews formal choreography, emphasizing instead "movement choices [that] are intersubjective and emerge under the conditions of the moment. . . . The making of the dance is the *subject* of the dance." Contact improvisation is thus itself a collaborative medium although a more obviously corporeal one than other aspects of the WTO collaboration were. Still, it allowed for a unique kind of adjacency to the WTO fieldwork as the dancers followed a light structure of ethnographic prompts in their improvisation. This in turn catalyzed a dialogic and improvisatory process of "collective hunchwork" between anthropologists, filmmakers, and dancers as both dance and film developed, producing certain "moments of fascination" that posited "generative possibilities for social inquiry through co-imagining and making."

Another project in this vein is Keith Murphy's work on the "ethno-charrette" which drew together elements from design as well as improvisational theater. In the classic design charrette—an intensive session of collective problem solving—Murphy saw interesting affinities with group improvisational work. "Both are organized precisely to eschew planning, to distribute responsibility to the group rather than invest it in individuals, and to encourage participants to provide one another some of the necessary materials—ideas, propositions, hunches, critiques—for manipulation in the design process. Both presume that all of the participants are working toward a common goal, though that goal exists as a kind of 'formless sense' for most of the process—a formless sense that allows for multiple interpretations—and only takes on a more concrete and mutually understood form as the group's work progresses." Together with George Marcus, Murphy conceptualized the ethnocharrette as an experimental venture to run ethnographic material through a design studio process. The design of the ethnocharrette was itself iterative, as were the outcomes; the first iteration produced slideshows, the second material artifacts based on ethnographic work, and the third ethnographic pamphlets. In all cases, prototypes were produced that could inform further ethnographic projects. The design studio intervention was not without its frustrations and frictions but Murphy judged the ethnocharrettes to be successful overall, especially for the groups "whose members were most adept at 'letting go'—of their fast held ideas about what 'counts' as ethnography, of their predilections toward autonomy, and of their resistance to playful engagement. By truly surrendering some autonomy to the whims of the group, something more than the sum of individual contributions, and much more creative and interesting, was likely to emerge."

This mode of collaboration is, generally speaking, very visible in the projects collected here that are positioned at the interstices of anthropology and the arts, particularly *Ethnographic Terminalia* and the Hamdy-Nye graphic novel.

6. Collaboration takes the form of an atelier in which a core group of collaborators work together over time on a series of projects, which may or may not be related to one another.

The *Ethnographic Terminalia* Collective (ETC) is the best example of this mode of collaboration among the projects assembled here and one whose pathbreaking work at the juncture of art and anthropology since 2009 has inspired many. ETC formed at least partly as a response to the annual meeting of the American Anthropological Association and the limited forms of anthropological research presentation that event could support. The first ETC exhibition was synchronized with, but offsite from, the 2009 AAA meetings in Philadelphia, featuring a range of multimodal installations based upon anthropological fieldwork. Although the ETC coalesced as an intentionally disruptive supplement to American anthropology's largest annual gathering, the group rapidly evolved into a curatorial atelier with an even more ambitious and varied effort to bridge collaborative art worlds to multimodal work in anthropology. They note that anthropology has much to gain from engaging the practices and norms of the art world where "a practice of distributed authorship and actions" is more common. In their reflection for the volume, the ETC emphasizes that "negotiating our collective work has resulted in a necessary annual re-invention of our process and has resulted in different curatorial outcomes." It has been accompanied by a constant process of artistic, analytic, and existential reflection on the work of the collective: "Over the years of working together we have grappled with questions such as: Whose curatorial vision is brought to life? Who supports this vision by completing the mundane yet necessary administrative tasks? Who should the members of the collective be, and how is this decided? Who co-authors? Who is a first-author? How does an emerging art-anthropology collective bridging creative practice and the merit-economy of the academy find its way to relative success in each? Can I finish my dissertation and do this work off the side of my desk? What kind of job should I try to get? Can I get tenure?" In their series of projects, they have experimented with a variety of formats ranging from large group exhibitions taking a "cabinet of curiosities" approach; "anchor artists" generating a thematic curatorial concept with an open call for submissions; invited projects by collaborating artists and anthropologists; smaller presentations of a single artist in a large institution; a curatorial design collaboration between the ETC and anthropologists; and collaborative, rapid-prototype publication workshops.

We would also note that the Anthropology of the World Trade Organization group, the Fortuns' collaborative network, and the Matsutake Worlds Research Group all have atelier-like qualities even though they are more focused on single projects or on a chain of related projects. Then again, one might provocatively ask: What differentiates a "research network" from an "atelier" in the context of collaborative ventures? Diversity of projects? Proximity to the arts? Intimacy of collaborative relations? Much depends on a group's own language of identification and mission and we do not argue for a strong analytical distinction between them.

7. Collaboration engages events and social movements with the primary objective of creating political effects.

The final mode we would highlight has been historically important in anthropology dating back to the public anthropological work of Boas on race, Mead on sexuality, and many anthropologists working in direct opposition to colonialist and imperialist ventures, especially since the Vietnam War. A focus on political effects creates unique opportunities for collaborative engagement with social movements and communities. What has been more difficult to gauge, and not infrequently contested by the conventional norms of university-based scholarship, is to what extent direct political action can advance theoretical and ethnographic scholarship in anthropology and related fields. Queer and feminist anthropology has long made political action a core part of its intellectual mission. Faye Ginsburg's work (1991, 1993) with indigenous media activists as well as Terry Turner's Kayapo Video Project (1992, 1995) certainly stimulated theoretical debate in the anthropology of media. In the context of 1990s and 2000s anti–free trade, neoanarchist, and participatory democracy movements, we have seen an efflorescence of activist political anthropology that has also produced insightful immersive ethnographies of activism (e.g., Graeber 2008). Most recently, scholarly participation in movements opposed to antiblack violence (e.g., Williams 2015) and in defense of indigenous sovereignty (e.g., Simpson 2014) have contributed greatly to contemporary theoretical and methodological debates in the discipline, generating renewed calls to decolonize the institutions, ethics, and knowledge forms of anthropology (e.g., Todd 2018). The de facto antipolitical condition of the disciplinary mainstream remains and is constantly reinforced both by weak professional leadership and by institutional disincentives to public political engagement in many universities and colleges. However, we live in unsettled and active political times and as we consider collaborative anthropology today, we see political modes of collaboration diversifying and intensifying. Recent collaborative ventures in online publication—for example *Allegra Lab* (http://allegralaboratory.net), *Anthro(dendum)* (https://anthrodendum.org), and *Footnotes* (https://footnotesblog.com)—have explicitly positioned themselves not only as fora for new models and temporalities of anthropological publicity but also an engines of youth-forward disciplinary challenge and reinvention in the cases of conversations like #anthrosowhite and #hautalk.

Many of the groups featured in this volume are strongly informed by broader political and social movements. For example, like EDGI, the Fortuns' research network is clearly committed to improving data transparency and infrastructure related to environment and health issues. The *Limn* collective is actively engaged in Open Access politics both inside and outside of anthropology. Boyer and Howe view their podcast as an intervention within the broader climate action movement, allied with environmental justice goals, and meant to widen the audience for research and arguments sculpted in critical environmental humanities.

The Revelry of Collaborative Anthropology

In slight tension with the idea that what we have gathered here is a collection of exceptions was the concept that emerged from our conversations at Irvine, "collaborative analytics," which seemed to capture our sense of a collaborative ethos among the various collaborative partnerships represented in the room. Collaborative analytics served as a marker for the new forms of thinking that could emerge from collaborative partnerships which transcended division of labor large-scale cooperation and instead risked individual autonomy and epistemic authority in the context of group work. In a way the emergence of the concept was the proof of its own proposition as we all sought to articulate the broader lessons for collaborative anthropology that could be objectified not only based on our individual projects but also on the ensemble of projects as a whole. In one of the breakout sessions, George Marcus, Craig Campbell, and Sylvia Yanagisako worked more intensely on this concept as George captured it in a subsequent write-up (Marcus 2017). George reported that he made "as strong a case as possible for collaborative analytics extending to subjects of research, especially when these were experts and analysts of their own conditions. What kind of experiments in the field, or in relation to it, could be conducted to elicit this dimension of collaborative analytics or concept work that connects or aligns anthropologist and subject, affecting both the forms and nature of claims to anthropological knowledge explored ethnographically?" George saw that the concept of collaborative analytics could "have radical implications for ethnographic reporting going forward, posing anew the ideals of polyphony and dialogics in ethnographic representation. Yet, this time around, these ideals are posed not so much as a problem of representation or ethics but as a problem of analysis itself. What form, in this light, can anthropological questions give knowledge once the concept of collaboration as ethnographic method becomes powerful, explicit, and diverse enough?"

In a response to these comments, Craig weighed in with the observation that

> not all collaborations produce a collaborative analytic. As with children's parallel play, many collaborations turn out to be built on a division of

labor ... which is fine but there is no point calling that a collaborative analytic. There is something of a dialectic in a collaborative analytic, as seen through probes and reconnaissance missions that search for anecdotes, elaborations, and clarifications from other collaborators. As I think Keith [Murphy] said, a lot of it is built on hunchwork, groping toward the figure of something. The interdependence of participants in a collaboration produces specific and ephemeral ecologies where meaning, work, and identity are negotiated. Earlier, I was thinking about cultivating a collaborative scene, but I now see a logic to the notion of cultivating a collaborative analytics: where the opportunity to probe is fostered.

We find that this exchange helpfully shows how a collection of exceptions can also constitute a collaborative ethos. The dialecticism internal to collaborations that seek, as most do, to extend beyond the capacities of self, to search and grope and probe toward designs or insights or messages in an interdependent way, means that every instance of collaborative anthropology is necessarily unique in its configuration of participants, practices, and outcomes. At the same time, there is a similar desire and willingness to feel one's way forward together, to conceive anthropology as an ecological rather than an individual enterprise. In a time of neoliberal ruins, this seems like an orientation toward knowledge making that befits the zeitgeist of returning to, and reimagining, models of collective action and being.

For this reason, we predict that collaborative anthropology has a bright and kaleidoscopically diverse future ahead of it. And, although we recognize the many pragmatic and institutional obstacles that thwart its centralization in anthropology and the human sciences today, we would suggest that those of us who are involved in PhD programs should at least begin the conversation with colleagues as to the intellectual benefits of offering more focused attention to and training in collaborative research and writing practices. We do not see the experiments with collaboration presented here as demanding drastic change so much as inviting an openness to new kinds of playful commitment. Collaboration is obviously already thriving in anthropology despite the institutional and professional norms that defend the solo research model. Yet, regarding pedagogy, we advocate, and some of us practice, teaching that looks beyond or alongside the individual student projects of ethnographic case development and toward collaborative futures: for example, the studio and design–oriented classes offered by Murphy, or the platform development assistance nurtured by the Fortuns, among others. We have found that such teaching does not overwhelm the considerable challenges of career-making first fieldwork projects, and indeed offers students an anticipatory awareness of future opportunities of collaborative experimentation.

As one of us mentioned in the workshop, these collaborative exceptions may be nothing more than supplements to conventional academic practice, "but it's obvious that they revel in their supplementarity." This is a reminder that one of the great benefits of collaborative anthropology is that it brings interruptive joy into the routines of professional academic life. The *Limn* group speaks for many of us when they write, "What remains at the heart of the endeavor is the desire to find places of thought and inquiry that escape the more stultifying aspects of normal university life, and sustain the pleasure of intellectual engagement without disappearing from the view (of our colleagues, and to some extent the university as well) entirely." Although, as promised, this is not a manifesto for collaborative anthropology, we do feel that anthropology is better for its supplemental revelries.

REFERENCES

Appadurai, Arjun. 1990. "Disjuncture and Difference in the Global Cultural Economy." *Theory, Culture and Society* 7:295–310.

Boyer, Dominic. 2015. "Reflexivity Reloaded: From Anthropology of Intellectuals to Critique of Method to Studying Sideways." In *Anthropology Now and Next: Essays in Honor of Ulf Hannerz*, edited by Thomas Hylland Eriksen, Christina Garsten, and Shalini Randeria, 99–110. New York: Berghahn Books.

Boyer, Dominic, James D. Faubion, and George E. Marcus, eds. 2015. *Theory Can Be More Than It Used to Be: Learning Anthropology's Method in a Time of Transition*. Ithaca, NY: Cornell University Press.

Boyer, Dominic, and Cymene Howe. 2015. "Portable Analytics and Traveling Theory." In Boyer, Faubion, and Marcus, *Theory Can Be More Than It Used to Be*, 15–38.

Clifford, James, and George E. Marcus, eds. 1986. *Writing Culture: The Poetics and Politics of Ethnography*. Berkeley: University of California Press.

Estalella, Adolfo, and Tomás Sánchez Criado, eds. 2018. *Experimental Collaborations: Ethnography through Fieldwork Devices*. New York: Berghahn Books.

Faubion, James D., and George E. Marcus, eds. 2009. *Fieldwork Is Not What It Used to Be*. Ithaca: Cornell University Press.

Ginsburg, Faye. 1991. "Indigenous Media: Faustian Contract or Global Village?" *Cultural Anthropology* 6 (1): 92–112.

——. 1993. "Aboriginal Media and the Australian Imaginary." *Public Culture* 5 (3): 557–78.

Graeber, David. 2008. *Direct Action: An Ethnography*. Chico, CA: AK Press.

Hamdy, Sherine, Coleman Nye, Sarula Bao, and Caroline Brewer. 2017. *Lissa: A Story about Medical Promise, Friendship, and Revolution*. Toronto: University of Toronto Press.

Holmes, Douglas. 2000. *Integral Europe: Fast-Capitalism, Multiculturalism, Neofascism*. Princeton, NJ: Princeton University Press.

Holmes, Douglas, and George E. Marcus. 2005. "Cultures of Expertise and the Management of Globalization: Toward the Re-Functioning of Ethnography." In *Global Assemblages: Technology, Politics, and Ethics as Anthropological Problems*, edited by Aihwa Ong and Stephen J. Collier, 235–52. Oxford: Blackwell.

——. 2006. "Fast Capitalism: Para-Ethnography and the Rise of the Symbolic Analyst." In *Frontiers of Capital*, edited by Melissa S. Fisher and Greg Downey, 33–56. Durham, NC: Duke University Press.

——. 2008. "Collaboration Today and the Re-Imagination of the Classic Scene of Fieldwork Encounter." *Collaborative Anthropologies* 1 (1): 136–70.

Konrad, Monica, ed. 2012. *Collaborators Collaborating: Counterparts in Anthropological Knowledge and International Research Relations*. New York: Berghahn Books, 2012.

Lamphere, Louise, and Michelle Zimbalist Rosaldo, eds. 1974. *Woman, Culture and Society*. Stanford, CA: Stanford University Press.

Lassiter, Luke Eric. 2005a. *The Chicago Guide to Collaborative Anthropology*. Chicago: University of Chicago Press.

——. 2005b. "Collaborative Ethnography and Public Anthropology." *Current Anthropology* 46 (1): 83–106.

Lynch, Barbara D. 1982. *The Vicos Experiment: A Study of the Impacts of the Cornell-Peru Project in a Highland Community*. Washington, DC: USAID.

Marcus, George E. 1995. "Ethnography in/of the World System: The Emergence of Multi-Sited Ethnography." *Annual Review of Anthropology* 24:95–117.

——. 2017. "Introduction: Collaborative Analytics." Theorizing the Contemporary, Cultural Anthropology website. July 27, 2017. https://culanth.org/fieldsights/1170-introduction-collaborative-analytics.

Matsutake Worlds Research Group. 2009. "A New Form of Collaboration in Cultural Anthropology: Matsutake Worlds." *American Ethnologist* 36 (2): 380–403.

Middleton, Townsend, and Jason Cons. 2014. "Coming to Terms: Reinserting Research Assistants into Ethnography's Past and Present." *Ethnography* 15 (3): 279–90.

Price, David. 2016. *Cold War Anthropology: The CIA, the Pentagon, and the Growth of Dual Use Anthropology*. Durham, NC: Duke University Press.

Rofel, Lisa, and Sylvia Yanagisako. 2019. *Fabricating Transnational Capitalism: A Collaborative Ethnography of Italian-Chinese Global Fashion*. Durham, NC: Duke University Press.

Schnegg, Michael. 2014. "Anthropology and Comparison: Methodological Challenges and Tentative Solutions." *Zeitschrift für Ethnologie* 139:55–72.

Simpson, Audra. 2014. *Mohawk Interruptus: Political Life across the Borders of Settler States*. Durham, NC: Duke University Press.

Stocking, George W., Jr., ed. 1974. *The Shaping of American Anthropology, 1883–1911: A Franz Boas Reader*. New York: Basic Books.

Strathern, Marilyn, ed. 2000. *Audit Cultures: Anthropological Studies in Accountability, Ethics and the Academy*. New York: Routledge.

Todd, Zoe. 2018. "The Decolonial Turn 2.0: The Reckoning." *Anthro(dendum)*. June 15, 2018. https://anthrodendum.org/2018/06/15/the-decolonial-turn-2-0-the-reckoning/.

Turner, Terence. 1992. "Defiant Images: The Kayapo Appropriation of Video." *Anthropology Today* 8 (6): 5–16.

——. 1995. "Representation, Collaboration and Mediation in Contemporary Ethnographic and Indigenous Media." *Visual Anthropology Review* 11 (2): 102–6.

Williams, Bianca C. 2015. "Introduction: #BlackLivesMatter." Hot Spots, Cultural Anthropology website. June 29, 2015. https://culanth.org/fieldsights/688-introduction-blacklivesmatter.

1

HOW DO WE COLLABORATE?

An Updated Manifesto

Douglas R. Holmes and George E. Marcus

In the early 2000s, we published a number of essays championing collaborative relationships growing out of contemporary projects of ethnography that we knew of (e.g., Holmes and Marcus 2005a, 2005b, 2006). We evoked ready-made concepts like "para-ethnography," and "epistemic partners" that resonated because they were relevant in projects of ethnographic research which increasingly crossed into and through the realm of corporate, bureaucratic, and activist organizations, and, more broadly, cultures of expertise (Knorr-Cetina 1999).

For us, this partnership was an evolution of our participation in the Late Editions project of the 1990s (Marcus 1992–2000, vols. 1–8), which operated both in the moods of fin-de-siècle assessment of global transitions as well as in the styles of critical thinking that favored dialogic modes of representation and writing. In our participation in the making of the first volume of this project (*Perilous States* 1992), we spun off our dialogic relationship with Doug's proposal of "illicit discourse" (Holmes 1993, 255–82) in a memorable chapter on catching an undertone of European Union politics (which led to his project on the rise of extreme right movements [Holmes 2001]). George's take on it was "complicity" (Marcus 1998b) as a means of characterizing the complexity of anthropologists' key subject relationships in localities that had multisited trajectories.

This chapter is a considerably changed version of "Collaborative Imperatives: A Manifesto, of Sorts, for the Reimagination of the Classic Scene of Fieldwork Encounter," by Douglas R. Holmes and George E. Marcus, in *Collaborators Collaborating: Counterparts in Anthropological Knowledge and International Research Relations*, edited by Monica Konrad (Oxford: Berghahn Books, 2012), 126–44.

In this chapter, we go behind the scenes focusing on the background of our long-term collaboration lasting until the very present, conducted through a steady cumulative conversation (conducted both by means of periodic quite long weekend phone calls, as well as encounters at various meetings and seminars), to reflect on the value of such a sustained process, mundanely identifiable as friendship, through a certain history of our discipline, which required an adaptation not necessarily of anthropological method, but of thinking about anthropological method.

Our collaborative efforts have focused on *aligning* our work with the analytical endeavors of our subjects, of various epistemic partners who have created a series of unusual challenges for us. The very traditional process as ethnographers of "translating" their cultures pulled us into unconventional challenges of shifting questions of research across anthropologist-subject relationships. We were left with no compass for ethnography except for the second-order, "third," para-ethnographic spaces that we forged out of our own parallel conversations that problematized anthropological assumptions of method just as we pursued it in separate projects. It is this complexity of participation and perspective in contemporary projects that our own decades-long collaboration regulated, so to speak, in each of our very separate endeavors of inquiry. To be clear, we did not do collaborative or comparative work on the same or similar subjects, as Dominic Boyer and Alexei Yurchak have done (see this volume), in their own years-long collaborative friendship; we did sustained collaborative and analytic work of a second-order nature on problems and opportunities suggested by ethnographic research practices and subjects themselves.

These reflexive subjects, found and defined in our separate projects, similar to, but substantially different in our thinking from the classic informant, come to serve as our collaborators, as they creatively navigate significant anthropological questions of our time. They come to see themselves as literally doing this, and in our own conversations (Doug and George) we construct or invent the analytics to identify and relate to them in this way. They are epistemic partners: figures who have assimilated and adapted our interpretative modalities to differentiate new forms of information, data, and intelligence. They experiment with the expressive idioms that shape and contour emerging aesthetic, religious, and political phenomena. They wrestle with current intellectual, emotional, and ethical imperatives, just as we do. In our own conversations, we create the stage designs, so to speak, translations, and analytic identifications in which such conversations can take place in fieldwork.

In other words, we are not merely concerned with the anthropology of particular phenomena but rather with the anthropology that operates *within* them.

> How do we pursue our inquiry when our "subjects" are themselves engaged in intellectual labors that resemble, approximate, or are entirely

indistinguishable from our own engagements as ethnographers? How do we create alliances with figures who are continually questioning the nature of information, the creation of social facts, and the framing of cultural knowledge? These reflexive figures who we encounter within the ethnographic scene are skeptical about analytical conventions, about the value of data and the procedures by which data are gleaned. We argue that we must treat these individuals as epistemic partners with whom we collaborate in the production of anthropological knowledge. Our analytical interests and theirs can be pursued simultaneously and we can share insights and thus develop a common exchange at a second-order, reflexive level. We can pursue this kind of alliance even if the ultimate aims of our analyses are different, if not opposed.

> Douglas Holmes, from the abstract submitted
> for our contribution to this volume

Refunctioned ethnography [a project proposed by Holmes and Marcus in their mid-2000s writings] has a more complicated cast of characters than the conversations traditional between the ethnographer and native subjects or informants. In contrast to the bilateral encounter over a camp table, ethnography for present situations is normally if not invariably constituted by the *ethnographer*, multiple *subjects* in some relation to one another (what relation may be self-evident, or may have to be discovered by the anthropologist) and liaisons. The contours of ethnographic fieldwork are determined by the relations the ethnographer establishes with the liaisons and the subjects who provide the material critical to the construction of her project. Rather than a sequence of interviews, refunctioned ethnography is much more like what in theater would be an ensemble production, which works through synchronization, or perhaps better, a film montage, in which relations among disparate and apparently disconnected items are established.

> David A. Westbrook, *Navigators of the Contemporary: Why
> Ethnography Matters* (2008)

How Do We Gain Access?

Issues of access have always been a key preoccupation of fieldwork. Often difficult, time consuming, and vexing, these difficulties have conventionally been understood as an inevitable and necessary aspect of the initial episodes of fieldwork, which are to be overcome by virtue of the familiarity and rapport that develop in due course.

By contrast, we argue that *access* is, in fact, an unrelenting challenge of many of the projects that anthropologists are pursuing today. We also think that the problems of access encompass key creative challenges of contemporary fieldwork, the means by which we continually align our research with the unfolding preoccupations of our subjects and the issues at stake in the domains and settings we seek to investigate: hence the basis of collaboration, the means and methods by which we *sustain* inquiry over time. Indeed, access increasingly involves the strengthening of weak ties (after Mark Granovetter's classic article, 1973), and this achievement requires imagining a project together that draws from mutual repertoires, but slightly more from shared future-oriented problem discourses that are so present in contemporary anthropology (and elsewhere). For example, parsing the term "public" or "publics" opens field conversations in a variety of ethnographic research contexts today. Anthropology's sensitive wordsmithing in the field (once evoked, and critiqued, as its art of translation; see Asad 1986) is what has both provoked our conversations and provided us with access and the recognition of epistemic partners in the specific settings of fieldwork (and sometimes beyond). Much of the sustained critical discussions among anthropologists themselves today depends on to what extent and in what contexts the results of shared concept work in the field holds up within the discipline's own distinctive history of thinking. Conversations within the field join disciplinary conversations in unsuspected and strategic ways, rather than conventionally being a primary source of anthropology's data isolated for its own expert concept work.

The Spaces of Collaboration

Constituting scenes of fieldwork out of real life, so to speak, materializes for many of us today by the conceptual work that we do with latter-day key informants, who as epistemic partners, instead, define the imaginary and plot of our own inquiries. Hence projects emerge out of a series of collaborative imperatives:

1. Our methods, that is, the practices of ethnography, have been assimilated as key intellectual modalities of the present. Epistemic partnership depends on anthropologists recognizing something like the practice of ethnography among subjects and negotiating this third form as part of the research relationship, to be described explicitly as a technique of the method of fieldwork. Finding a kind of training language for this enhancement of ethnographic method has been a key interest of our long-term collaboration. The contest inside bureaucracies of various kinds and policy-making circles is precisely for interpretations

of emerging realities, and regardless of winners or losers, there are those perspectives in play that parallel the curiosities of ethnographers in particularities, the conditions of lived ordinary experience, and a sensitivity to the rules of informal culture that dominate governing rationalities and formalisms. There is hardly a demand for ethnography itself to duplicate or to operate independently of these para-ethnographic tendencies and desires within its scenes of fieldwork. What is left for it to do? Ethnography advances today by deferring to, absorbing, and being altered by found reflexive subjects—by risking collaborative encounters of uncertain outcomes for the production of ethnographic knowledge in the forms that have in the past been regulated by the disciplinary communities that propel anthropologists into fieldwork.

2. Within the epistemic communities that we seek to explore, our subjects are themselves fully capable of doing superb ethnography in their own idioms. Within their own situated discourses, the basic descriptive function of ethnography is very likely to be already exercised (artifactually, books and memoirs emerge every day now from within, so to speak, that explain, with a strong edge of critique, how the most complex and strategic contemporary processes, institutions, and organizations operate and have their own cultures). Anthropologists are not needed to add critique, moral injunction, or higher meaning to these accounts.

3. We must therefore relearn our method from our subjects as epistemic partners, from a careful assessment of how they engage our world and our time intellectually. This presumes motivation, intent, purpose, curiosity as well as intellectual appropriation on the part of subjects who agree to become part of, or cooperate with, ethnographic inquiry.

4. Against the prevailing theoretical tides of the first two decades of this century, the ethnographic subject has returned forcefully and persuasively. Put indelicately, the subject is back and fully in our poststructuralist faces. We want this subject to perform a deferred intellectual operation for us that we cannot do under the established imaginary of the ethnographer's relation to subject as informant. This renegotiation of the rules of engagement with the dialogic, epistemic subject in ethnographic research opens the intellectual space for a rethinking of collaboration beyond the older understanding of it as the subject responding to, cooperating with, and tolerating the ethnographer's more or less overt agendas.

What we are describing here is neither style nor fad, nor is it a mere emendation or add-on to the compendium of practices available to the anthropologist.

There are two common senses of collaboration to which we take exception in developing ours in this chapter. One is the sense of collaboration long implicitly embedded in anthropological fieldwork, concerning the anthropologist in relation to a less powerful and formally silent subject in traditional ethnography. This sense has been the source of much critique since the 1980s and is the basis today of restating the ethics of research by recognizing as a norm of research practice these long-embedded collaborative relations. In our rethinking of fieldwork relationships, we have a sense of the dynamics of power and the intellectual standing of the reflexive subject. For us, collaboration is overt, epistemic, and mutually invested in.

The other sense of collaboration is a heightened contemporary ideology of practice in which all projects of fieldwork define themselves. This is collaboration that defines the pervasive condition of the contemporary social situation that the (still usually lone) ethnographer wants to work within. Both ideologically and tangibly, it is collaboration of the collaboratory of the information age and the operating ethos of the organizations (corporations, universities, NGOs, etc.), institutions, and arrangements that define the processes that anthropologists study worldwide. It is the ether of spaces of fieldwork today. Of course, ethnographers must blend into this ideological order as the condition of doing fieldwork research, but in so doing, they cannot quite avoid the once deprofessionalizing move of going native. This is the problem of not just appearing to go along with the collaborative milieu in order to do ethnography, as we have known it, but responding to the imperatives to work collaboratively within the reimagined classic Malinowskian scene of fieldwork. Being marginal natives or strangers in a world that constitutes itself as collaborations all the way down just will not do. Ethnographers need to construct models of fieldwork as collaboration for themselves that let them operate with their own research agendas inside the pervasive collaboratories that define social spaces today.

As against these two senses of collaboration—atoning for the past sin of not recognizing collaboration in traditional fieldwork, going along with collaborations as the environment of research so as to be in control of one's research as the still lone ethnographer—we want to distinguish another that remakes classic fieldwork which we refer to here and that escapes, on the one hand, atonement for the once silenced subject and, on the other, does so without becoming an artifact of the contemporary collaboratory of the global information age which seemingly restructures all organizational environments alike.

For us, then, the figure of the para-ethnographer fundamentally changes the rules of the game for collaboration and the mediation of ideas and sensibilities encompassed by and within the ethnographic exchange. We have no interest in collaboration as a division of labor among the investigators who control the design of a project or as the basis for the blending of academic expertise or as gestures to a canonical interdisciplinarity. The corrective is, again, to fully integrate our subjects' analytical acumen and insights to define the issues at stake in our project as well as the means by which we explore them.

So here is our profoundly simple ethnographic observation: these found experimental discourses in scenes of fieldwork everywhere today, and impelled by the ideological push for new arrangements and paradigms in established organizations as being collaborative, presume a master interlocutor to whom these reflexive stories are addressed. The interlocutor can be real (a family member, a colleague, a patient, a client, or someone else) or figurative (the market, the public, and so on), but our point is that there is an emphatic presumption of positions into which ethnographers can easily insinuate themselves. Again, the space of collaboration is created for the ethnographer prior to his or her arrival on the scene and the ethnographer is a figure whose presence is anticipated.

We argue that collaboration represents not merely some new or revamped practice to be added to the repertoire of methodological tools available to an ethnographer; rather, we view collaboration as fundamental to what we have termed a refunctioning of ethnography (Holmes and Marcus 2005a, 2005b, 2006). Key to this refunctioning is engaging, as it were, the para-ethnographic practices of our subjects, drawing on their analytical acumen and their existential insights to recast the intellectual imperatives of our own methodological practices. Working amid and on collaborations significantly shifts the purposes of ethnography from a descriptive-analytic function for which it has settled to a deferral (*not* necessarily deference) to a subject's modes of knowing, a function to which ethnography has long aspired. This act of deferral, as a distinctive methodological premise, is thus generative of different collaborative configurations by which, we believe, the architecture of a refunctioned ethnography gains coherence.

A Short History of Thinking Together into an Era of Collaborative Imperatives

The Late Editions project of the 1990s, produced under George's editorship at Rice University (see Marcus 1992–2000) was a decade-long experiment and response to the then current intense critique in the academy of realist and documentary representation (e.g., Clifford and Marcus 1986), yet at a time—the fin-de-siècle—when there was an equally intense intellectual and public interest precisely in documentary accounts of the century's legacy and new (even millennial) futures emerging. Through collective and interdisciplinary editorial deliberations—call this a collaborative project indeed, although collaboration at that time was not the pervasive ideological figure that it is now—under agreed topical frames, participants were asked to develop conversations with selected, cooperating subjects throughout the world, and to produce dialogical writings for a series of annuals until the year 2000 (there were eight of them; see Marcus's Addendum, this volume).

What this series did for George and Doug (who was a participant in the project over the years), as a by-product of the specific intentions of the series, was to cast their attention critically to the present conditions and classic ideology of fieldwork relationships in anthropological ethnography as the compass and scale of such research was changing markedly through the 1990s. While the Late Editions project, because of its origins among anthropologists, did ask its interdisciplinary contributors/reporters to exercise something like an ethnographic sensibility, we never presumed that we were producing a paradigm for the rethinking of ethnographic fieldwork itself; we were responding rather to counterposed theoretical critiques and documentary urges of the times.

Yet one legacy of the Late Editions project was to focus George and Doug's joint attention on the scene of fieldwork as a site of problematization in the disciplinary projects that each of them was pursuing at the time. For George, the problem was how to rethink the dynamics of fieldwork relationships in the context of a paradigm of multisited ethnography, which he was trying to articulate (Marcus 1998a). Having grown up in anthropology on the study of elites, George thought through a revised scene of fieldwork in terms of a trope of complicity (Marcus 1998b) in which the ethnographer allied with the subject as intellectual partner in coming to terms with the understanding of a shared common object of curiosity elsewhere. George's conceptual work was fed by the coevolving research of Doug on shifting political trends in Europe that required him to think differently about the dynamics of fieldwork than he had in his earlier research in northern Italy. Doug's fieldwork at the site of the European Parliament led to scenes of fieldwork elsewhere that coalesced as an account of the poorly understood social and cultural strength of neofascism in contemporary Europe (see Holmes 2000). The key point here is that this latter shift in his research developed because of his rethinking of the dynamics of the fieldwork encounter, reported on in the Late Editions series as a conversation with Bruno Gollnisch of Jean-Marie Le Pen's movement (see Holmes 1993).

George and Doug's shared efforts of the 1990s have led them to further develop after 2000 a reimagination of the scene of fieldwork encounter as collaboration, according to this explicit topical fashion and ideological imperative of the present.

Since 2000, the project vehicles for George and Doug's joint reimagining of the scene of fieldwork have been increasingly posed in terms of collaboration in which the first section of this chapter has been couched. George completed a work, *Ocasião*, with a Portuguese aristocrat (Marcus and Mascarenhas 2005) that on the face of it looked like another in the genre of reflexive, coproduced ethnography popular after the critiques of the 1980s when anthropologists were licensed to write explicitly dialogic works as ethnography. But, for George, there were different principles at work in his epistolary exchanges with Mascarenhas. While much is learned in *Ocasião* about the world of the contemporary Portuguese aristocracy, the roles of anthropologist and subject in this text are never settled; there is a game of mutual deferral (and deference) and appropriation going on that explores unformed norms of collaboration implicit in ethnography where the fiction of the ethnographer's authority is mutually acknowledged but shifts in its assumption between anthropologist and subject. There were elements in this relationship, and Doug's earlier ones, that seem distinctively characteristic of ethnography as collaboration today.

Since 2000, George and Doug have each developed a project or vehicle in which to probe more systematically the changing scenes of fieldwork, themed as collaboration, that they had been reimagining together previously. In Doug's case, it is an ambitious ethnography of central banking (see Holmes 2014a). In George's, it is a reconsideration of the pedagogy of graduate dissertation projects that strategically bring students into careers of ethnographic research which has collaboration as an institutional agenda, and more recently, his atelier projects with Luke Cantarella and Christine Hegel, and especially at the World Trade Organization in 2013 (see Hegel and Cantarella, this volume).

By the mid-2000s, for both George and Doug, there were new dimensions and qualities to the dialogic properties of fieldwork in the context of ethnographic research projects of nontraditional compass and scale. While these were very clearly issues about collaborative research norms in fieldwork, of a different character than had been exposed in various earlier critiques of Malinowskian (or Boasian) fieldwork, the articulation of what these protonorms at play in contemporary (now routine) multisited research are, and what their implications for the future of anthropology's distinctive and signature mode of inquiry are, are only now being addressed in what we consider to be an explicitly ideological era (or perhaps just fashion?) of collaborative knowledge-making endeavors of all kinds. Certainly, then, it is an era of ethnography of collaboration as a pervasive social condition in the problems and sites where anthropologists have the ambition to develop their research (it permeates, for example, the sites of fieldwork in the range of examples that we offered previously, and indeed in the other chapters in this volume), but to what extent is it necessary to conceive ethnography itself in its doing as collaboration, different from the way this trope has been buried in the humanistic professional craft culture of method of the past?

Work in Progress

What are we working on now? We have brought to our collaboration new challenges, which have pushed our conversation on to unfamiliar terrains. They echo many of our earlier preoccupations, but we also have made new forays, notably George's engagement with questions of design, gentrification, and curation, in his going-concern projects with Keith Murphy, Luke Cantarella, and Christine Hegel (see Marcus's Addendum, and the chapters by Murphy, and Hegel and Cantarella, this volume).

Here are two very abbreviated examples illustrating our efforts to delineate what is at stake anthropologically in the enigmatic and vexing materials drawn from Doug's current research. Both cases return us to long-standing preoccupations while further amplifying and refining the bases of our collaboration. The first addresses a particular aspect of "cultures of expertise": domains in which data, information, and intelligence underwrite institutional organization and action and how these settings can be investigated ethnographically. Specifically, we examine how an abstract quantitative model has guided central bankers as they have sought to navigate the predicaments posed by the financial crisis (and now the Covid-19 pandemic). Broadly, our purpose is to show how "thin," indeed, austere ethnographic materials can yield something recognizable as "thick description." But, in this particular case, there are unusual institutional maneuvers that require the actors themselves—central bankers—to impart to their quantitative analyses relational meanings in order to animate policy. In other words, they "thicken" their high-level mathematical reasoning rhetorically to render their interventions effective as policy.

The second focuses on another of our abiding interests: how an "anthropology," an illiberal anthropology, operates *within* fascism, a contemporary fascism that unfolds ethnographically (Holmes 2019). For this foreshortened account, we are interested in the opening gambit, the delineation of research questions under the sway of the para-ethnographic. In this case, the question is provoked by political activists who seek to reawaken a virulent past in order to animate a new, illiberal Europe: "How and why have the most discredited ideas and sensibilities of the modern era—ideas that yielded the indelible horrors of the twentieth century—become persuasive, compelling even, in the new century?" (Holmes 2019, 85). This, as it happens, is a realignment of the original "illicit discourse" that inspired our collaborative endeavors in the early 1990s (Holmes 1993).

The two cases are compelling for us insofar as they represent distinctive experiments conducted in vivo, experiments that we have sought to render accessible ethnographically. Both experiments are fundamentally future-oriented requiring us to align our analyses with the institutional predicaments and, at times, disquieting aspirations of our subjects. The projects are thus para-ethnographic by design—contingent on the intellectual acumen of our subjects, on their theoretical insights, and on their methodological practices and constantly in motion.

For central bankers, the future is, in the first instance, a *technical* problem—"the intertemporal problem"—upon which the basic challenge of monetary affairs hinges: By what means is the value of money to be anchored over time? (Goodhart 1975). By addressing this fundamental question of monetary affairs, central bank personnel perform an exploration of the cultural exigencies of money and credit. What follows is a stylized representation of the technical analysis—guided by a series of macroeconomic equations—employed by central bankers to address the behavior of prices over time. What is striking about this technocratic practice is that, for it to "work," the solution must be translated into a different idiom and communicated to an audience in order for it to assume a performative efficacy (Austin 1961; Searle 1969).

The quantitative model examined herein is drawn from a commentary on Michael Woodford's book *Interest and Prices: Foundations of a Theory of Monetary Policy* (2003), by Stanley Fischer, former vice chair of the Federal Reserve (2014–17) and prior to that governor of the Bank of Israel (2005–13). Fischer is an academic economist and a central banker, a theorist, and a practitioner. Fischer's account encompasses a technical representation of macroeconomic relationships governing the operation of monetary policy that has come to be known as "forward guidance" (Fischer 2016). Here are three key equations by which central bankers think and act systematically upon the future:

$$x_t = E_t x_{t+1} - \sigma(\hat{i}_t - E_t \pi_{t+1} - \hat{r}_t^n) \tag{1}$$

$$\pi_t = k x_t + \beta E_t \pi_{t+1} \tag{2}$$

$$\hat{i}_t = \bar{i}_t + \phi_\pi(\pi_t - \bar{\pi}) + \phi_x(x_t - \bar{x})/4 \tag{3}$$

Where

x_t is the output gap, $\hat{y}_t - \hat{y}_t^n$;

$\hat{y}_t^n$ is an exogenous variable, representing variations in the natural rate of output;

π_t is the rate of inflation;

$\hat{i}_t$ is the interest rate;

$\bar{i}_t$ is an exogenous, possibly time-varying, intercept of the Taylor Rule.

(Fischer 2016, 13)

These symbolic representations seem to frustrate or defy conventional anthropological scrutiny. Yet there are translational modalities built into the operation of the model that can be aligned within a relational framework that renders them recognizable and fully susceptible to anthropological analysis. The model seeks to impart by means of forward guidance policy interventions by which to act upon the future by means of shaping expectations prospectively. The intriguing feature of this model—a key imperative of central bank policy more broadly—is that, for it to work, it must be rendered persuasive to the public. The public—as market participants—must be persuaded by the solutions derived from the model to achieve intended policy outcomes (Yellen 2013).

The process of translation performed by the personnel of central banks reveals an acute anthropology of pricing—the key dynamic of market economies—the behavior of which is understood in relation to expectations, expectations susceptible to persuasion by means of official communications. The figures who craft speeches, reports, graphic images, and other written documents apply their rhetorical acumen to the high-level mathematical reasoning and quantitative analysis perform this representational labor (McCloskey1985). They model the economy and the financial system with language establishing a radically communicative and relational dynamic at the center of monetary affairs (Holmes 2014a). Here is a very abbreviated statement demonstrating how the Monetary Policy Committee (MPC) of the Bank of England sought to make its intentions decipherable, intentions derived from the three equations that underwrite the forward guidance framework. "At its meeting on 1 August 2013, the Monetary Policy Committee (MPC) agreed its intention not to raise Bank Rate from its current level of 0.5% at least until the Labour Force Survey (LFS) headline measure of the unemployment rate had fallen to a 'threshold' of 7%" (https://www.bankofengland.co.uk/-/media/boe/files/inflation-report/2013/monetary-policy-trade-offs-and-forward-guidance.pdf, 5, accessed May 20, 2020).

Simply put, the bank is communicating its intentions to hold to a policy—a very stimulative policy—unchanged until some point *in the future* when the unemployment rate in the United Kingdom crosses a threshold, at which point the bank will consider raising interest rates to restrain prices—inflationary forces—building in the economy. As the audience for these communications in the summer of 2013 assimilated policy intentions as their own personal expectations, they did the work of monetary policy (Merton 1948).

How does this work anthropologically? "Central bankers seek to endow the future with discernible features that we—the public—can reflect and act upon, animating or curtailing our propensities to produce, consume, borrow, and lend" (Holmes 2014b, 24). Policy interventions—in this case forward guidance—depend on rhetoric: "Central bankers, rather than predicting the future, seek to create elements of a tractable future. They do this with words. They use language to explore, promulgate, and sustain the ideas that animate our economic future, as well as the structures of feeling, the sentiments, expectations, and desires that make them real" (Holmes 2018, 85). By aligning our ethnography with the experiments pursued by the personnel of central banks, we can observe how "thin" technocratic representations can yield "thick" description, capable of imparting performative outcomes (Austin 1961; Callon 2007; MacKenzie 2006; MacKenzie, Muniesa, and Siu, 2007).

Alignment in Extremis

The other aspect of Doug's current research that we are examining is prompted by the use of a single term: "fascism." And this usage was and is the result of a series of alignments and realignments with the trajectory of emerging forms of political activism.

Over the course of many years, we have observed the accretion of political agendas that are termed—far too simplistically—the "extreme right," "the nationalist right," or "the populist right" to yield a contemporary fascism: a fascism enacted in our midst (Berezin 2019; Brubaker 2017; Mazzarella 2019). As we began to discuss the extremism emerging around us as *fascism*, a fascism of and in our time, a fascism that has distinctive contemporary features that are not fully nor necessarily congruent with its historical manifestations, a series of acute anthropological questions emerged. In the abbreviated account that follows we focus on how the para-ethnographic reconfigures these questions—classic questions on the nature of activisms and our relationship to them—in surprising and potentially productive ways.

If what we are encountering is indeed fascism, then we are confronted with one overriding question: How and why have the most discredited ideas and sensibilities of the modern era—ideas that yielded the indelible horrors of the twentieth century—become persuasive, compelling even, in the new century? (Holmes 2019, 63). We take the position that it is not their alien nature that makes the ideas that animate contemporary configurations of fascism dangerous, but rather their proximity to conventional, indeed glorified, values that underwrite the European intellectual tradition. Crucially, anthropological modes of thought are implicated, fully implicated, in the story.

The sensibilities of the Romantic tradition, folkloric styles, and ethnological methods make fascism available to us in deeply held convictions concerning the nature of human collectivities that are aligned with distinctive understandings of individuals' capacities to think, feel, experience, and act. Fascist activists understand culture. Indeed, they have sought to resolve a key cultural conundrum: Can those rich and varied symbolic endowments that constitute convention and tradition be recast to animate a distinctive configuration of modernity, a conceptualization of modernity that veers away from the assumptions of the European Enlightenment? If we address this challenge, we can begin to understand fascism's contemporary seductions, particularly for the young.

What is at stake in this illiberal anthropology? It is comprehensive intellectual stance—predicated on the strident and relentless discrimination of cultural affinity and difference—that compelled us to align our ethnography with the fears and aspirations of a diverse community of unruly activists thereby allowing us to confront a formidable, profound even, constellation of political outlooks and sensibilities albeit couched in prosaic and seemingly harmless language that anthropologists know well. "If contemporary fascism can colonize just about every expression of identity and attachment, every aspect of truth, beauty, virtue, and depravity, if fascism can acquire and assimilate new meanings and affective predispositions from the motifs and metaphors of diverse folkloric traditions and from countless genres of popular culture, and if fascism has the capacity to merge, fuse, and synthesize what would otherwise be considered incompatible elements, then the tasks we face are daunting" (Holmes 2019, 85). Grappling with the unspeakable—confronting the anthropology within fascism—reveals an inchoate scene of and for the ethnographic encounter and our disquieting place in it. Complicity anticipates vexed forms of collaboration frustrating an ethical stance that removes us from the scene of encounter (Marcus 1999). Michel Foucault anticipated the alien and for some, the distasteful basis of this claim: "Last but not least, the major enemy, the strategic adversary is fascism . . . and not only historical fascism, the fascism of Hitler and Mussolini—which was able to mobilize and use the desire of the masses so effectively—but also the fascism in us all, in our heads and in our everyday behavior, the fascism that causes us to love power, to desire the very thing that dominates and exploits us" (2004, xiv–xv). Collaboration, like the related issue of access, is under these conditions fraught and unrelenting.

Para-Ethnographic by Design

Our own collaboration has been about a restatement at an especially important moment in the discipline's development (after Writing Culture, in the wake of the era of expanding globalization, in the aftermath of the critical theory period as well as in the afterglow of the diverse research "projects" that emerged in the 2000s). And our collaboration is also characteristic of the discipline's particular development at the moment in which collaboration is itself a characteristic/ tendency/outgrowth of the pursuit of the classic method. Crucially, in our work we have sought to capture both "varieties" of collaboration—one that evokes the present/recent past and the other which wrestles with the emerging present/ future. Our take on collaboration is thus informed by our incessant restatement and commentary on the classic method understood prospectively.

The expanded, perhaps limitless space of para-ethnography comes with an unusual stipulation. Ethnography itself, its practices, its modes of thinking and acting, must have an open architecture permitting the appropriation of those formal and informal modalities that animate the lives of diverse ensembles of players and characters with whom we can or must collaborate. The craft of para-ethnography is to create or identify situations where this can happen, settings where such found relations of collaboration can be enhanced. Alternatively, we have experimented with scenography, various modes of curation and simulation to evoke these circumstantial dynamics disrupting the naturalism assumed to mediate the classic field situation.

Our collaboration traces the historical adjustments by which anthropology has moved from the intellectual preoccupations of a resolute field science to modes of inquiry increasingly attentive to "second order" realms of knowledge— to "observing observers observing"—as primary sites of investigation (Holmes, Marcus, and Westbrook 2006).

We both did sustained collaborative work in which the fundamental analytical problems and methods we deployed were recommended or advocated by our subjects: our epistemic partners. We constructed or invented the analytics to relate to these counterparts and thereby gain access to realms in which emergence and experimentation were the key, indeed relentless, cultural preoccupation. We aligned our conversations with inchoate struggles unfolding around us though largely under the radar of the conventional anthropological gaze. We suspected that the great anthropological ideas of our time are being formulated elsewhere largely outside the disciplinary control or knowledge of academic departments. As suggested at the outset, our collaboration is not merely concerned with the anthropology of particular phenomena, but rather with the anthropology that operates *within* them.

A final and fair question is this: How rare is the financial technocrat or the fascist activist in routine creations of scenes of fieldwork today? Are we drawing too much from unusual cases of serendipitous advantage and fanciful construction? That is, how valid is it, or how far can the relationship with central bankers or fascists be used as a simulacrum to think about the schematics and dynamics of changing fieldwork situations today especially in relation to para-ethnographically inclined reflexive subjects and counterparts? At stake are de facto norms in play in many fieldwork projects today about relationships that can be called collaborative which badly need articulation, discussion, and debate. While there are perhaps several genres or designs at play (a number are represented by the collection of exceptions that is this volume), we believe that the dynamics of collaboration we have described in George and Doug's relation to research projects gives us at least a working imaginary for refunctioning ethnography.

REFERENCES

Asad, Talal. 1986. "The Concept of Cultural Translation in British Social Anthropology." In *Writing Culture: The Poetics and Politics of Ethnography*, edited by James Clifford and George E. Marcus, 141–64. Berkeley: University of California Press.

Austin, John L. 1961. *Philosophical Papers*, edited by J. O. Urmson and G. J. Warnock. Oxford: Oxford University Press.

Berezin, Mabel. 2019. "Fascism and Populism: Are They Useful Categories for Comparative Sociological Analysis?" *Annual Review of Sociology* 45:345–61. https://doi.org/10.1146/annurev-soc-073018-022351.

Brubaker, Roger. 2017. "Why Populism?" Theory and Society 46 (5): 357–85.

Callon, Michel. 2007. "Performative Economics." In *Do Economists Make Markets? On the Performativity of Economics*, edited by Donald MacKenzie, Fabian Muniesa, and Lucia Siu, 311–57. Princeton, NJ: Princeton University Press.

Clifford, James, and George E. Marcus, eds. 1986. *Writing Culture: The Poetics and Politics of Ethnography*. Berkeley: University of California Press.

Fischer, Stanley. 2016. "(Money), Interest, and Prices: Patinkin and Woodford." A speech given at "A Conference in Honor of Michael Woodford's Contributions to Economics," cosponsored by the Federal Reserve Bank of New York, Columbia University Program for Economic Research, and Columbia University Department of Economics, New York, New York, May 19, 2016. Accessed May 25, 2020. https://www.federalreserve.gov/newsevents/speech/fischer20160519.htm.

Foucault, Michel. 2004. Preface to *Anti-Oedipus: Capitalism and Schizophrenia*, by Gilles Deleuze and Félix Guattari, translated by Robert Hurley, Mark Seem, and Helen R. Lane, xiii–xvi. London: Continuum.

Goodhart, Charles. 1975. "'Monetary Relationships: A View from Threadneedle Street' and 'Problems of Monetary Management: The U.K. Experience.'" In *Papers in Monetary Economics*. Vol. 1. [Sydney?]: Reserve Bank of Australia.

Granovetter, Mark. S. 1973. "The Strength of Weak Ties." *American Sociological Review* 76 (6): 1360–80.

Holmes, Douglas R. 1993. "Illicit Discourse." In *Perilous States: Conversations on Culture, Politics and Nation*, edited by George Marcus, 255–82. Late Editions, 1. Chicago: University of Chicago Press.

———. 2000. *Integral Europe: Fast Capitalism, Multiculturalism, Neofascism*. Princeton, NJ: Princeton University Press.

_____. 2014a. *Economy of Words: Communicative Imperatives in Central Banks*. Chicago: University of Chicago Press.

_____. 2014b. "Communicative Imperatives in Central Banks." *Cornell International Law Journal* 47 (1): 15–61.

_____. 2018. "A Tractable Future: Central Banks in Conversation with Their Publics." In *Uncertain Futures: Imaginaries, Narratives and Calculation in the Economy*, edited by Jens Beckert and Richard Bronk, 173–93. Oxford: Oxford University Press.

_____. 2019. "Fascism at Eye-Level: The Anthropological Conundrum." *Focaal: Journal of Global and Historical Anthropology* 84 (2019): 62–90.

Holmes, Douglas, and George E. Marcus. 2005a. "Cultures of Expertise and the Management of Globalization: Toward the Re-Functioning of Ethnography." In *Global Assemblages*, edited by Aihwa Ong and Stephen J. Collier, 235–52. Oxford: Blackwell.

———. 2005b. "Refunctioning Ethnography: The Challenge of an Anthropology of the Contemporary." In *The SAGE Handbook of Qualitative Research*, edited by Norman Denzin and Yvonna Lincoln, 1099–113. 3rd ed. Thousand Oaks, CA: Sage.

———. 2006. "Fast Capitalism: Para-Ethnography and the Rise of the Symbolic Analyst." In *Frontiers of Capital*, edited by Melissa S. Fisher and Greg Downey, 33–56. Durham, NC: Duke University Press.

Holmes, Douglas, George E. Marcus, and David A. Westbrook. 2006. "Intellectual Vocations in the City of Gold." *Political and Legal Anthropology Review* 29 (1): 154–79.

Knorr-Cetina, Karin. 1999. *Epistemic Cultures: How the Sciences Make Knowledge*. Cambridge, MA: Harvard University Press.

MacKenzie, Donald. 2006. *An Engine, Not a Camera: How Financial Models Shape Markets*. Cambridge, MA: MIT Press.

MacKenzie, Donald, Fabian Muniesa, and Lucia Siu. 2007. Introduction to *Do Economists Make Markets? On the Performativity of Economics*, 1–19. Princeton, NJ: Princeton University Press.

Marcus, George E., ed. 1992–2000. Late Editions: Cultural Studies for the End of the Century series (vol. 1, *Perilous States*; vol. 2, *Technoscientific Imaginaries*; vol. 3, *Connected*; vol. 4, *Cultural Producers in Perilous States*; vol. 5, *Corporate Futures*; vol. 6, *Paranoia within Reason*; vol. 7, *Para-Sites*; vol. 8, *Zeroing in on the Year 2000*). Chicago: University of Chicago Press.

———. 1998a (1995). "Ethnography in/of the World System: The Emergence of Mulit-Sited Ethnography." In *Ethnography through Thick and Thin*, 79–104. Princeton, NJ: Princeton University Press.

———. 1998b (1997). "The Uses of Complicity in the Changing Mise-en-Scène of Anthropological Fieldwork." In *Ethnography through Thick and Thin*, 105–32. Princeton, NJ: Princeton University Press.

Marcus, George E., and Fernando Mascarenhas. 2005. *Ocasião: The Marquis and the Anthropologist, a Collaboration*. Walnut Creek, CA: AltaMira.

Mazzarella, William. 2019. "The Anthropology of Populism: Beyond the Liberal Settlement." *Annual Review of Anthropology* 48:45–60.

McCloskey, Deidre. 1985. *The Rhetoric of Economics*. Madison: University of Wisconsin Press.

Merton, Robert K. 1948. "The Self-Fulfilling Prophecy." *Antioch Review* 8 (2): 193–210.

Searle, John. 1969. *Speech Acts: An Essay in the Philosophy of Language*. Cambridge: Cambridge University Press.

Westbrook, David. 2008. *Navigators of the Contemporary: Why Ethnography Matters.* Chicago: University of Chicago Press.

Woodford, Michael. 2003. *Interest and Prices: Foundations of a Theory of Monetary Policy.* Princeton, NJ: Princeton University Press.

Yellen, Janet. 2013. "Communications in Monetary Policy." Speech presented at the Society of American Business Editors and Writers 50th Anniversary Conference, Washington DC, April 4, 2013.

2

IMAGINATION, IMPROVISATION, AND LETTING GO

Keith M. Murphy

This chapter is a reflection on collaboration in three modes—my research interest in face-to-face collaboration, my own collaboration with George Marcus as co-organizer of a series of "ethnocharrette" events at the University of California, Irvine, and the results of collaborations between participants in those events. Before getting there, though, I'd like to begin with a few words about the general status of collaboration in anthropology.

The different subfields of anthropology tend to display different general orientations to collaboration and sharing. In archaeology, and to some extent biological anthropology, collaborative research is more or less treated as a given. Students typically first put archaeological methods to use in field schools, under the guidance of more advanced students and professional archaeologists. While they are in the field, they work together in teams, collecting data that contributes to a larger site-based project, and in the lab they work alongside one another, in consistent contact with others. Training in linguistic anthropology is often lab-based as well, with participants sharing their data—in the form of recordings and transcripts of language in use—in order to widen the scope of possible interpretations and analyses beyond what the fieldworker herself will conjure on her own.

Sociocultural anthropology, though, has been less amenable to weaving collaboration into the subfield's methodological fabric. The figure of the lone anthropologist still dominates the subfield's imaginary, and basic collaborative practices like data sharing (in this case, sharing field notes) are not common. Of course, this is not to say that collaboration is, or has historically been, absent in sociocultural anthropology. While they are unevenly scattered across space and time, there are plenty of notable examples. For instance, the Six Cultures study by Beatrice and John Whiting (Whiting 1963), Marjorie Shostak's (1981) collaboration with Nisa, and more recently the Matsutake Worlds project (Matsutake Worlds Research Group 2009) and the Center on Everyday Lives of Families (Arnold et al. 2012)—a project that crossed subfields and disciplines—all represent quite distinct ways of reconfiguring the traditional model of the singular and elevated ethnographer (see also contributions to this volume). Despite these and other examples that work against the traditional grain, sociocultural anthropology has yet to fully accept collaboration as a basic condition of its continued development.

One reason for this may be that, as the collection of examples just mentioned illustrates, there is no single sense of collaboration that is widely or evenly applied. For some, collaboration is about fieldwork and data collection, either with multiple researchers working in the same field site, or multiple fieldworkers in different sites contributing to a single project. For others, collaboration may be about writing together, or thinking together, or sharing data and discussing it as part of a team. This fundamental unspecificity of the category itself calls into question what collaboration even refers to, or whether it is even possible to abstract it from the activities it steers and supports, or from the institutional evaluation regimes that either grant it prestige or view it as all but worthless. In other words, maybe collaboration isn't even really a coherent thing that looks more or less the same in different contexts.

In my own professional work, I study designers and designing, and I teach courses about improvisation, two very collaborative fields. I have been closely examining collaboration, in one form or another, from the very start, though always with a view toward how other groups do it, not anthropologists. I am, of course, reluctant to say that I have figured out collaboration in any definitive sense. But I do think that after spending so much time around people who stress collaboration in their own lifeworlds, and after trying to create conditions for productive collaborations in graduate student training, a few thematic keywords that matter have emerged: imagination, improvisation, and letting go.

Collaborative Imagining

My first bit of ethnographic research ended up orbiting, if not entirely centering on, collaboration in architectural design interactions. I spent six months at a Los Angeles architecture firm observing and video-recording a team of architects working together to finalize the plans for a large scientific building for a university in the American Southwest. Though I had not started the project intending to look at collaboration per se, it quickly became a topic of concern: How do these three architects, each tackling different aspects of a very large and complicated structure, come to see and construct their shared project together, and what sorts of practical actions help facilitate that creative process? That second subquestion was critical. It became apparent very quickly that collaboration could not simply be reduced to "multiple individuals working on the same thing," because each of those elements—the "multiple," the "individuals," the "working," and the "same thing"—were obviously in need of further exploration.

One of the ideas that emerged from this project was the concept of "collaborative imagining" (Murphy 2005). As I originally conceived it, collaborative imagining was a cognitive operation that was different from traditional ways of treating cognition for at least two reasons: first, because from the collaborative imagining perspective, the objects of imagination exist—or are stimulated by—phenomena largely outside of an individual's own mind (or at least one's brain); and second, because collaborative imagining is not a lonely action, but is always done with, and supported by, the simultaneous and sequentially ordered actions of others. Thus, for example, when the team of architects I worked with convened to discuss some aspect of the unfolding design, their work was irreducibly facilitated by—that is, it absolutely required—the presence of a range of publicly available media, including not just talk, but also architectural drawings, hand gestures, computer screens, architects' scales, tracing paper, pencils, and so much more. And when all of this was brought into the action and combined in different configurations, it was put to use to collectively constitute invisible but present objects for the group to imagine together.

Take, for example, an extended pencil tracing out a three-dimensional doorframe in the space just above the plan laid flat before the architects; a vertical hand in a "karate chop" form, mimicking a swinging gate at the front of a loading dock drawn on the plan; and an embodied enactment of looking through a chain-link fence for security when one of the architects questions the use of that material. To be sure, these are all very small details that do not themselves amount to much in light of the grander architectural project in which they are embedded. But at the same time, they do actually constitute the most basic building blocks of collaborative creativity, the "minor motions" (Murphy 2015) that allow collaboration to work in real time: a constant and ongoing mutual provision of raw materials for members of the group to take up, consider, evaluate, and transform as needed (cf. Goodwin 2018).

Of course, this kind of collaborative imagining is relatively easy to see in architectural interactions, because such interactions tend to be rather narrowly constrained in terms of topics, artifacts, and workspaces. Nevertheless, I have come to realize in the many years since I completed that research that not only is collaborative imagining a useful way to understand how collective conversational interaction works, or how imagining functions as a kind of social action, but it is also useful for understanding how collaboration in general actually plays out in multiple contexts and at multiple scales beyond the level of face-to-face interaction. Thus, from another point of view, I went into the architecture studio to study hand gestures, but I came out with something to say about collaboration.

My next project, a study of design in Sweden and its relations with politics there (Murphy 2015), while not explicitly concerned with collaborative imagining, did rely on the concept to help explain how disparate groups of people, widely distributed over space and time and working on unconnected projects, come to reproduce and maintain "Swedish design," even without really trying. Designers design objects like chairs and tables, journalists and researchers routinely attach a particular political narrative to these objects that connects them to long-standing social democratic values (like equality and care), and institutions like the Nationalmuseum in Stockholm and the furniture store IKEA display these objects in ways that help visitors experience the connections between objects, discourses, and political values firsthand. All of this in concert helps craft a collaboratively imagined vision of the Swedish welfare state in which political values are materialized in the everyday world. This is a scaled-up version of the original idea of collaborative imagining, in which the collaborative creativity is spread across different social domains, unorchestrated but still aligned in loose harmony, with some groups worrying the forms of Swedish design, others its language, and still others the logic of its links to state politics. It is multiple individuals all working on the same thing, but in a vastly different mode and with vastly different consequences.

Design Charrettes

In late 2010 I had the opportunity to join a small group of designers at Syracuse University. The group was known as COLAB, and we were tasked with devising and carrying out projects that used design and design thinking to build bridges between the university, the surrounding community, and industry in new and (it was hoped) productive ways. We also included research and pedagogy as central components of our mission. Among the activities we regularly organized were charrettes, each with a different theme or purpose.

There is some (mostly inconsequential) debate about where the term "charrette" comes from, and which discipline owns the concept (both industrial designers and architects claim it as their own, as do urban planners). The basic form of a charrette, regardless of which discipline is employing it, is this: a number of designers, and typically other stakeholders, gather together for a short period of time—sometimes a few hours, sometimes over a period of days—to work intensively together on a specific design problem. The goal is not necessarily to produce a final workable solution, but rather to prototype possible solutions that can be further developed as part of a longer design process. Charrettes share some qualities with brainstorming sessions and workshops, and in some cases look quite similar to hackathons (Irani 2015; Jones, Semel, and Le 2015), but they tend to stand out because they are quick, messy, and collaborative by design.

As a researcher interested in collaboration, I had participated in and observed a small number of charrettes, but my time with COLAB was the first opportunity I had had to help organize them, in this case, mostly for various groups of university students. As I followed the lead of my more experienced colleagues, I grew particularly interested in the wider potential of the charrette form: a balance of imposed structure, individual intent, and social pressure that seemed likely to lead to interesting results as participants collectively organized themselves for accomplishing imaginative creative work. And as COLAB ran our charrette events over the course of several months, indeed something more did emerge from our students' efforts, more than individual work or mere brainstorming would produce. I do not want to overstate it, though. Charrettes, or segments of charrette events, are often difficult, silly, frustrating, and fruitless. Nonetheless, all of that can be overshadowed when great things are created from the combined efforts of the group.

Improvisation

As it happens, this general feeling was familiar to me. In college and for a short time in graduate school, I was heavily involved in improvisational theater as an actor, trainer, and director. I also regularly teach a course to undergraduates in which we explore theories of social interaction through improvisational performances (I train the students in very basic improv techniques). The sense I experienced with charrettes—that great things are created from the combined efforts of the group—was very similar to what can happen in a good improv comedy scene. Individual contributions matter, but if it is done well, the whole produced from the constituent parts can feel absolutely sublime.

The basic premise of improvisational theater is that a small group of actors, without any specific preparation, script, or foreknowledge, performs scenes for an audience typically based on information provided by the audience just before the start of the scene. These scenes may be short (a few minutes) or longer (about fifteen minutes or even more), but they should emerge from the back-and-forth interactions of the improvisers onstage. Rather than relying on a script, though, the improvisers are trained to follow a small set of rules that help guide their participation in the emergent scene. Among these rules, and perhaps the most important, is "yes, and," which both encourages improvisers to always agree with what their fellow actors have said, and asks them to add information to build on their fellow actor's previous contribution. Because the improvisers cannot plan out a scene beforehand, they must instead plan it out as they go, in real time, collaboratively imagining and simultaneously enacting a compelling and coherent scene; and in order to do that, the actors must provide one another with the scene's raw materials on the fly, for immediate or near-future elaboration, transformation, or extension.

For example, one actor onstage can greet her fellow improviser with "Good morning, mother, I'll need to borrow the car again today." This minor motion, just a simple utterance, gives the second actor a lot of material to work with, including a time of day, a relationship, an implied location (in the home), an implied backstory (the "again" indicates this has happened before), and a potential conflict. Add to that any mimed body language, tone of voice, and other paralinguistic features that accompany the utterance, and the first actor has rapidly transformed a blank canvas into a vibrant set of features for her partner to elaborate and expand upon. Scene building in this manner works best if the actors trust one another, and listen carefully to each other, and try to work as a collective, rather than as individuals.

Design charrettes function in very similar ways to improvisational theater. Both are organized precisely to eschew planning, to distribute responsibility to the group rather than invest it in individuals, and to encourage participants to provide one another with some of the necessary materials—ideas, propositions, hunches, critiques—for manipulation in the design process. Both presume that all the participants are working toward a common goal, though that goal exists as a kind of "formless sense" for most of the process—a formless sense that allows for multiple interpretations—and only takes on a more concrete and mutually understood form as the group's work progresses. And both request, if not require, that individuals let go of their own preferences and desires so that a will of the group can emerge (cf. Dumit 2017). These are, I would argue, critical aspects of all collaborative activities.

The Idea of an Ethnocharrette

In 2011 I returned to the University of California, Irvine from Syracuse, at which point George Marcus and I began talking in earnest about creating new opportunities to help our graduate students engage ethnographic materials beyond received traditional forms, with particular reference to design. The two of us approached this possibility from different perspectives and with very different stakes in the endeavor. Marcus's main concern was exploring new ways to transform ethnography both conceptually and in practice, and using design as one path for getting there. My own interest and expertise was design, and in particular exploring designing from a critical ethnographic point of view. After spending several months casually discussing possibilities, we landed on the idea of, essentially, shoe-horning design pedagogical techniques into our existing training regimes.

This was an idea Marcus had been contemplating for some time. While working at Rice University, he had noticed over the years that architecture students who enrolled in his classes always seemed to approach and analyze ethnography differently—in a good way—than students coming from a more traditional liberal arts background. He speculated that perhaps there was something specific in the practical ways that architecture students were trained and expected to work that led them to view ethnography from productively oblique angles. If that was the case, perhaps importing some of these techniques into anthropological training could push a new generation of ethnographers in otherwise unexplored directions.

The most iconic pedagogical form in architecture, art, and design education is the critique or "crit" (Murphy, Ivarsson, and Lymer 2012). At the end of a given project (or at other intermediary points), students are asked to present their designs to a public audience, usually made up of fellow students, instructors, and outside critics. The form of the crit varies, of course, but in general students will offer a brief verbal description of their work—usually plans, sections, and other drawings, along with 3D models—often including a few prepared words on their process. They then step aside so that the critics—professors and practitioners brought in for the event—as well as other students, can comment on what is good and what is not good about the drawings and models the students have created. In most cases, students work on individual projects, but they tend to do so in shared studio spaces in which they are in constant and consistent interaction with one another. So, while the designs they produce are not strictly the result of collaboration, they are nonetheless supported by collaborative conditions throughout the entire process.

However, as a mechanism for reconfiguring some of the basics of ethnographic training, the crit did not seem like the best option for us to borrow. There were some upsides to the form, like an emphasis on creativity, some aspects of collaboration, and a potential value in public performance and critique; but there were also some downsides, the most obvious being that the project—that is, whatever the students actually work on—would be difficult to replicate for anthropology graduate students, given the wide variation of field sites, topics, and field languages in anthropology.

The charrette, though, seemed like it might actually work. In terms of its form, the charrette is self-contained, flexible in length, and still offers most of the features of design pedagogy we were looking for. We decided to try it, calling our version the "ethnocharrette," an inartful phrase that has nonetheless stuck. The only question was, What was this thing about?

Ethnocharrettes Take Form

In a previous essay (Murphy and Marcus 2013, 263), Marcus and I described the ethnocharrette in this way: "The *ethnocharrette* is an augmentation of the charrette form tailored to the needs of ethnographers. The idea behind initiating the *ethnocharrette* was simple enough: What happens if we ask ethnographers to run ethnographic material through a design studio process? How would they think? What would they produce?" Thus far, I have been using the vague phrase "ethnographic materials," partly because we've tried a number of different versions of the ethnocharrette, and partly because we have not settled on what really matters in this process.

So far, there have been roughly three formations of the ethnocharrette, typically with multiple events within each formation. The first was the most free-form and chaotic, and consisted of two events (for more on this, see Murphy and Marcus 2013). For both events, we assembled groups of graduate students, mostly from anthropology but a few from other departments, and gathered them together for a full day of activities. They were split into groups of four or five participants, and everyone worked with the same material, published ethnographic monographs that everyone was asked to read ahead of time (Desjarlais 1997; Masco 2006). The task the groups were assigned was relatively simple: working with an explicitly experimental attitude, collaborate in groups to see another anthropologist's ethnographic material—in this case, the book and what is represented in it—from some unexpected angle, and then deconstruct those materials and reconfigure them into something we have never seen before. These instructions were intentionally nondescriptive. We provided significant structure for the event—three stages of specific lengths, with specific tasks in each stage—but left the "What are we actually doing?" part open-ended to see what the groups would collaboratively imagine. They were told they needed to produce a slideshow at the end, and receive critique of the slideshow, but otherwise they were allowed to do what they liked.

The results were quite good, in our eyes. In keeping with the experimentalist attitude, we had no specific expectations, but in both events the groups produced and presented imaginative ethnographic tools and reworked ethnographic worlds. However, one clear takeaway was that, for most of the participants, collaboration within this type of activity was difficult. The students were not prepared to work in teams, unsure of what they needed to produce, and they did not want to disrespect the authors and the ethnographic realities represented in their books. Indeed, there was a strong individualist bias that seemed to run through much of the feedback we received, a preference for working alone at least part of the time, for producing something like a written document, and for treating existing books as inviolable artifacts.

After running these first two events, we realized that we were not sure what the best end product really should be. But it was clear to us that, despite the resistance of the participants, continuous collaboration was one of the critical conditions we were striving for (and that the resistance to this was likely engendered by our own design of the events). To help us further consider what this form could do for us, we convened an all-day workshop composed of seasoned ethnographers with a range of backgrounds to provide us, the organizers, with our own critique session. We presented what we had done in our first two events and invited some of the students who had participated to speak. One of the critical results of this workshop was the insight that the ethnocharrette process should somehow involve *iteration*, a collaborative creation and transformation of *versions* of whatever it was we wanted students to produce, and that this versioning could afford new kinds of contemplation. So we instigated the second iteration of the ethnocharrette itself.

This second formation embedded the ethnocharrette within the structure of ongoing courses, rather than running them as stand-alone events—and the second of these events marked a turning point for the form. For their final projects, students in a proseminar course on anthropological theory were assembled into groups and assigned one of the theorists they had read during the quarter. Each member of the group was asked to bring in some physical, tangible (or otherwise sense-able) object from their field sites. These two things—theoretical texts and ethnographic artifacts—served as the raw material for collaborative production, and they were asked to find unexpected or uncanny connections among the various ethnographic worlds they planned to study for their dissertation fieldwork, and with the theoretical texts they were assigned. In addition, rather than producing a slideshow, students were asked to construct physical objects based on their collaborative work and using whatever materials they could find. What the groups ended up creating looked more like fantastical art projects than anything else, but the narratives they crafted to accompany their physical objects, and to trace out their unexpected connections, were often quite profound. Moreover, the resistance to collaboration seemed to all but disappear during this event. There could be a number of reasons for this, including a much shorter schedule (just a few hours), familiarity among the groups, and the satisfaction of making a real, physical thing rather than just a slideshow. However, by the end of this event we felt that the product itself was almost incidental. It was the process, and what we hoped it would stimulate, that really mattered the most.

The third ethnocharrette iteration was also the most ambitious. This formation, officially titled Formal Play, involved forty-five participants, including graduate students, professors, and postdocs, all from a range of disciplines, split into eight separate groups of four or five people. We wanted participants to work together to playfully undermine the norms of ethnographic data and the genre of ethnography itself—the idea being that individuals will all have different senses of what those norms are, and how they matter, and those differences would motivate each group's process. The main conceit of the event was for participants to embrace *arbitrariness* as a mechanism for producing odd ethnographic forms, which would themselves challenge what we take for granted as the right way to represent and interact with the worlds we study.

Arbitrariness was introduced in a few different ways. First, groups were tasked with compiling a collection of photographs by asking strangers on campus to send the group the very last photograph that they took on their phones (each group had its own email address for this task). Once that collection was made, groups were then asked to find similar images using databases of stock photography (how they determined what was similar was up to each group's participants). Finally, they were asked to use these two image collections to produce ethnographic pamphlets—an odd form that does not yet exist, and whose properties would challenge dominant modes of ethnographic representation. The goal was not to produce usable materials, or to posit this activity as an actual field method, but rather it was to encourage groups to explore collaboratively what, in fact, an ethnographic pamphlet, composed of arbitrary but meaningfully linked images, could possibly be, what it could possibly do in the world, and how it could change how we conceive of ethnographic data.

This event was the longest we had ever organized (one and a half days), which gave the groups ample time to explore ideas and possibilities. At first, nearly everyone resisted the idea of an ethnographic pamphlet, which we expected. Ethnography has developed as a genre of nuance and detailed description, woven together with complex arguments that demand time and patience of the reader. A pamphlet, in contrast, is typically simple and cheap, its contents focused on one point or set of points, and as objects they are easily consumed and discarded. So, in many respects, ethnographic monographs and pamphlets are antithetical forms, which leaves the concept of an ethnographic pamphlet an inherent contradiction. But when tasked with working together to overcome that contradiction and imagine what this form could look like, how it would work, and who would possibly use it, the groups all collaboratively produced a range of intriguing pamphlet prototypes, including posters, 'zines, flyers, and brochures that each tackled some corner of the social world that the groups collectively decided deserved some illumination.

Despite producing amazing results, the Formal Play ethnocharrette did not go off without hitches. The biggest difficulty we faced was one that we were already familiar with from previous ethnocharrettes: people, especially people trained in the social sciences and allied fields, often have a difficult time working together. Note that this is not to say that they have a hard time *collaborating*. Instead, it is a resistance to the basic real-time practice of laboring with and laboring alongside other people who may not entirely agree with you, or may not see the world from your perspective. To some degree, academics are experts in "thinking with" one another, so long as that thinking happens in specified forms, usually through noncommittal consultative activities, like workshopping a paper for feedback. But when "thinking with" becomes "making with," as it does in the ethnocharrette, the stakes begin to shift and the accountability involved in doing the work shifts too; Patrick Jagoda (2016, 202) calls this "critical complicity." For better or worse, when groups gather to "create together" as something more than a collection of individuals, participation is never simple or neutral. Instead, participants all become jointly complicit in the process and outcome of the work. While most of the groups in the Formal Play ethnocharrette worked quite well together, some participants actively resisted our activities, describing them (negatively) as "something I'd make my students do." This line of thinking is revealing: it demonstrates a recognition and acceptance that there is pedagogical value in group work, but also a moralized evaluation that such group work is "not for me"—perhaps because shared accountability is difficult for those of us who have grown accustomed to being accountable only to ourselves. In contrast, the most successful groups were those whose members were most adept at "letting go" of their fast-held ideas about what "counts" as ethnography, of their predilections toward autonomy, and of their resistance to playful engagement. By truly surrendering some autonomy to the whims of the group, something more than the sum of individual contributions, and much more creative and interesting, was likely to emerge.

Reconstituting Collaboration

A recent book on "design for social innovation" describes "collaborative organizations"—basically any social groups that engage in collaboration—as "characterized by *freedom of choice* (their members can freely decide whether, when, and how to join or leave the group) and *openness* (they present a positive attitude toward 'others': other people, other ideas, other organizations)" (Manzini 2015, 83, original emphasis). This is just one particular representation of how collaboration works, but this sort of framing is very common. It is also largely misguided.

First, these renderings of collaboration miss something significant. One of the things I have emphasized here is the role of imagination in supporting real-time collaboration, and in particular an active kind of imagining that a group performs together. This imagining can take many forms, including hunches, propositions, enacted possible scenarios, and more, but regardless of the form, one of its main purposes is to project a shared sense of an ending or goal. This goal will not be conceived in exactly the same ways by all participants, of course, but because they are all working with the same basic stimuli, there are still limits to the possible variation in how participants understand what the group is working toward. It is precisely this threshold between difference and similarity in imagining the action of the group that makes the collaboration worthwhile and productive. After all, if everyone were imagining exactly the same thing, there would be no reason to assemble the group in the first place.

Second, these renderings overemphasize a decidedly liberal character that often is not really relevant to on-the-ground collaborative projects. In fact, this liberal characterization often obscures the necessity of individuals to submit, at least partially, to the group. To argue that collaboration is inherently improvisational, as I am doing here, is to argue that group creativity is always conditional and shaped through the gradual transformation of raw materials that participants provide for one another and with which they imagine a shared goal. This is not about an individual exercising freedom of choice in terms of how they contribute, but about working within constraints to help guide creativity. Moreover, the constraints of accountability and critical complicity mean collaborators cannot simply get up and leave a collaboration, as Manzini's (2015) definition implies, without causing severe disruption or destruction. Instead, the integrity of the collaboration fundamentally relies on commitment, trust, and empathy among participants, all of whom are invested in creating something together by means of the contributions they all provide.

Third, successful collaboration is less based in openness to others (though openness does matter) than it is in reflexivity about one's own personal constraints and commitments. In other words, and perhaps counterintuitively, participants should spend some time unraveling their own priors and preconceptions before accepting what others have to say. After all, I can be open to hearing other ideas while still affirming that my contributions are obviously the best. Letting go of that position, though—which actually is a precondition for being truly open to others—is a much more difficult, and much more necessary, challenge than simply subscribing to an ideology of openness.

So what does this mean for anthropology? As I outlined at the start, different kinds of collaboration are already quite commonly, if not consistently, practiced throughout the general field. However, should the discipline more fully embrace collaboration as a fundamental orientation to how we work—especially in as-of-yet unseen forms, and beyond what is currently de rigueur—I would suggest that rather than focusing on simply doing things together, we pay extra attention to the roles played by imagination, improvisation, and letting go in conditioning collaboration more generally. Perhaps this means embracing the speculative alongside the empirical in designing and conducting fieldwork. Or maybe it means renovating the very idea of fieldwork itself, modeling it more after an improvised theatrical scene or set of scenes rather than a field study with roots in the life sciences (cf. Murphy 2017). And probably most importantly, many things will have to be let go (or at least put to the side), including not just our individual sense of ownership over the research we do, but also more fundamental facets of anthropology, like the figure of the lone anthropologist, the expectations of solo authorship, the kinds of expertise that tend to matter for ethnography, and the ways in which graduate training and mentorship tend to work (of course, many other things too). While reasonable people can disagree as to whether collaboration is actually inherently valuable to anthropology, I don't think that disagreement prevents us from exploring how collaboration might send anthropology in new worthwhile directions.

REFERENCES

Arnold, Jean E., Anthony P. Graesch, Enzo Ragazzini, and Elinor Ochs. 2012. *Life at Home in the Twenty-First Century: 32 Families Open Their Doors.* Los Angeles: Cotsen Institute of Archaeology Press.

Bakke, Gretchen, and Marina Peterson, eds. 2017. *Between Matter and Method: Encounters in Anthropology and Art.* London: Bloomsbury Press.

Desjarlais, Robert R. 1997. *Shelter Blues: Sanity and Selfhood among the Homeless.* Philadelphia: University of Pennsylvania Press.

Dumit, Joe. 2017. "Notes toward Critical Ethnographic Scores: Anthropology and Improvisation Training in a Breached World." In Bakke and Peterson, *Between Matter and Method,* 51–72.

Goodwin, Charles. 2018. *Co-Operative Action.* Cambridge: Cambridge University Press.

Irani, Lilly. 2015. "Hackathons and the Making of Entrepreneurial Citizenship." *Science, Technology, and Human Values* 40 (5): 799–824.

Jagoda, Patrick. 2016. *Network Aesthetics.* Chicago: University of Chicago Press.

Jones, Graham. M., Beth Semel, and Audrey Le. 2015. "Negotiating Commitment in a Context of Volatile Sociality." *Journal of Linguistic Anthropology* 25:322–45.

Manzini, Ezio. 2015. *Design, When Everybody Designs: An Introduction to Design for Social Innovation.* Cambridge, MA: MIT Press.

Masco, Joseph. 2006. *The Nuclear Borderlands: The Manhattan Project in Post–Cold War New Mexico*. Princeton, NJ: Princeton University Press.

Matsutake Worlds Research Group. 2009. "A New Form of Collaboration in Cultural Anthropology: Matsutake Worlds." *American Ethnologist* 36 (2): 380–403.

Murphy, Keith M. 2005. "Collaborative Imagining: The Interactive Use of Gestures, Talk, and Graphic Representation in Architectural Practice." *Semiotica* 156 (1/4): 113–45.

——. 2015. *Swedish Design: An Ethnography*. Ithaca, NY: Cornell University Press.

——. 2017. "Art, Design, and Ethical Forms of Ethnographic Intervention." In Bakke and Peterson, *Between Matter and Method*, 97–115.

Murphy, Keith M., Jonas Ivarsson, and Gustav Lymer. 2012. "Embodied Reasoning in Architectural Critique." *Design Studies* 33 (6): 530–56.

Murphy, Keith M., and George E. Marcus. 2013. "Ethnography and Design, Ethnography in Design . . . Ethnography by Design." In *Design Anthropology: Theory and Practice*, edited by Wendy Gunn, Ton Otto, and Rachel Charlotte Smith, 252–68. Oxford: Berg.

Shostak, Marjorie. 1981. *Nisa: The Life and Words of a !Kung Woman*. Cambridge, MA: Harvard University Press.

Whiting, Beatrice 1963. *Six Cultures: Studies in Child Rearing*. Oxford: John Wiley and Sons.

3

ETHNOGRAPHIC REENTANGLEMENTS IN THE COLLABORATIVE ECOLOGIES OF FILM AND CONTACT IMPROVISATION

Christine Hegel, with contributions from Luke Cantarella

There is only one body at first, lunging ever-so-slowly forward and then reaching around to pluck a tiny box from a pocket. Joined by another, tilting over at an awkward angle to take the box, but then leaving it after all, melting into a heap of dirt beneath them both. Their bodies comingle with a third, and then a fourth, and they all grasp hands and arms, levering over and around one another— gently in one moment, with more force in the next. Suddenly, one body, wobbling in midturn, is ensnared by arms that stretch and lift and hold aloft before delivering to the side of the heap. A head appears between them, the body follows, and slinks heavily forward. These four move around and through one another, torsos taking unexpected shapes, forming a many-armed and many-legged beast.

There is no other way to describe this scene of movement except by recounting its shapes, the placement of limbs, and the way bodies folded into one another and then lifted away and back again, charting a deliberate collision course. The dancers were improvising intimate responses to one another's gestures for the making of a video installation piece entitled *Trade Is Sublime*. What was particularly remarkable about this piece, one of many that the dancers developed over the course of two days of shooting, was that they had all just met one another. Each joined the project with experience in contact improvisation, a dance form that eschews both choreographic direction and music. Contact improvisation is reliant on an ecology of collaboration that emerged during the early 1970s, circulating through a small but coherent group of practitioners and hubs like Movement Research in New York City (cf. Albright and Gere 2003; Novack 1990). Their prior training in the form meant that they didn't need rehearsal to begin to move in concert, but rather initiated a physical call-and-response that evolved with little discussion. Their collaboration took the form of testing another's strength and heft and flexibility, through which a silent rapport emerged and gradually built into a covert lexicon of iterated gestures. They coembodied an emergent knowledge comprising rules invisible to outside observers.

The scenic designer Luke Cantarella and I were interested in the way this movement tradition could be used in the design of an intervention at the World Trade Organization (WTO). The intervention, initiated and coordinated by George Marcus, was part of an experiment in creating a second act, following and derived from a three-year (2008–10) collective project of ethnographic research inside the WTO Geneva headquarters by an international team of anthropologists (see Abélès 2011; and Marcus 2016). They produced studies of a number of WTO processes and values, including the negotiation of trade agreements at various stages, multicultural and cooperative values, attitudes toward trade, and consensus making on the transnational level and with the aid of the secretariat.[1] Though their access was unprecedented, the ethnographers left with an unfulfilled appetite for situations of participant observation. Stimulated by discussions in anthropology of the introduction of design and studio interventions into scenes of ethnographic fieldwork (see, for example, Rabinow et al. 2008), George proposed to Pascal Lamy, then director-general, a follow-up project in the form of an art installation. The aim was to communicate with members of the WTO secretariat and delegates through an aesthetic intervention closely informed by the previous research. The director-general, who had long been partial to bringing more art into the décor of the WTO villa, agreed. Jae Chung, an anthropologist and professor at Aalen University as well as an accomplished member of the original team, joined our second-act experiment.

We (Christine, Luke, George, and Jae), then, conceived *Trade Is Sublime* as a return to the site of fieldwork with an installation piece that would allow George and Jae to find new and alternate reverberations in the ethnographic material. Moreover, the piece would be targeted at the WTO community as a means to unlock latent or unarticulated sense making in their daily discourse. Our proffer to artful intervention was to adopt the language of a monument, which relies on grand metaphor, seeking to capture and represent, in perpetuity, some essential quality of an event or a person (or in this case, an institution). This experiment was intended to extend the use of metaphor perhaps further than anthropologists tend to use it in their imaginaries by creating a metaphor in material form for display at the Centre William Rappard (CWR), the home of the WTO in Geneva. The overarching aim was to engage in a lateral analysis (Maurer, 2005) of the core principles of the institution, its inner workings, and the public's perception of it.

The project took about six months from conception to installation, although George had been involved in developing ideas with groups of artists even longer than this. The making of *Trade Is Sublime* entailed working with more than eighteen key collaborators from indie filmmaking, theater, and contact improvisation. It involved at least two months of conceptual work, culminating in a proposal presented to key decision makers at the WTO for approval. We then solicited external funding to support hiring a team of designers and professional dancers, for equipment rental, and to cover ancillary costs. The concept continued to evolve as we prepared for the film shoot, and involved developing materials (a score and a structure, discussed later on) that derived from the ethnographic data George and Jae had compiled and on which they had written; these materials would guide our creative process. We hired a small company of dancers, a director of photography, and a production design team and crew who developed and prepared a sound stage at Pace University replete with scenic, lighting, sound, and costume elements. We shot the majority of the footage over the course of two days in early 2013 and then assembled and edited the footage in postproduction to create three short video documents. These videos were then prepared for looping play on monitors nested in hand-built scale-model replicas of the CWR. The completed installation was comprised of these scale-model video pieces— framed as "proposals for a monument to trade"—and exhibited for two weeks in a public passageway at the CWR for visitors to encounter and watch. During the exhibition period, the aim was to elicit responses to the proposals in a variety of ways (a voting process, observation, unstructured interviews, etc.). In titling the piece *Trade Is Sublime*, we intended to create an honorific, aesthetically beautiful portrayal of the potential aspirations of the organization. In other words, we were not attempting to produce an ethnographic representation of the WTO, using the data at hand for veracity. The point was to shift, momentarily, away from grounded theories of the institution and investigate latent or unarticulated knowledge that might be unearthed through an imaginative collaboration.

In this chapter, we have two interconnected aims. First, we consider the underlying rules and habits of different creative domains as a way to understand how they condition collaboration. Ecologies of collaboration, as we call them, form where they are needed, and these ecologies vary in the way they divide and conjoin effort. Second, we use our experiment to consider how external collaborative ecologies might be integrated into and assimilated to anthropological analysis. The dynamics of metacollaboration with artists already immersed in cultures of collaboration as part of their craft are of equal interest to us as the generative dynamics of the initial studio phase of production. In so doing, we reflect on how the forms of rigor and play present in the collaborative ecologies of film and contact improvisation generated new openings and insights in an ongoing ethnographic project.

Our decision to assimilate modalities of collaboration in artistic mediums rests on a fundamental belief that fieldwork and anthropological analysis are likewise deeply creative. But collaborations with artists and performers deliberately bend social analysis through processes of imaginative making. Our experiment in outsourcing an interpretive practice to nonanthropologists was a way to disrupt the linear propulsion of social science knowledge generation about a particular institution (the WTO) and the future of global trade. Moreover, as the trend toward anthropological collaboration across and in creative fields continues to grow, our aim here is to think carefully about the implications for anthropology when integrating into or borrowing from existing collaborative ecologies.

Collaboration

The workshop that spawned this collection of essays came on the heels of the 2016 Society for Cultural Anthropology meetings, with the theme of collaboration as object and as method. There has long been a trend toward explicitly framing fieldwork as a collaborative undertaking with interlocutors in field sites, not only as a way to reformulate the power dynamic between anthropologists and those with whom they work but also as a way to disrupt institutional and Western-centric claims of expertise. Since the 1980s, this trend has been particularly notable in dialogic, polyphonic, and self-reflexive modes of ethnographic writing aimed at acknowledging and facilitating convergences between knowledge traditions. Textual experiments have had limited success in fomenting a radical shift in the politics of anthropological representation, notes Lassiter (2001), who advocates for pushing the dialogic approach to ethnographic endeavor further into what he terms "reciprocal ethnography."[2] Although situated within a broad set of epistemological concerns, these efforts foreground representational politics. Parallel to this, research efforts that bridge the social and life science fields continue to multiply (cf. Fortun 2004; Matsutake Worlds Research Group 2009; Montoya 2011); less concerned with questions of representation and power, such collaborations tend to be rooted in a desire to achieve reliability and validity through complementary expertise. The collaborations entailed in *Trade Is Sublime*, on the other hand, most closely align with projects situated between anthropology and art or design (cf. *Ethnographic Terminalia*, Hamdy and Nye, and Murphy, this volume; Gunn, Otto, and Smith 2013; Schneider and Wright 2010). These experiments may be motivated by similar concerns as the models just mentioned, but attune to emergent social life and affective registers by taking multimodal and multisensory approaches through artistic collaboration.

Whether collaborations are across or outside of the academy, they inevitably pose tricky questions about how to work together. How will decisions be made, especially concerning the kinds of data that should be collected, how they will be disclosed, and to whom? Will collaborators play similar or complementary roles, working in hierarchical or nonhierarchical modes? What forms of analysis will result? Such decisions are sometimes shaped by the funding entity, which may require making distinctions between roles (principal researcher or coresearchers, research assistants, lab manager, etc.) with research activities differentiated and hierarchically allocated.[3] The fact that anthropology lacks standardized collaborative arrangements and norms suggests that our commitment to collaboration is still evolving and unstable. This situation also offers opportunities for more imaginative and creative experiments.

It is increasingly clear that the single lead-researcher model is limiting. Emerging forms of collaboration, like those just noted, are integral to expanding how and what we can know through social inquiry. But as a discipline we are not yet at the point where we have decided that the limitations of independent research modalities outweigh the benefits of cooperation. As Anna Tsing notes, and graduate programs implicitly maintain, ethnographic immersion, which requires a kind of responsiveness that can be impeded by multiresearcher arrangements, continues to be a hallmark of our discipline (Matsutake Research Group 2009, 381). Moreover, solving the challenges that arise in cross-disciplinary collaboration requires an investment of energy in communication about process. She describes some of the concerns that arose with collaborative writing among team members investigating interconnected aspects of the matsutake mushroom market:

> Perhaps creative collaboration is associated with feminist scholarship in part because it requires a labor of emotional intimacy, entailing close hours and long years of negotiation and great care over procedural matters. Who takes the lead? Whose insights take precedence? Whose style works? These questions are never settled. When things go well, the experience is delightful; when disagreements arise, everyone feels crushed. This is because there is no easy complementarity among roles. No a priori standards set the frame. Questions, methods, and goals are worked out in the process. This open-endedness makes collaboration in creative authorship an intriguing—but also terrifying—possibility for ethnographic research and writing. (Matsutake Worlds Research Group 2009, 381)

The Matsutake Research Group is perhaps a unique collaborative entity in its effort to engage in different arrangements of cowriting across disciplines.

Despite this more experimental aspect of the project, it moves, like many multi-investigator projects in the social sciences, in familiar directions—from observation through discourse to textual representation. In other words, our collaborative working arrangements, even when they cross disciplinary borders, follow a fairly standard trajectory and gravitate toward the commonalities that exist between disciplines. Examples of collaborative work in anthropology tend to reaffirm the thinking that collaboration expands the possibilities for research and analysis when it avoids disrupting or radically reorganizing the general flow of research.

Trade Is Sublime was an undertaking that infiltrated and engaged the collaborative ecologies of indie filmmaking and contact improvisation as a way to create a temporary adjacency to research on the WTO in a form that might foment new questions and understandings about the project both for its investigators and its subjects. It was disruptive in the sense that its outcomes were decidedly unknown and the project didn't promise forward motion on the research; instead, it aimed to create material and situated opportunities for lateral thinking. The idea was to work according to the rules of these alternate ecologies and in so doing to temporarily cede intellectual control over the project. Out of this, we hoped to generate something aesthetically beguiling yet relevant to denizens of the WTO, whose routine experiences and interactions in the institution are generally restricted to highly rationalistic and technocratic discourses. When those very discourses are offered in a provocative form, legitimated in the name of art, could the painstaking ethnography following our second-act provocation generate more reflexive engagement than the original research generated?

Why a Designed/Art Intervention

Luke and I have collaborated on several projects with George that were intended as adjacencies to ongoing research. These are what George has called para-sites (2000) and what we together have come to refer to as productive encounters (Cantarella et al. 2015; Hegel et al. 2019). These projects rely on design-based processes and entail collaboration between researchers and designers and other creative makers who play roles in conceptualizing, prototyping, and implementing projects, anchored, and in some relation to, ongoing or reference-specific ethnographic research. While our projects take various forms, in the case of *Trade Is Sublime* we focused on an intervention in the form of an aesthetic proposition. Why an art intervention, and in particular why an art intervention in the form of proposals for a monument to trade? George sensed that a "second-act" project at the WTO should take an aesthetic form in large part because the CWR had recently undergone a major renovation. Older murals, from when the building housed the International Labor Organization (ILO), had been unearthed and now graced the hallways. Additionally, George witnessed the enthusiasm of those in the Office of the Director-General for expanding the presence of art at the CWR in a general remodeling project that was transforming the gloomy, dark halls of the CWR.[4] Although works of art were becoming more present at the WTO, delegates and those in the secretariat seemed not to be paying much attention. Art was in view as part of the internal politics of remaking the institution for the future, yet it was simultaneously insignificant or external to the modes of discourse that had real stakes in that context.[5] Art, then, appeared to be an exciting space in which to intervene. In this medium, our experiment could be a provocation hiding in plain sight.

Although, as Schneider and Wright have noted, anthropology has suffered from an anti-aesthetic sensibility and even "iconophobia" (2010, 2), experimental work emerging in the space between anthropology and art in recent years has contributed to eroding that phobia. Unlike anthropologists working in the vein of socially engaged art (cf. Lippard 2010), collaborating with artists in a field site (Feld 2010) or using art making as a way to integrate affective and analytic registers (Ossman 2010), we were placing a new art piece into the terrain of an institutional art collection on a hunch that this gesture could provoke forms of reflective comment within the institution, and perhaps even restart fieldwork conversations by broadening the range of possible questions. Indeed, this was a primary purpose of Jae Chung in the project. One of the most accomplished ethnographers of the earlier research at the WTO, Jae saw our installation as embedding the means to ask questions that may have been difficult to articulate earlier, and might have remained so without this kind of provocation.

In developing the concept and design of the piece, we had a series of extended conversations by email and Skype with George and Jae about their field research, in which they ruminated on leftover questions, parts of the data that felt underexamined or unresolved, barriers to access within the institution, and so forth. These conversations eventually led us to a broad concept for an art installation and we settled on designing a series of proposals for a monument to trade. We were interested in the monumental because it allowed a way of stepping back from the WTO as a complex and embattled institution and of thinking symbolically about its ideals and hopes. We researched other monuments to trade, including the monuments to Peace and Justice that frame the entrance of the CWR, monuments at stock exchanges and trade commissions around the world, and monuments to shuttle traders in Russia. George was particularly interested in incorporating performance into the piece, which prompted us to think about performances that are meant to monumentalize. Annual performance rituals (feast day parades, pageant plays, graduation ceremonies) serve as cultural anchors to reify community values. George and Jae were curious about the fact that the WTO seemed to lack distinct community practices. Grand-scale multimedia performances, such as the halftime show at the Superbowl or opening ceremonies of the Olympic Games, were among our reference points as rituals that operate at the national and supranational level to monumentalize both an event and an entity. However, nothing so dramatic or communal would seem to fit within the formal, bureaucratic confines of the CWR.

Instead, we concurred that the piece should be framed as a series of proposals because they are inherently conditional; they suggest potential futures, provoke imagining, and invite a response. They also represent the form of communicative overture in which the WTO trades. By offering choices or options, an audience is incentivized to weigh in. In the world of architecture or urban planning, it is typical to request proposals for designs that may be subjected to public comment before a finalist is selected. We envisioned the delegates and secretariat as not merely an audience for this art piece but as a kind of selection committee charged with determining which proposal best exemplified the WTO in its current or future (possible) incarnation. It was also at this point in the development process that we decided to incorporate materials produced by the WTO about itself, and specifically, a brochure articulating ten key aims and principles of the organization. This brochure, produced by the publications department at the organization, asserts that the organization is an infrastructure in which "everyone has to follow the same rules" and "no decision is taken until everyone agrees," and is committed to policies and practices that "allow trade to flow more freely."

The precise design and how to implement it developed quickly from this point, with the three assertions just mentioned serving as the framework for the piece. We were interested in collaborators who had no stake in making a particular political statement for or against the institution. We thought of the piece as neither *for* the WTO, as if they commissioned it, nor *against* the WTO, as a piece of oppositional art. Having considered performance traditions related to the monumental spectacles referenced earlier, we determined that contact improvisation would be particularly generative for our purposes. Contact improvisation grew out of choreographic traditions in modern dance in which practitioners perceive movement as a field of open signifiers. At its core, contact improvisation is negotiated physical practice; the ascription of meaning, from the smallest gesture to a complete piece, is left to the audience. For contact improvisers, there is no external subject that movement illuminates; bodies are subject to gravity, movement choices are intersubjective and emerge under the conditions of the moment, and the making of the dance is the *subject* of the dance. On some level, this is similar to the "negotiated practice" of cowriting that Tsing describes. As a creative practice, the goal is a kind of flow state in which conflict and harmony co-occur.

To bring improvisational performances to the CWR as proposals for a monument, they would need to be captured on film for portability. Each of these creative mediums—contact improvisation and film—entail internal, preexisting collaborative ecologies. Our goal was not to ask dancers or filmmakers to do ethnography with us, or interpret elaborate data sets using their mediums, or cowrite with us. Instead, we were infiltrating these collaborative ecologies for a process of design and implementation that would operate on the terms of these ecologies.

Borrowing the Rules

To produce an adjacency to George and Jae's research that was accountable to the rules of the filmmaking and contact improvisation required translating insights and questions from their ethnographic work into forms that were legible to our collaborators. A translational process is inherent in work across disciplines, and in our case, the process was facilitated by Luke's expertise as a designer and Christine's background as a performer. These knowledge sets helped us transform the ethnography into languages and workable forms that would be legible to dancers and designers. Our translational work included developing two types of documents—a structure and a score—that could instigate creative decision making for the design team and the dancers.

Designers are comfortable working in information-poor environments. A design, whether the medium is scenic design, graphic design, product design, or any other medium, can begin with suppositions and propositions around a loose concept. In our case, we created renderings of a version of the installation based on conversations with George and Jae before bringing other collaborators onboard. Armed with this first-draft concept, Luke made a site visit to Geneva to survey potential venues at the CWR for the installation and to identify logistical issues regarding the project. His interactions with high-level members of the secretariat as well as with workers in the building maintenance department during the survey were also influential in our thinking about the politics of the installation and informed our aesthetic choices as well as our approach to solving logistical problems.

These initial design renderings also operated as an aesthetic sounding device for the production design of the films, relaying partial information to be edited and clarified. Key visual elements of the CWR—long, white-and-gray hallways; clean, polished surfaces; orderly rows of open doors—would eventually be referenced in the production design. We had decided that the installation would contain three films, each linked to one of the three assertions about the WTO.[6]

After the drawings of the production design were complete, we generated a chart that we referred to as the structure of the three films, which outlined the distinct types of physical actions and tonal quality, or "beauty language," for each. To return to the idea of translation as part of collaboration: the structure was a translational medium that bridged our anthropological curiosities, articulated as values and attributes of institutional culture and filmmaking. We presented it as a storyboard, on which narrative filmmaking typically relies, yet comprising an assemblage of words that juxtaposed stylistic references with ethnographic observations. In preproduction meetings, we relied on this structure to further develop visual and audio ideas with our designers and the director of photography (cinematographer). The structure (figure 3.1) was the key text for the designers, with whom we shared little of George and Jae's ethnographic data or writing about the WTO.

While designers can work from generalized or categorical information, dancers rely on more detailed instructions often organized in a score, a form of dance writing "usually relating to physical, bodily or movement notions, rather than being narrative or psychological" (Millard 2016). As such, the score was a second

Action	Frame	Actors	Beauty language	"Rule"
Exchange transfer leaderless coordinated ideal cooperative following	A harmonious enclave	2 (at a time) [in/out of space]	Minimalist formal pattern-making geometrical "fase" - de keersmaeker jeff wall	Everyone has to follow the same rules
Exchange thrashing negotiation "peacocking" seeking consensus	The box interrupted	4	Surreal subjective skin performative Crewdson	No decision is taken until everyone agrees
Gliding flowing currents nature processes	The open sea	None	Natural organic 'goldsworthy'	Allow trade to flow more freely

FIGURE 3.1.   Structure: *Trade Is Sublime* (2013)

translational document that was intended to allow us to infiltrate contact improvisation on its terms. The score included prompts in the form of rules and action statements that are typical in improvisation to build movement phrases. At the same time, these prompts related back to our anthropological queries about the WTO as an institution, including the culture of the secretariat and processes involving delegates. Therefore, the score prompted the exchange of commodities (in this case, boxes filled with sand as trade objects that the dancers would circulate), designated rules and procedures, and suggested the tensions inherent in reaching consensus. The score contained prompts like this:

> Objective: Establish order.
>> Rule #1: Only two traders in the Interior space at one time.
>> Rule #2: Everyone must follow.
> Objective: Exchange commodities one at a time.
>> Rules #1 & #2 still apply
>> Rule #3: Sand must remain in the box (avoid spilling)
>> Rule #4: One gesture is established to be used consistently (throughout all segments) to indicate that an exchange is complete.

For designers, rules take the form of specifications that guide their work and limit deviations, accidents, or mistakes. Specifications derive from conversations with the director, from the limitations of the physical space, and from the design concept; they have an internal logic and entail both creative and practical elements of a design process. By contrast, contact improvisation relies on rules, often arbitrary, to embed constraints into a piece that disrupt their normative impulses. The effort to negotiate challenges, and attention to and use of failure, are integral to the performance material.

Moments of Fascination

Over the course of two days on set, we produced more than ten hours of footage, which we would ultimately distill down to two three-minute films. Jae was unable to be in New York for the filming, but George was on set both days with Luke and me and the entire team. The first day we shot *Everyone Has to Follow the Same Rules*, moving the next day to *No Decision Is Taken Until Everyone Agrees*. Given the evolving nature of our process, we decided halfway through the second day that the third film, *Allow Trade to Flow More Freely*, would be filmed outside the studio; this was both a logistical necessity because we were short on time, and a rethinking of the film's structure and score.[7]

For our two filming days on set, there was no storyboard, script, or even rehearsal per se, only the design structure and the dance score and ongoing discussions about various ways to interpret these documents. What unfolded was a highly responsive and intersubjective process that rarely pointed back to the ethnographic data in any direct way; Luke, George and I increasingly ceded creative authority to the team. The film crew worked through the structure we had given them by setting up shots; when the director of photography (DP) began shooting a take, the performers worked and reworked through corresponding prompts in the score. The sound designer selected scratch music to play, building a series of increasingly complex sonic fields in response to the movement the dancers were creating and to which, in turn, they responded physically.[8] The lighting designer operated in a similar vein, laying out color fields for each take that evoked a mood and delineated areas of action and then reacting to the movement improvisation by varying lighting cues within takes and for subsequent segments.[9] The DP and his two additional camerapersons moved around and over the set, at one point filming from a suspended camera above the stage and at other times capturing footage from the sides or in slow front dolly shots (see figures 3.2 through 3.6).

The shoot was dialogic and improvisatory, and creative decisions were emerging as a form of collective hunchwork between the dancers and the film crew. Both the film crew and the dancers were developing a formal aesthetic language that generated an internal feedback loop and making decisions inspired by, but

FIGURE 3.2.   Preparing the stage for a shot

FIGURE 3.3. DP Rodin Hamidi working with the dancers on spacing

FIGURE 3.4. Shooting footage for "No Decision Is Taken Unless Everyone Agrees"

FIGURE 3.5. Dancers holding a position while the next shot is set

FIGURE 3.6. Dancer Jesse Zarritt exiting the stage

not tethered to, the frameworks we provided. By day two of the shoot we were shifting into shooting footage that evoked increasing levels of tension, disagreement, and possible chaos. This set of conditions yielded what we have come to call "moments of fascination" for us and George, and there are three such moments from the filming of "No Decision is Taken Unless Everyone Agrees" worth examining. The first was a captivating take focused mainly on one dancer, Kayvon Pourazar. Staring intently into and then away from the camera, barefoot and dressed in a disheveled suit, Kayvon barely moved as he rotated a small box around his body, forcing other dancers away. His gestures, focused and uncompromising, illuminated tensions posed by the film: How do people truly negotiate? How does a body of individuals make consensus-based decisions? How do they resist the pressure to do so? Kayvon harnessed the tangled complexity of these questions, embodying them before the camera. In conjunction with this series of gestures that pointed (in our reading) toward the anxieties around trade, Kayvon also generated a movement series that evoked a kind of organizational ennui; his hands seemed to bring to life a cup of coffee, slowly stirred, and his eyes conveyed some combination of submission, inertia, and resignation. Kayvon was not privy to the ethnographic findings of Jae and George and was generating movement passages based on the score and in response to the aesthetic choices of the design team. What was emerging, unexpectedly, was a rendering of the very observations Jae and George had made in the field. Kayvon's embodiment provoked a kind of reckoning with the profoundly human interiority of this institution.

Another moment of fascination was a series of takes in which two of the dancers responded to the prompt "One trader must break away from established rules and make a distinct performance ('peacocking')." The dancers, Jesse Zarritt and Nami Yamamoto, stood in piles of mulch that seemed to bind their feet in place and took turns holding forth in expressive, spasmodic solos. There was a wildness to their movement, guided by pulsating music, but also a sense of unwanted constraint; the two dancers had tacitly determined to contain themselves to a designated spot. The "peacocking" prompt was based on an observation made by Jae that WTO delegates from less powerful countries would periodically stand and pontificate during committee meetings and, in her words, "peacock." Her interpretation of these moments was a provocative rejoinder to the WTO's assertion that "No Decision Is Taken Until Everyone Agrees" because it highlighted the relatively weak position of these members; a delegate might be fully aware that his perspective would not sway a committee vote yet would use his speaking rights as a member to speak out against historical and current injustices against his country. As we watched the dancers' embodied interpretation of this ethnographic observation, we found it immediately odd and funny—the notion that delegates might stand and flail in this way was delightfully preposterous. At the same time, these movement pieces had a sense of raw urgency and profound complaint that we found riveting. What could this suggest about the formal rule-bound processes for negotiating and creating consensus at the WTO—what forms of silencing did they engender, and how did the silencing systematically embed itself in particular bodies? On the other hand, what would it look like if an institution like the WTO allowed for such complaint, for such rawness? Could it reckon with uncontained oppositional energy?

As we sat in front of the monitors during these takes, George moved back and forth between the present unfolding of the shoot and the past and future of ethnographic encounter, between apprehending the footage and reflecting on questions about the WTO that enframed the entire project. As the performers worked, the DP was attending to whether they were in frame and whether the light was creating interesting shapes; by contrast, George was zeroed in on gestures and noting how they subverted or indexed institutional norms. Some of his commentary filtered outward to the film crew and the dancers. But more importantly, this intermediary form was acting on George in the moment, fomenting new questions and making submerged insights evident.

Another moment of fascination illustrates the tangential analytic capacity of this collaboration. At the start of the day, we had to decide how to transform the set (consisting of three adjacent light-colored walls and a glossy white floor) to set the tone for the second film. One idea that Luke floated was to film around the perimeter of the set; in other words, to set the performance around the back of the set rather than on it. Another idea that we began to play around with was "exploding" the tightly contained interior; breaking the walls apart to create dark shadowy spaces between them. This design quandary set up a series of considerations relating back to how we might visualize and materialize our institutional subject. If we were suggesting that the interior of the set was the WTO itself, and we positioned the performance external to the set, would that evoke bilateral trade deals that occur outside the purview of the organization? If so, would it raise questions for viewers about how bilateralism weakens the institution? Or questions about how the institution seeks to incorporate bilateral trade relations into its mission? If we ruptured the interior to allow for murky zones of entry and exit, would that highlight some of the very ruptures and dim interstitial zones currently straining the cohesion of the organization? The design problems were an avenue for asking different questions about the ethnographic subject. One could argue that contact improvisation (and the filming thereof) is a clumsy tool for social analysis; for us, this clumsiness was vital to its ability to create moments of fascination, exposing things that rested deep in the seams and far out on the margins of the ethnographic frame.

Reflection

Because *Trade Is Sublime* would be installed at the WTO to engage the secretariat and delegates in a discussion about the present and future of the institution, George was particularly attuned to the recognizability and resonance of the finished piece. Hence, the footage, both during the filming and later in the editing room, was another kind of sounding board. As Holmes (2013) has suggested, ethnography is an exercise in finding alignment between our anthropological curiosities and the curiosities of the communities we study. As we edited, George, Luke, and I focused on compositional questions as well as on how the piece might align with the concerns and understandings of those in the institutional community. Did the moment of "peacocking," for instance, go too far in its sense of uncontrolled fury? Or was there something in that gestural language that would be readable to delegates—would it be recognizable to them as a form of their frustration at inequity among nations at an institution that claimed that all member states had an equal say in decision making? Would the highly formal tone of the first film resonate with a generalized sense of alienation among the secretariat?

Later, when the piece was on exhibit and George and Jae were reconnecting with their interlocutors and making new connections, some of these questions were indeed answered. There isn't room here to thoroughly examine this aspect of the piece as a "conversation object" (Kester 2013) placed provocatively in the field. But *Trade Is Sublime* provoked varied responses among the inner public of the institution, perhaps in large part because the exhibition was held in the tense final weeks before a shift in leadership, as Director-General Pascal Lamy was preparing to leave and Roberto Azevêdo was appointed to lead the WTO. As the films took on a life of their own, offering up images that we could not have predicted, they carved out a space for analysis through a highly metaphoric and gestural language. They also provided fodder for doing the kind of empathic work that ethnography involves—a means by which we, and George and Jae in particular, could try to imagine and see into the experience of those for whom it was intended.

In conclusion, holding ourselves accountable to the collaborative ecologies of film and contract improvisation enforced alternate forms of rigor and a commitment to serious play that were both critical for how George and Jae reentangled themselves in existing and new relations at the WTO. We have our forms of rigor in ethnographic research—length of time in the field, linguistic fluency, accurate and extensive field notes, and so on—and processes of vetting that limits dissemination to work deemed valid after peer evaluation. Subjecting ourselves to standards of rigor found in other traditions is a process by which we might reassess our disciplinary understanding of how to cultivate the conditions for good research. For instance, participant observation is a means to tap tacit knowledge through a kind of parallel embodiment. By contrast, participation in the tradition of contact improvisation entails a way of sensing others, seeing and being seen, and negotiating relationality in a direct and physical modality. The way the dancers attuned to one another, the nearness of their experience, highlighted the relative distance of ethnographers from the emergent knowledge of interlocutors. Moreover, filmmaking, even in an improvisational project like ours, entails very particular kinds of rigor. Each component (camera angle, lighting, sound, clothing, and properties, in addition to the action itself) is carefully attended to before each shot; in the editing phase, minuscule variations in the footage are assessed, and the film may be cut and recut multiple times. This is not to say that ethnographers don't pore over their fieldnotes and write and rewrite their analyses, but rather to suggest that leaning into the rigors of filmmaking allowed us to see and care about different things in an ongoing project of social inquiry.

Moreover, the making of *Trade Is Sublime* articulated a space and time not merely for creative thinking but also for serious play. We took the process seriously and operated on a relatively large scale in terms of the investment of time and money in order to hire and work with professionals; the development of three complete films from conceptualization through the design, filming, and editing of the films; the creation of a multimedia art installation by a predetermined deadline; and a two-week exhibition at a major intergovernmental organization. These multiple elements contributed to what we were able to accrue from the project at various points during the production and exhibition. The stakes were high: what we exhibited at the CWR would put the reputation of the prior research, including the efforts of others on the multi-investigator team, on the line. The culminating product of our collaborative work would need to generate shared interpretive interest among the WTO secretariat to such an extent that it would reignite the ethnographic project. The improvised understandings of the dancers (and designers) and the edited representation of their work would need to travel as provocations for new questions and conversations with former contacts from the original WTO research project. Our installation, as a highly visible intrusion into the terrain of the institution, felt risky because neither its precise form nor its reception would be clear until we were months into the project and on-site at the CWR. Jae arrived in Geneva as the installation went live, at which point Luke, George, and I focused on tracking its impact on the institutional community and Jae's second-act research in the field. What George found is that *Trade Is Sublime* worked in subtle ways to illuminate the ethnographic concerns that remained for both of them. At the same time, it elicited new responses that helped them realign their interests with how the WTO had continued to evolve two years after the original research. Although, or perhaps because, we allowed *Trade Is Sublime* to emerge through nonlinear creative collaboration, it produced unexpected resonances that extended the life of the ethnographic project. It also reinvented the field by recentering it around the installation; as an object, it voiced a set of anthropological concerns that actively interpellated informants.

This form of collaboration was intended to open a side door back into a field site and in so doing reconfigure the return to ethnography. It served intermediary roles of lateral analysis during production, but at its core it operated in the tradition of what Kester (2013) has called "conversation pieces," to reinstigate connections, forge new dialogic opportunities, and elicit responses in various forms in the site. Whether and how *Trade Is Sublime* would achieve that was interlaced with each creative and logistical decision. Importantly, the development and making of the piece, as well as its integration into the field site, were ongoing diagnostic practices through which we tested out suppositions, first in the studio and later in the field. Thinking of the installation as a sounding board made us invest personally in each email, phone call, and conversation with members of the secretariat as we negotiated the terms of its presence. It revealed spaces of bureaucratic flexibility and fortitude, and we saw both alliances and camps that did not align with the formal organizational structure. It allowed Jae and George to see some of the limits of the institutional commitment to transparency. And one afternoon, over coffee with a member of the publications department who had contacted us to discuss the piece, we heard how deeply the cold formality of the first film (*Everyone Has to Follow the Same Rules*) resonated with this man's sense of being simultaneously contained by and disconnected from the institution. The adjacency of *Trade Is Sublime*, and the relatively unfamiliar rules and norms of collaboration to which we adhered in its making, generated plenty of moments of miscommunication and confusion but also spaces of empathy within and toward an unwieldy and increasingly tenuous institution.

NOTES

We are deeply grateful to all our creative collaborators on *Trade Is Sublime*, to the Center for Ethnography in the School of Social Sciences at the University of California, Irvine and the University of California Institute for Research in the Arts (UCIRA) for funding, to George Marcus and Jae Chung for instigating and guiding the project, and to the members of the WTO secretariat who facilitated the installation of the piece at the Centre William Rappard in Geneva.

Some elements of this chapter, including figure 3.6, were previously published in Luke Cantarella, Christine Hegel, and George E. Marcus, *Ethnography by Design: Scenographic Experiments in Fieldwork* (Bloomsbury Press, 2019).

1. The original research aims are detailed by Marc Abélès (2008) at http://www.iiac. cnrs.fr/article1249.html (accessed August 12, 2017).

2. More broadly, Lassiter and others have continued to advocate for approaches to anthropological research that are genuinely collaborative from inception to implementation, taking up questions initiated by and for local populations to address situated issues (aligned with the aims of public anthropology), in lieu of research that originates in the academy for the purpose of scholarly advancement.

3. See, for instance, Brenneis's (2006) astute analysis of how NSF funding forms shape anthropological research.

4. The renovation phases of the WTO are described here: https://www.wto.org/english/ thewto_e/cwr_e/renovation_e.htm. Among the series of artworks that had been commissioned in the months preceding our June 2013 installation were a series of forty abstract paintings of trade routes and a series of paintings in which artists used trade materials (coal, salt, etc.) as a paint medium.

5. We can contrast the inconsequentiality of art in this context to the perception of anthropology as consequential. The previous director-general, Pascal Lamy, invited the anthropologist Marc Abélès to organize the initial study, which can be construed as an effort that recognized the capacity of social science to identify submerged and potentially tenuous facets of institutional culture at the WTO. In fact, Marcus has noted, the directness of this effort may have impeded the researchers' ability to penetrate the discrete and codified world of the organization (Marcus 2016).

6. The work of the choreographer Anna Teresa de Keersmaeker and the photographer Gregory Crewdson was particularly influential as we developed our thinking about how to filter institutional monumentalizing language through movement and film.

7. This film was shot on location on the Long Island Sound and the Quinnipiac River. Rather than using contact improvisation to embody the notion of free-flowing trade, we collected footage of the same exchange objects (white boxes filled with sand) flowing with the currents and tides on these waterways.

8. Scratch music refers to temporary soundtracks used during filming that set a tone or rhythm to guide the direction, which are replaced with alternate compositions in the editing phase.

9. The costume designer's work was less improvisational, although she made minor stylistic changes for the second film in response to the aesthetic and tonal shift in that film.

REFERENCES

Abélès, Marc, ed. 2011. *Des anthropologues à l'OMC: Scènes de la Gouverance Mondiale.* Paris: CNRS Press.

———. 2008. "Anthropology of the World Trade Organization." Institut Interdisciplinaire d'Anthropologie du Contemporain website. http://www.iiac. cnrs.fr/article1249.html.

Albright, Ann Cooper, and David Gere. 2003. *Taken by Surprise: A Dance Improvisation Reader.* Middletown, CT: Wesleyan University Press.

Brenneis, Don. 2006. "Reforming Promise." In *Documents: Artifacts of Modern Knowledge,* edited by Annelise Riles, 41–70. Ann Arbor: University of Michigan Press.

Cantarella, Luke, Christine Hegel, and George E. Marcus. 2015. "A Week in Pasadena: Collaborations toward a Design Modality for Ethnographic Research." *Field: The Journal of Socially-Engaged Art Criticism* 1 (Spring): 53–94. http://field-journal.com/issue-1/cantarella-hegel-marcus.

Feld, Steven. 2010. "Collaborative Migrations: Contemporary Art in/as Anthropology." In Schneider and Wright, *Between Art and Anthropology,* 109–26.

Fortun, Kim. 2004. "From Bhopal to the Informating of Environmentalism: Risk Communication in Historical Perspective." *Osiris* 19:283–96. http://www.jstor. org.wcsu.idm.oclc.org/stable/3655245.

Gunn, Wendy, Ton Otto, and Rachel Charlotte Smith, eds. 2013. *Design Anthropology: Theory and Practice.* London: Bloomsbury Press.

Hegel, Christine, Luke Cantarella, and George E. Marcus. 2019. *Ethnography-by-Design: Scenographic Experiments in Fieldwork.* London: Bloomsbury Press.

Holmes, Douglas. 2013. *Economy of Words: Communicative Imperatives in Central Banks.* Chicago: University of Chicago Press.

Kester, Grant H. 2013. *Conversation Pieces: Community and Communication in Modern Art.* Berkeley: University of California Press.

Lassiter, Luke Eric. 2001. "From 'Reading over the Shoulders of Natives' to 'Reading alongside Natives,' Literally: Toward a Collaborative and Reciprocal Ethnography." *Journal of Anthropological Research* 57 (2): 137–49. http://www. jstor.org.wcsu.idm.oclc.org/stable/3631564.

Lippard, Lucy R. 2010. "Farther Afield." In Schneider and Wright, *Between Art and Anthropology,* 23–34.

Marcus, George E. 2000. Introduction to *Para-Sites: A Casebook against Cynical Reason,* edited by George E. Marcus, 1–102. Late Editions: Cultural Studies for the End of the Century, vol. 7. 2nd ed. Chicago: University of Chicago Press.

———. 2016. "A Chronicle of Art (and Anthropology) at the World Trade Organization . . . in Five Not-So-Easy Pieces." *Field: The Journal of Socially-Engaged Art Criticism* 3 (Winter): 39–71.

Matsutake Worlds Research Group. 2009. "A New Form of Collaboration in Cultural Anthropology: Matsutake Worlds." *American Ethnologist* 36 (2): 380–403. http:// www.jstor.org.wcsu.idm.oclc.org/stable/27667568.

Maurer, William. 2005. *Mutual Life, Limited: Islamic Banking, Alternative Currencies, Lateral Reason.* Princeton, NJ: Princeton University Press.

Millard, Olivia. 2016. "What's the Score? Using Scores in Dance Improvisation." *Brolga: An Australian Journal about Dance* 40:45–56.

Montoya, Michael. 2011. *Making the Mexican Diabetic: Race, Science, and the Genetics of Inequality.* Berkeley: University of California Press.

Novack, Cynthia Jean. 1990. *Sharing the Dance: Contact Improvisation and American Culture.* New Directions in Anthropological Writing. Madison: University of Wisconsin Press.

Ossman, Susan. 2010. "Making Art Ethnography: Painting, War and Ethnographic Practice." In Schneider and Wright, *Between Art and Anthropology,* 127–34.

Rabinow, Paul, George E. Marcus, James D. Faubion, and Tobias Rees. 2008. *Designs for an Anthropology of the Contemporary.* Durham, NC: Duke University Press.

Schneider, Arnd, and Christopher Wright, eds. 2010. *Between Art and Anthropology: Contemporary Ethnographic Practice.* New York: Berg.

4

VARIATIONS IN THE WAYS THAT COLLABORATIONS SURROUND AND EFFECT ETHNOGRAPHIC RESEARCH PROJECTS

Addendum to Chapters 1–3

George E. Marcus

This brief personal account describes, first, two experiences in collaborative projects, one through the 1990s and the other briefly in 2009–10, that have made an impression on me about how ethnographic work builds collaborative contexts these days. Then, I provide a commentary on my part and perspective in collaborations with four others represented by chapters in this volume: with Doug Holmes (with whom I have coauthored an account of our sustained collaborative friendship); with Keith Murphy around trying to introduce a design-influenced pedagogical form that teaches the still largely solitary model of ethnographic research in a collaborative, studio form (what we have called "the ethnocharrette"—a term that seems to have appealed to readers and users); and with Luke Cantarella and Christine Hegel in an atelier model of artistic collaboration across ethnographic projects based on scenic studio design and workshop methods.

Facing the heightened assessments of change brought on by the self-consciousness in the 1990s of a fin-de-siècle, or more grandly, the coming of a new millennium, I proposed to the University of Chicago Press a series of annuals (a form certainly now outdated by new media technologies)—called Late Editions—that would try to document changes by recruiting those with specific ethnographic experience to enter new sites and familiar ones as well as to document change under the sensibility of the fin-de-siècle or millennial grand turning point. The challenge in the 1990s, when critiques of realist forms of representation were current, was not to use documentary voice or description, but rather to experiment with the representation of situated dialogue and voice.

Eight edited volumes, each with a distinctive topic, were produced (Marcus, 1992–2000). There were regular members of the project along with some new ones added each year. The paradigm was for writers to return to sites of expertise and fieldwork, to produce conversations that might be turned into representation-sensitive *entretiens* as a signature form of the series. The key event each year was a collective editorial meeting, based at Rice University, to assess work in the past year and plan new volumes. Cumulatively, these proved to be deep seminars on the nature of dialogics as a documentary form in the framework of fieldwork-like expeditions of inquiry into recent pasts and near futures. The series itself was not a commercial success, though there remains a range of extraordinary documents in dialogic form through the volumes that captures various dimensions of that transition. The collective editorial meetings taught us much about the benefits of sustained collaborative relationships and the imaginaries they created for influencing the way that ethnographers pursue projects of individual research. So the Late Editions experience remains one prominent personal source for thinking about how collaborations, however they emerge or come about in whatever new and emerging media, might influence the expanded possibilities of the classic ethnographic research paradigm after the 1980s.

My second formative experience in collaborations was a brief association with ARC (Anthropology Collaboratory for Research on the Contemporary) at the University of California, Berkeley. By the early 2000s, I had become interested in how those pursuing ethnographic research might relate to those with parallel concerns in arts and design disciplines, whose methods were collaborative in nature (e.g., the studio, the workshop, the stage), and who made things or performed things, and wrote only secondarily or as an enhancement to the former. Specifically, I was interested in collaborations between the habitual loners/owners of ethnographic research and those habitual collaborators who made things, performed, and designed things and spaces. For a while, I joined with Paul Rabinow, who was rethinking the core anthropological research paradigm in related ways (see Rabinow et al. 2009). While I did not participate in the actual work of the ambitious Anthropological Collaboratory for Research on the Contemporary (ARC) that he and his students established at the University of California, Berkeley (see the chapter by Collier, Kelty, and Lakoff, this volume, for an account of an entirely different offshoot of this project), I did participate in some of its formative discussions.

One discussion in particular was significant for me. It had to do with the version of ARC as a lab or atelier model in which the fruit of ethnographic-style research on various topics, done by individual scholars or teams in the world, would be brought back for rich treatment and discussion in the space and resources (e.g., a beautifully designed online platform) that the collaboratory offered for experiment and discussion among those who worked there. But I wondered at that point whether the pull of the worlds investigated might not be greater in centrifugal force, and whether relations of the field might not become intellectually stronger or more powerful in their draw than the collaborative relations of the studio, lab, and medium for scholarly communication that the ARC website created. The ARC should be more than a successful formula for a more worldly seminar. It suggested the means to change media and relations of research. This would require new forms of reception, experiment, and participation in fieldwork-staged collaborations found in the field and organized as performances that would find their way back to the lab, the seminar, the research group in reverse interventions. This tension of collaborations from fieldwork falling into the sites of still individualistic research immersion fascinated me as a productive problem for locating/designing a modality for rethinking the sorts of participations in ethnographic research projects, from fieldwork to reporting them, that the introduction of a notion of the collaboratory might evoke.

I myself have never produced a platform, a studio, or website by which research projects could be defined—and perhaps eventually be challenged—by their diverse centrifugal field investigations in the world. Rather, I have remained interested in how the participations in classic fieldwork projects could be transformed by the interventions of studio/design disciplines through long-term working relationships on shared projects.

So, with these inspirations, I want to briefly represent three collaborative projects in which I have been engaged that change the way that ethnographic research projects are typically produced in anthropology. One is with and through the long-term research projects of Douglas Holmes, entangled with a lateral continuous collaborative friendship that we have cultivated (see Holmes and Marcus, this volume). As we recount in the chapter for this workshop volume, ours is a very long-term and consistent project on concept work (beginning in a contribution of his to the first volume of Late Editions on "illicit discourse") that tries to radically rethink the subject of ethnographic research as somehow equivalent to ethnographer/anthropologist. This evocation works particularly well for the sort of research that Doug has been doing for many years. What is transacted conceptually or theoretically in the field is more important than what is transacted in the collective of academic anthropological knowledge making. It requires a strong third source. of authority to pull off this shift toward para-ethnography and make it matter in a sustained way in *the* field. Our collaboration/friendship based on concept work and exploration over a long duration has provided this third space. Whatever critiques of such conceptual inventions might be made in professional reception, there is no doubt that our collaboration on concept work has created opportunity for access where there would otherwise have been none or little. So, simply, ethnographic insight and following through on it is greatly facilitated by, if not requires, the sort of third space, adjacent, sustained friendship/collaboration we have had, the basis of which has been to see anthropological thinking and concern in fairly exotic (for traditional anthropologists, at least) subjects.

A second collaboration has been over recent years with my colleague Keith Murphy, a linguistic anthropologist and performance artist (cf. improv comedy), whose ethnographic expertise is design, design disciplines and practices. We have been interested in how classic ethnographic training could integrate at key points the collaborative methods of design disciplines themselves. When and where in the formation of first projects of ethnographic research would it be stimulating and useful to introduce design/studio methods or workshops? Early on, we came up with an exercise, the ethnocharrette, based on the characteristics of studio production in design training: a rapid, collective production of protoypes emphasizing alternative imaginaries and conditions for already published and largely admired ethnographies; and the imaginative remaking of texts (we found working with produced published ethnographies difficult) to insert into the training of graduate students in their first projects of ethnographic research. It has not been easy to find ways to integrate compressed, studio exercises into the vested habits of thought and imaginaries that students produce under considerable pressure in defining ethnographic research and, most importantly, finding funding for it. We have been more successful in introducing ethnocharrette sessions as finales to seminars that involve reading and thinking through a variety of classic and very contemporary ethnographic texts. Currently, we are thinking that the best moment of intervention of the ethnocharrette as a creative, studio remaking of the ethnographic project, is in the postdoctoral period, when most initial ethnographic projects are considerably rethought, researched anew, and remade. It is perhaps an ideal experimental moment of collaborative remaking of the first ethnographic project. We'll see.

My collaborative work with Murphy has been, for me, a second personal modality of collaborative engagement—this time in the realm of pedagogy. Teaching ethnographic research is in its own milieu primarily mentoring and advising, and it is therapeutic. These practices are formidable in their influence on and shaping of individual projects of dissertation research. Any alternative must define a pedagogical niche, equally powerful, where collaborative invention enters the making of ethnography perhaps most cogently thought through the existing workshop/studio models developed in a variety of design disciplines. Murphy's chapter expertly considers the costs and benefits of moving basic anthropological training pedagogy in this direction.

Finally, a third mode of collaboration in which I have been involved is a relationship with the anthropologist/artist Christine Hegel and Luke Cantarella, a scenic designer/scenographer, formerly at the University of California, Irvine, and now in the theater department at Pace University. Over the past five years, we have been engaged together in a series of projects that concern the intervention of scenic-design thinking and imaginaries in ethnographic projects in various stages of development. See the website productiveencounters.com, and Cantarella, Hegel, and Marcus (2019) for a presentation of the projects on which we have worked. What we have attempted is perhaps the ideal model of how a collaboration—its own going concern—might insert itself into ethnographic work.

While our projects have been opportunistic to some degree, they have also provided a cumulative opportunity to define the relationship of collaboration, with an independent logic and trajectory toward ethnography in a systematic way. We have produced a book, *Ethnography by Design* (Cantarella, Hegel, and Marcus 2019), detailing how a particular design discipline—scenography as a discipline of theater—changes or provides a space of experiment within the relations of ethnography, across a number of projects unified only by the fact that we have taken them up successively and opportunistically as a team interested in the aesthetics of working design productions into settings of potential or ongoing ethnographic investigation. What we are trying to create are sources of substantive reception within the field of ethnographic research that risk the way the participant observer/marginal native doctrine of being in the field is conceived. What particularly fascinates me is the atelier context or effect on ethnographic thinking and imagination as our project experiences accumulate. The range of cumulative thinking in project experience becomes the most important source of ideas as new projects emerge or previous ones are rethought. It is this cumulative and serendipitous experience of collectively thinking new projects and rethinking older ones that is distinctive of a collaborative such as ours, as we conceive our "going concern" as it is inserted into, or gives rise to, the spaces of conventional ethnographic research. Circulations and iterations of an intervention designed for a particular project that begins as conventional ethnography are the most generative elements of this kind of collaboration. Such a designed intervention works with ethnographic expertise earned through participant observation and adds dimensions by multiplying strategically the relevant publics for ethnographic insights that always arise in a quite located way in relation to classic values of immersion, observation, and site-specific duration.

For this workshop volume, Hegel and Cantarella have written an account of our most important project. Following a three-year (2008–10) team ethnographic project (of which I was a member), on the bureaucracy that runs the World Trade Organization, I proposed to the director-general to produce a "second act" as an art/anthropology installation. The idea was accepted. Already having worked with Luke and Christine on one project in Orange County, California, I suggested we work together on an installation in the villa that houses the headquarters of the WTO. A partial account of our collaboration on this was published in the online journal *FIELD* (Cantarella, Hegel, and Marcus 2015). The responses to what we did were varied and complex—including puzzlement and some hostility by the bureaucrats who run the WTO (of course, they had earlier exhibited the same orientation toward ethnographers who were loose among them for a while), but elicited fascinated interest from members of trade delegations who passed by our installation. Accompanying us for the two weeks of the installation in 2013 was perhaps the most gifted and informed of the ethnographers from the original project, Dr. Jae Chung. Our sojourn at the WTO was Chung's opportunity to return to the field, renew previous relationships, and ask questions that perhaps were not so easy to ask or to be accepted the first time around (in 2010). Brilliantly reported and described by Hegel and Cantarella in this volume, the installation provided the context and opportunity to allow the experienced ethnographer to deepen engaged perspective and inquiry. For the experienced ethnographer, it provided the medium to pose an additional object of curiosity in the material environment of fieldwork, amid established relations and discovered newer ones. We might say that the value added to the return to the field of the most gifted ethnographer of the original project defined the value of our work to ethnography, quite aside from the usual hopes for how an installation might be diversely responded to by those who observe it.

For me, the most thrilling and intellectually challenging moment in this collaboration was the actual production of a score, composed by Christine and Luke, for contact improv dancers on the principles of trade (and what escapes them) as the organizing ideology of the WTO itself, one of the key post–World War II international organizations. Because of limited funding, this score was produced in a studio at Pace University in New York City on one Saturday, a few months before the actual installation at the villa headquarters of the WTO in Geneva, which Luke had carefully scouted out. There were three scenarios to the score, produced at Pace. The key element to me was how the insights of ethnography— as speculations, hypotheses, or provocations—were embedded in this studio making such that what was an artistic production would also be recognized as having ethnographic dimension by the denizens of the WTO when they saw it. Was there effective recognition and provocation built into the studio—enclosed in the faraway making of our intervention? The answer is yes and no—we had what I would say was a mixed result. While we produced clearly beautiful scenarios, the triggers built into them were not obvious in a way that ethnography perhaps has to be to attract an internal public at the site of previous research. What saved the project in this regard during the period of installation was the fact that it was occurring as a strange body in the WTO politic, copresent with the complicit continuation of the able return of standard ethnographic interview and observation by Dr. Chung.

In their chapter, Christine and Luke deal, in detail, with the making of the scores, under the title for them of *Trade Is Sublime*—which turned out to have been a provocative, and for some, a puzzling theme for the scenarios that dealt with the rules of trade as well as with trade's independence of the WTO moving like a force of nature. What impressed me was the level of collaboration and the improvisational creativity that the actual production of the scores as a work of theater art exhibited in its making. I found observing it absolutely thrilling. Reception at the highly political shrine to bureaucratic rationality that the WTO is was frankly, for me, a letdown. Did the installation once moved to the WTO and made available on screens create an internal public for what the earlier ethnography produced among its subjects? That requires a complex response, worth an essay in itself. But, in my view, it is the sort of essay or report as ethnography, or second-order ethnography, that this project should produce. And it would be a work of anthropological scholarship based on different principles expected of standard ethnographic reporting and insight. Here, collaborative strategies would redefine the forms of what counts as knowledge that would come from ethnographic inquiry—that were discussed in our Irvine workshop as, I believe, its primary contribution. Passing earlier ethnographic insight and argument— itself produced through an unusual team ethnography through the kind of glorious (to me) collaboration that produces performance—and then back again to the scene of ethnography where both performative installation and the best remnant of the earlier ethnography is at play, is a kind of lab for understanding the differential impact of the effects of collaborative practices in a very difficult space to operate either as art or anthropology.

REFERENCES

Cantarella, Luke, Christine Hegel, and George E. Marcus. 2015. "A Week in Pasadena: Collaborations toward a Design Modality for Ethnographic Research." *FIELD: A Journal of Socially Engaged Art Criticism* 1 (1). http://field-journal.com/issue-1/cantarella-hegel-marcus.

———. 2019. *Ethnography by Design:Scenographic Experiments in Fieldwork*. London: Bloomsbury

Marcus, George E., ed. 1992–2000. Late Editions: Cultural Studies for the End of the Century series (vol. 1, *Perilous States*; vol. 2, *Technoscientific Imaginaries*; vol. 3, *Connected*; vol. 4, *Cultural Producers in Perilous States*; vol. 5, *Corporate Futures*; vol. 6, *Paranoia within Reason*; vol. 7, *Para-Sites*; vol. 8, *Zeroing in on the Year 2000*). Chicago: University of Chicago Press.

Rabinow, Paul, George Marcus, James Faubion, and Tobias Rees. 2009. *Toward an Anthropology of the Contemporary*. Durham, NC: Duke University Press.

5

FUNCTION AND FORM

The *Ethnographic Terminalia* Collective
between Art and Anthropology

The *Ethnographic Terminalia* Collective

Trudi Lynn Smith, Kate Hennessy, Stephanie Takaragawa,
Fiona P. McDonald, and Craig Campbell

Since 2009, the *Ethnographic Terminalia* Collective (ETC) has staged projects in North American cities (Minneapolis, Denver, Vancouver, Chicago, New York, San Francisco, Montréal, New Orleans, Philadelphia, and Washington, DC) that explore intersections between art and anthropology. Much of our work has been manifest in the organization and curation of exhibits alongside the annual meetings of the American Anthropological Association (AAA), and has been inspired by emergent interdisciplinary art practices (Schneider and Wright 2010). Our projects have been "para-sites" (Marcus 1998) used to draw anthropologists from the conference venue into arts and cultural spaces in local host cities—a tactic designed to create multidirectional public conversation within local communities. To date, we have worked with over 150 artists and anthropologists in public art galleries, project spaces, artist-run centers, museums, and commercial galleries to build exhibits that generate creative critiques of ethnographic research and representation and create public conversation. Through this work, we have fostered dialogue around the roles and responsibilities of anthropologists, curators, and artists who exhibit and produce culture in multiple media including new media, sound, photography, drawing, painting, performance, installation, sculpture, and film.

Our curatorial mode builds upon critique that argues for the potential of a more experimental anthropology that activates creative practice (Grimshaw and Ravetz 2005; Schneider and Wright 2006, 2010, 2013; Smith 2014; Taussig 2011). At the core of this experimental curatorial model, we find ourselves engaged with multiple modes of collaboration. Over ten years of working together, we

FIGURE 5.1. *Ethnographic Terminalia*, Denver, 2015. Aeolian Politics. Installation View. Emmanuel Gallery, Denver. Photo by Trudi Lynn Smith.

have collaborated with one another by negotiating responsibilities, ideas, and our interpersonal relationships. In addition to the nuanced collaborations within our collective, we have collaborated with artists, anthropologists, curators, and institutions. This has enabled us to create and install projects that engage disciplinary discourses and that explore new forms of knowledge dissemination to reach audiences and wider publics beyond the discipline of anthropology. Our curatorial project came into being, and has been sustained, through these endless but mutually inspiring negotiations and the tangible evidence of collaboration in practice. The ways in which our collective functions and dysfunctions has found expression in multiple forms.

More broadly, we have worked to expand our curatorial practice beyond the metaphor of border zones to theorize the way that exhibition can be a disruptive encounter (De Angelis et al. 2015), one that offers alternative interpretive tools and knowledge (Centre for Imaginative Ethnography 2015). The rise in curatorial projects that bring art and anthropology together has pushed us to identify an urgent need to address curatorial experiments: How is anthropology served by curation? How has collaboration in this space driven creativity and experimentation with form and content? Through our collective practice, intersecting with contemporary art worlds and the anthropological community, we join Tarek Elhaik (2015) in asking, How does collaborative work in art and anthropology point us toward, and provide a setting for, new forms of curation yet to be imagined?

In 2016, as the *Ethnographic Terminalia* Collective, who are the equal authors of this chapter, (Trudi Lynn Smith, Kate Hennessy, Fiona P. McDonald, Stephanie Takaragawa, and Craig Campbell), we drafted a statement defining our collective work in this way:

> The *Ethnographic Terminalia* Collective (ETC) is a leaderless coopera-
> tive. We make decisions on a consensus basis and attempt to share duties
> and obligations equally. Where possible we curate, write, and make
> things together. While we each maintain individual research, art, and
> curatorial programs, the ETC aims to operate with a collective voice.
> (*Ethnographic Terminalia* Collective Statement)

Getting to this statement took us years of collaboration to define how we would work among ourselves and with artists and anthropologists (Mol 2010). In this chapter, we present some examples of the collaborations we have created, their expressions in art and exhibition as well as in the collective practices of knowl-edge making and communication. We start with our beginnings in order to high-light some challenges encountered along the way. We suggest that embracing the challenge of creative collaboration, and all the work it entails, has pushed us outside of convention and forced us to repeatedly reinvent our process.

Beginnings

The *Ethnographic Terminalia* Collective came to life in a small bar in downtown San Francisco in 2008, during the annual meeting of the American Anthropo-logical Association. Stephanie Takaragawa, Kate Hennessy, Craig Campbell, and Adam Fish (then graduate students) drank beer, ate popcorn, listened to Led Zeppelin, and wondered how the experimental works that they were engaged in producing could ever find a place within the conventions (literally and other-wise) of anthropological presentation. The idea of finding a space outside of the annual meeting of the American Anthropological Association (AAA) was raised.

The first exhibition was held the next year in Philadelphia at Crane Arts. It was curated by Craig Campbell and Fiona P. McDonald, with Anabelle Rodri-guez of Temple University, and co-organized by Stephanie Takaragawa and Kate Hennessy. The exhibition featured the work of seventeen artists, including Trudi Lynn Smith, who was invited to join the curatorial group going forward. In this first curatorial effort, we described the exhibitors as an "ad hoc international group of ethnographers, anthropologists, and artists," the goal being to disrupt

expectations for anthropological projects and celebrate work that defied classifi-
cation. The Ice Box Gallery at Crane Arts was an impressive industrial white cube
space that was provided to us for one month at no cost. Over the course of the
exhibition, we were surprised by the number of people who left the familiar territory of the AAA convention center and crossed the city to attend our opening
event. Their enthusiastic response to our exhibition was profoundly encouraging.
We learned that there was both a desire and an expectation from participants and
visitors for us as a newly formed collective to continue our unique experiment.

The notion of a formal collective emerged as we came together to initiate
our 2010 exhibition in New Orleans. We struggled to define roles and responsibilities, and productive ways of communicating and working together across
distance and time zones (at that time, Canada, the United States, and the United
Kingdom). While we had all engaged in forms of collaborative anthropological
practices in our graduate work and early professional careers at that time, and
had been directly inspired by George Marcus's notion of the "para-site," we did
not primarily draw references for collective work from anthropology, where a
single-author model dominated, and collaboration with community and alternative forms of knowledge sharing was undervalued and poorly documented
(or underrepresented). Building on our collective experience and training, we
looked instead to art history and models of collaboration in art making as well

FIGURE 5.2. *Ethnographic Terminalia*, Philadelphia, 2009. Ice Box Gallery,
Crane Arts, Philadelphia. Photo by Fiona P. McDonald.

FIGURE 5.3. *Ethnographic Terminalia*, New Orleans, 2010. Installation view of Candy Chang's *I Wish This Was*, which was launched in the ET2010 exhibition. Photo by Fiona P. McDonald.

as the strong discourse that existed around curation more generally. We also just fumbled forward, negotiating and developing in search of something that felt right.

Seeing Collaboration

Collaboration is more common between artists—a practice of distributed authorship and actions. These are long-standing practices, from medieval guilds to the work of the Guerrilla Girls. In our present moment (2020), a thriving mix of collaborative and collective approaches are circulating global contemporary art worlds such as those seen in the recent work of Superflex, Postcommodity, Ladies Invitational Deadbeat Society, and Leisure. These examples are oriented toward activism and social practice that strive to address issues of unpaid labor, underrepresented artists, and feminist art interventions.

Collaboration is also linked to the idea of social dimensions of participation (Bishop 2006). Multiple authorship can be a foundation for collaboration between communities of audiences and the artists and we drew inspiration from a wide variety of art movements that draw on participation. For example, Fluxus encouraged participation of people from outside of art worlds, and art practices by feminists' call for fundamental reorganization of art institutions (Molesworth 2010). It is also important to note that we were all influenced as graduate students by a burgeoning of discussions of practices that emerged in the late 1990s and early 2000s such as "relational aesthetics," process-driven practices, dialogical practice, participatory art, social practice, activism, and more (see Bishop 2006, 2012; Kester 2009, 2011; and Bourriaud 1998, 2002). The art theorist Grant Kester (2011) attributes the present vigor of these arrangements to a "complex and contradictory mixture of cultural and geopolitical forces" of neoliberal capitalism and the rise of fascism on the one hand, and the "triumph of immaterial labour" and the spread of socialism on the other (7). To Kester, the tension between these two futures creates a "profusion of contemporary art practices concerned with collective action and civic engagement" (7). As we show in the examples toward the end of this chapter, these practices in art have set the scene for our collective to create new relationships between artists, anthropologists, and publics.

Ethnographic Terminalia as a project is inspired by experimental events and social structures happening within collaborative art worlds. We are also influenced by visual and multimodal work in anthropology that seeks to address the role of the visual in anthropology (as generative rather than subordinate to textual knowledge production) and changing media ecologies (Collins, Durrington, and Gill 2017) that may challenge disciplinary boundaries (Chin 2017). We draw on the creativity and ideas from anthropology and art and bring them into a distinct, collaborative entity of *Ethnographic Terminalia* projects. It raises the question, of course, of how these arrangements are worked out in practice and how these practices shape our work together.

Function, Form, and the Necessity of Reinvention

Over the years of working together, we have grappled with such questions as Whose curatorial vision is brought to life? Who supports this vision by completing the mundane yet necessary administrative tasks? What is a collective, and who should the members of the collective be, and how is this decided? Who coauthors? Who is a first author? How does an emerging art-anthropology collective bridging creative practice and the merit-economy of the academy find its way to relative success in each? Can I finish my dissertation and do this work off the side of my desk? What kind of job should I try to get? Can I get tenure? With each annual exhibition we were forced to negotiate these questions again and again while facing the inevitability of being human: illnesses, childbirth, complications of family life, relocations, and the precariousness of the academy.

A direct expression of these human and more-than-human relationships was our annual reinvention of what we could collectively achieve. Our work has thus been dependent on access to and possibilities for collaboration with a venue and seeking out the people on the ground who support that venue's functioning; we have worked with—and learned from—artist-run centers, commercial galleries, project spaces, museums, community organizations, conference centers, and a range of public spaces. The spaces available to us and the willingness of gatekeepers in those spaces to be involved have in part determined what is possible to curate.

In addition to the search for appropriate spaces and finances, the tangible outcomes of our collaborations each year—the aesthetic and ethnographic form that our curatorial work has produced—have depended on the availability and initiative taken by individual members of the collective. After some negotiation and reflection on division of labor and creative leadership in the first two years of exhibition, we moved by the third year to a model in which two or three members of the collective would lead that curatorial initiative, supported by the rest of the collective. This would shift each year as individual members or partners proposed new initiatives that they wished to develop. Our projects have included large group exhibitions taking a "cabinet of curiosities" approach (Philadelphia, 2009; New Orleans, 2010); invited "anchor artists" generating a thematic curatorial concept with an open call for submissions (Montréal, 2011; San Francisco, 2012; Washington, DC, 2014); invited projects by collaborating artists and anthropologists (Chicago, 2013); smaller presentations of a single artist in a large institution (New York, 2013); a curatorial design collaboration between the ETC and anthropologists (Denver, 2015); and collaborative, rapid-prototype publication workshops (Vancouver, 2015; and Minneapolis, 2016), and to conclude the curatorial work of the collective work, we organized a group show of invited dynamic, interactive projects (Vancouver). Since 2014, while the rotating division of curatorial and administrative labor persists as a productive model, we have moved away from the "lead curator" model and embraced a process in which all the ETC projects, including this chapter, are credited to the collective as a whole, better reflecting our desire to work as a *leaderless cooperative* with no ranking of authorship.

While the failures within exhibit installations make for good stories (from unrealistic installation plans to technological malfunctions), it is relational failure that is an important (and often underexposed) part of collaborations like *Ethnographic Terminalia*. Consisting of multiple collective members' ideas and labor, the shape of each project is variegated. With that can come disagreement or misunderstandings. The challenge of disagreement, as much as consensus, is central to the process of decision making and advancing an idea. We make use of audio and video conferencing as well as texting and emailing from diverse settings, and time zones, each of us bringing different ideas about what makes good anthropology, art, and exhibition. The failure to agree and related experiences such as the power of miscommunication (Skype glitches, loud cafes, and instant messaging) can be seen as difficult but generative sites of creation.

In the remainder of this chapter, we highlight four examples of curatorial collaboration that the collective has engaged in since 2009. In particular, our projects in Montréal (2011), Chicago (2013), Denver (2015), and Vancouver (2015). We choose these as four examples that demonstrate how curatorial collaboration has functioned, and the forms that these collaborations have produced.

Field, Studio, Lab: Montréal, 2011

In 2011, three of us traveled to the Art Gallery of Ontario (AGO) to witness the Panamanian artist Humberto Vélez's performance piece entitled *The Awakening*, a collaboration with the Mississauga New Credit First Nation and Toronto's Urban Runners parkour artists. The work, commissioned by the Art Gallery of York University and curated by the AGYU assistant director Emelie Chhangur, was developed in a series of residences between 2009 and 2011 that culminated in a performance in which members of the Mississauga New Credit and parkour artists staged an art ceremony that took over the AGO's Walker Court. It was led by Humberto Vélez (see the video here: http://humbertovelez.com/toronto/toronto-slideshow/).

According to the artist's website, "The Awakening is the culmination of a sustained relationship between Humberto and the people of Toronto and surrounding area" (Vélez 2011). While at the AGO, we watched runners rappel off the museum's iconic Frank Gehry architecture, we paused as we smelled sweetgrass smoke filling the space, and we joined in the round dance that concluded the public ceremony. Vélez had recently accepted our invitation to anchor our group exhibition at Montréal's Eastern Bloc Centre for New Media and Interdisciplinary Art, and we were filled with ideas about how his work could inform our curatorial approach for the 2011 ETC exhibition. In addition, we received great support and engagement from Emelie Chhangur whose curatorial work saw Vélez's project into existence in Canada.

The exhibition in Montréal in 2011 was a departure from the cabinet-of-curiosities open-call model of curation that we had used in our first two exhibitions.

Early in 2011, we had decided to develop a curatorial framework inspired, in part, by our anchor artist, Vélez. The exhibition would come to be named *Field, Studio, Lab,* and feature creative works being made that test the boundaries of those spaces. These were sites that we as curators traversed in our own respective work, and at that moment in time, some of us were conducting fieldwork, some were deep into studio practice, and others were developing labs for research.

At that time, we wrote:

> These three locations—the field, the studio, the lab—comprise both their own communities of practice, and form sites of inquiry and production for artists and anthropologists. The field, studio, and lab are not only places where knowledge is produced, or ethnographic data gathered, but are spaces of everyday life and local cultural production; they are generative sites of encounter, negotiation, conflict, celebration, failure, disappointment and revelation—all of which can unsettle (or ossify) discursive, disciplinary, and methodological boundaries.

On the opening night of the exhibition, the curator Emelie Chhangur traveled to Montréal to publicly present video documentation of *The Awakening* and host a

FIGURE 5.4. *Ethnographic Terminalia,* Montréal, 2011. *Field, Studio, Lab.* Installation View. Photo by Rachel Topham. Reprinted by permission of the photographer.

conversation with Mississauga New Credit First Nation project participants via Skype. At the center of the gallery space, we exhibited video documentation of Vélez's earlier collaborative work, *The Fight*, a project in which he worked with three boxing clubs from Southwark (the location of the Tate Modern) and organized a series of multidisciplinary workshops to bring community groups in the area together. Five amateur boxing matches were choreographed by a street dance company with specially composed music and these were staged in the Tate's Turbine Hall and documented on video.

We see Vélez's work as important in various art worlds but, more importantly, it is grounded in practices at the heart of anthropology: working in communities, structuring knowledge, and creating representations of social relations. We wanted to bring these approaches from collaborative art practices that we saw as "anthropological" into anthropology worlds, into an exhibition that would be viewed by many anthropologists who attended the AAA meetings in Montréal. The idea of collaboration within projects trickled through the exhibition.

In another example, representatives of the Public Lab for Open Science and Technology, Jae Ok Lee and Byeongwon Ha, created a site-specific installation titled *Making Sense: Lab as Gallery as Field*. Representing Public Lab's mandate to turn everyday spaces and tools into sites of investigation and knowledge production, the installation presented a DIY spectrometer and a Roomba that had been hacked to be an indoor air pollutant mapper. A corner of the gallery was transformed into a lab where visitors were invited to use the tools and collectively generate real-time data about the gallery environment. In the course of the exhibit, the hacked Roomba was released to map and investigate the gallery space, generating visualizations about indoor air pollution such as Formaldehyde (*Ethnographic Terminalia* 2011). Where Vélez's *The Fight* intervened in institutional art spaces through long-term community engagement and performance, *Making Sense: Lab as Gallery as Field* performed citizen science in the gallery to model collaboration through experimental knowledge sharing, technological literacy, and a commitment to environmental justice.

The curatorial process in Montréal depended on building connections on the ground. Early on in planning the project in Montréal, we entered into a curatorial partnership with Erica Lehrer at Concordia University and the Center for Ethnographic Research and Exhibition in the Aftermath of Violence (CEREV), who together acted as an on-the-ground liaison with Eastern Bloc, the host gallery. Members of the *Ethnographic Terminalia* Collective traveled to Montréal to workshop installations being produced by CEREV graduate students for the exhibition. After the collective had agreed on the exhibition theme and articulated a statement in coordination with CEREV, we set a deadline and circulated

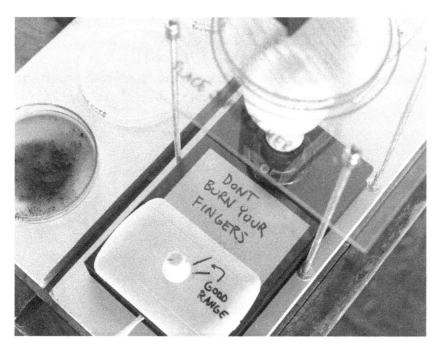

FIGURE 5.5. *Ethnographic Terminalia*, Montréal, 2011. *Field, Studio, Lab.* Details of Installation View, Public Lab, *Making Sense: Lab as Gallery as Field.* Photos by Rachel Topham. Reprinted by permission of the photographer.

an open call. Using various online collaboration and communication tools, we selected twenty-six projects from over seventy submissions. In the fall of 2011, we worked with the artists we selected for exhibition to develop iterations of their work that could be installed in Eastern Bloc's warehouse space. We made detailed installation plans and discussed, at length, how the works would sit together and what they could say. Installed in the gallery space, these works helped us begin to visualize the porous edges and ethical entanglements of the field, the studio, and the lab in art and anthropology.

Exhibition as Residency—Art, Anthropology, Collaboration: Chicago 2013

In 2013, the collective curated an exhibition at the Arts Incubator in Washington Park in Chicago that addressed the possibilities of collaboration in art and anthropology directly. We were inspired by the artist and Arts Incubator director Theaster Gates's social practice artwork (Becker, Yun Lee, and Borchardt-Hume 2015) and emerging collaborative projects taken up by anthropologists working with and as contemporary artists. *Exhibition as Residency—Art, Anthropology,*

FIGURE 5.6. *Ethnographic Terminalia*, Chicago, 2013. *Exhibition as Residency.* Installation View. Arts Incubator in Washington Park, Chicago. Photo by Rachel Topham. Reprinted by permission of the photographer.

Collaboration invited seven artist-researcher-anthropologist teams to Chicago for a weeklong residency in the Arts Incubator's Project Flex Space in which to realize their chosen project. In that week, visitors to the gallery were invited to observe the teams at work and to participate in scheduled workshops that invited collaboration from local residents and attendees from the annual meetings of the American Anthropological Association.

Collaboration in the exhibition, as a thread, was rendered visible in multiple media through the application of a range of methods. It took place across locations and distances, inside and outside of the gallery, and within and between the artist-anthropologist and curatorial teams. Collaboration was presented as an active, iterative process in which successes and failures were on display and produced in different forms in the course of the exhibition. Some of the projects attempted, with various degrees of success, to connect their work to the local community, creating, what Monique Scott recognized as "a space to reflect on the dialectics of race and class that transpire when predominately white artists take up residency in a predominately Black South Chicago neighborhood" (Scott 2014, 191).

One of the projects in particular, *Re-Connections: Coast Salish Knitting and Resilience in Chicago*, demonstrated collaboration in a series of scales, temporalities, and materialities. The team comprised the Coast Salish knitters and entrepreneurs Joni Olsen and Adam Olsen of the Tsartlip First Nation, and their mother Sylvia Olsen, a renowned knitter and historian; Andrea Walsh, professor of anthropology at the University of Victoria; and Trudi Lynn Smith, artist and anthropologist and a member of the *Ethnographic Terminalia* Collective. With support from the First Peoples' Heritage, Language and Culture Council in British Columbia, Canada, the group embarked on a project of reconnecting themselves with Coast Salish woven wool artifacts in the collections of the Chicago Field Museum that had been collected for the 1893 World's Fair. The knitters conducted research on the history of Coast Salish collecting in the colonial archive, and in response, designed and created a contemporary knitted garment in the gallery. The group also performed and videotaped a blanket ceremony at a replica of an 1893 World's Fair monument called *Bulls with Maidens*, which depicts a partially dressed Indigenous woman standing next to a bull. In the ceremony, the figure of the woman was covered with a blanket that the knitters had created on Tsartlip territory in British Columbia. The video and blanket were shown together in the gallery on the last day of the exhibition. The blanket was then gifted and accessioned into the Field Museum's contemporary northwest coast art collection, creating a material, discursive, and temporal connection across territories, institutions, and people.

FIGURE 5.7. *Ethnographic Terminalia*, Chicago, 2013. *Exhibition as Residency.* Workshop with members of the "Re-Connections: Coast Salish Knitting and Resilience in Chicago" team and members of the Committed Knitters. Arts Incubator in Washington Park, Chicago. Photo by Rachel Topham. Reprinted by permission of the photographer.

Within the Arts Incubator Project Flex Space, the team held a knitting workshop that invited members of the community to exchange knitting knowledge with the Coast Salish knitters. The team was thrilled to learn that the Arts Incubator is a regular meeting place for a group called the Committed Knitters, an organization that offers knitting workshops for incarcerated women and men in the Cook County Jail, and provides opportunities for maintaining community through knitting after release. The Committed Knitters joined the Coast Salish knitters for conversation and knowledge exchange in the Flex Space. Later, the team and some of the *Ethnographic Terminalia* curators and artist teams joined the Committed Knitters for another knitting meetup at a yarn store in downtown Chicago, again extending ETC's commitment to reaching broader audiences for reciprocal exchanges.

Aeolian Politics: Denver, 2015

In 2015, the *Ethnographic Terminalia* Collective worked with the anthropologists Cymene Howe and Dominic Boyer to present *Aeolian Politics*, an exhibition that transformed the fieldwork research and data of Boyer and Howe into a material installation. In contrast to the larger shows featuring many artists, the goal of this collaborative project was to translate the sensorial dimensions of wind into an exhibition form. Howe and Boyer stated that the rationale for their installation was to restore the wind to aeolian politics, to make "a visitor see, feel, and hear not just anthropolitics but ventipolitics, as well. To understand one, one must understand the other" (Boyer and Howe, Artist Statement, 2015). We embarked on a process of imagining and designing an exhibition that might realize Boyer and Howe's vision, and that kept true to their fieldwork data on wind-generated power in Mexico. The process transpired through Skype conversations, throwing out ideas, testing them and drawing them up, negotiating, changing, researching, stretching our ideas of what the work could be, changing, planning, and of course considering budgets. We settled on the design and construction of a structure in the gallery that would provide a visitor with the experience of both strong wind and soft wind, the two kinds of wind that Boyer and Howe so provocatively write about in their work and understood from the local context of the Isthmus Tehuantepec in Oaxaca, Mexico. One important aspect of our collaboration involved research into the quality of wind generation. At one juncture, all members of the collective found themselves together in Vancouver riding a bus across the city to a rental equipment warehouse for the film industry. We browsed through the aisles, pulling out giant and small fans to test out the quality of breeze, wind, sound, blast. One of us would stand in front of the gust of air, while the others looked and listened, inevitably asking, How does it feel? What is the right quality? What was the right or permissible amount of noise? Did this fan match our idea of what Boyer and Howe wished to translate? Where could we rent it in Colorado?

During installation and construction of the wind house in Denver, this iterative process continued. How could a structure be built to encompass and reveal wind? How could a projection be glitched to respond to the force of the wind? We worked with a local fabrication company, Paper Airplane, and developed engineering and architectural plans, acquired necessary permissions and approvals, and the structure came into existence while the details of public programming were also unfolding.

As part of the sonicscape of the gallery, we incorporated poetry and a recording of "The North Wind Whips" by the Binnizá (Zapotec) poet Victor Terán. Mr. Terán played an integral part in the exhibition programming as he joined an open group in the Emmanuel Gallery via video connection to discuss his poetry and engage with questions about poetry in anthropology. While gallery visitors had become familiar with Mr. Terán in the installation—a video of him performing a poem was a primary force in the gallery—his presence once again

FIGURE 5.8. *Ethnographic Terminalia*, Denver, 2015. *Aeolian Politics*. Installation View. Emmanuel Gallery, Denver. Photo by Trudi Lynn Smith.

transformed the space, where workshop collaborators were able to see, hear, and feel the exhibition and communicate with one of its interlocutors in yet another mode.

Terminus: Archives, Ephemera, and Electronic Art, Vancouver, 2015

The same year we were working on *Aeolian Politics*, we were presented with the opportunity to develop a project in Vancouver that connected art and anthropology at multiple venues within the academy and broader publics. In collaboration with the grunt gallery in Vancouver and the Twenty-First International Symposium on Electronic Arts (ISEA 2015), we presented an exhibition, public panel discussion, creative publishing workshop, and a performance. These events centered around *ARCTICNOISE*, a multimedia work by Geronimo Inutiq, curated by Britt Gallpen and Yasmin Nurming-Por, co-organized by Tarah Hogue and the ETC, and exhibited at the grunt gallery.

Our collaborative array was made possible by several factors. We had a longer time scale than our typical turnaround time of under a year; two of the ETC members live in Vancouver or nearby; and we were able to apply for funding in

FIGURE 5.9. *Ethnographic Terminalia*, Vancouver, 2015. Terminus: Archives, Ephemera, and Electronic Art. VIVO Media Arts Centre, Vancouver. Photo by Reese Muntean. Reprinted by permission of the photographer.

collaboration with the grunt gallery to help support the projects, making it possible to connect with a gallery's programming to cocurate/copresent an exhibition alongside other events.

In collaboration with Tarah Hogue, Glenn Alteen, and Karlene Harvey of the grunt gallery, we co-organized *ARCTICNOISE*, developed a format for a creative workshop, and hosted a public discussion. The workshop, *Terminus: Archives, Ephemera, and Electronic Art*, was held at VIVO Media Arts, off-site from the conference. The conference workshop was made from selections out of a call for presentations to respond to the main themes of *ARCTICNOISE*. Given that the workshop format was embedded within a scholarly conference, and our interest in experimenting with alternative forms of scholarly communication, we transformed the standard set of conference proceedings into a creative critique. Those presenting in the workshop provided us with a representation (set up as page spreads) of their presentation in advance. Inspired by Garnet Hertz's *Critical Making* project (2012), Michael Taussig's discussions of his field sketches (2011), and George Marcus's explorations of dynamic anthropological archives, studios, labs, and parasites, and the dialogic modes for ethnographic research, during the workshop itself participants and observers were all asked to document their questions, comments, doodles, tweets, and other responses. These were brought

FIGURE 5.10.   *Ethnographic Terminalia*, Vancouver, 2015. Terminus: Archives, Ephemera, and Electronic Art. Photo by Kate Hennessy.

together into a group-constructed analogue collage of responses to the day's presentations. Participants collaged their drawings, notes, Polaroids, and other contributions onto posters. At the end of the day, we photographed the posters and imported them into the skeleton proceedings/zine document that we had prepared in advance. We added photographs from the event, our introductory essay and acknowledgments, and printed the zine the next day. We handed out copies to workshop participants and to the public at the opening of *ARCTICNOISE* at the grunt gallery two days later. The zine and workshop documentation can be viewed at ethnographicterminalia.org/terminus/.

In this chapter, we have described some of the ways that the *Ethnographic Terminalia* Collective has functioned over the last decade, and some of the forms that our collaborative curatorial work has produced. We have emphasized that negotiating our collective work has resulted in a necessary annual reinvention of our process and has resulted in different curatorial outcomes. For example, our 2011 exhibition in Montréal, *Field, Studio, Lab*, was curated in response to an invited anchor artist, Humberto Vélez, and in partnership with Concordia University's CEREV. Inspired by Vélez's work grounded in anthropology worlds and transdisciplinary artwork, the exhibition prompted visitors to question the porous borders of these disciplinary spaces.

Taking a different approach, our 2013 exhibition in Chicago, *Exhibition as Residency: Art, Anthropology, Collaboration*, invited artists and anthropologists to collaborate on-site in the form of a residency. Collaborative art-making processes were on display, while projects such as *Reconnections: Coast Salish Knitting and Resilience in Chicago* endeavored to connect with local institutions and intervene in historical representations of Coast Salish peoples and their material culture. The challenge of connecting with the local community prompted the participating artists, visitors, and curators to engage in important discussions about the dynamics of race and power in art and anthropology.

In Denver in 2015, rather than curate a group exhibition from an open call or by invitation, the collective worked with the anthropologists Dominic Boyer and Cymene Howe to develop the installation *Aeolian Politics*. This iterative exhibition design process highlighted possibilities for collaboration between artist-curators and artist-anthropologists, as well as the potential for foregrounding the sensory dimensions of ethnographic work.

In yet another experimentation with alternative forms of knowledge representation, our 2015 workshop in Vancouver for the International Symposium on Electronic Arts resulted in a collectively produced rapid-prototype publication that was printed and freely distributed at a related exhibition of Geronimo Inutiq's *ARCTICNOISE*, co-organized with the grunt gallery. In Vancouver, we built on longer-term collaborations with local galleries and artist-run centers, and attempted to disrupt the conventions of academic conference proceedings by documenting and prioritizing the ephemera of scholarly and artistic gatherings.

Through this work, we have created new relationships between anthropologists, artists, exhibition spaces, funders, and institutions, and pushed for a greater place for curation in North American anthropology. We have underscored the importance of experimentation through collaboration in our curatorial process. Reflecting on Elhaik's provocation (2015), we wonder what forms of curation in anthropology are yet to be imagined. How will experimental modes of collaboration support the realization of new or underrepresented forms? In 2019, we made the decision to end our formal collaboration as a collective in curating projects, and are instead shifting our work together to archiving the projects we had created over ten years together. Through *Good Times and Bad Times*, often *Dazed and Confused*, we *Ramble On*.

REFERENCES

Becker, Carol, Lisa Yun Lee, Achim Borchardt-Hume, eds. 2015. *Theaster Gates*. New York: Phaidon.
Bishop, Clare. 2006. *Participation: Documents of Contemporary Art*. London: Whitechapel.

———. 2012. *Artificial Hells: Participatory Art and the Politics of Spectatorship*. London: Verso.

Bourriaud, Nicolas. 2002. *Relational Aesthetics*. Dijon: Les presses du réel, 2002.

Centre for Imaginative Ethnography (CIE). Accessed 2015. http://imaginativeethnography.org/.

Chin, Elizabeth. 2017. "On Multimodal Anthropologies from the Space of Design: Toward Participant Making." *American Anthropologist* 119 (3): 541–43.

Collins, Samuel, Matthew Durrington, and Harjant Gill. 2017. "Multimodality: An Invitation." *American Anthropologist* 119 (1): 142–53.

De Angelis, Alessandra, Celeste Ianniciello, Mariangela Orabona, and Michaela Quadraro. 2015. "Introduction: Disruptive Encounters—Museums, Arts and Postcoloniality." In *The Postcolonial Museum: The Arts of Memory and the Pressures of History*, edited by Ian Chambers, Alessandra De Angelis, Celeste Ianniciello, Mariangela Orabona, and Michaela Quadraro, 1–20. London: Ashgate.

Elhaik, Tarek 2015. "The Incurable Image: Curation and Repetition on a Tri-Continental Scene." In De Angelis, Ianniciello, Orabona, and Quadraro, *Postcolonial Museum*, 162–74.

Ethnographic Terminalia Collective and grunt gallery. 2015. Terminus: Archives, Ephemera, and Electronic Art. Vancouver: grunt gallery. Accessed April 27, 2017. http://ethnographicterminalia.org/terminus/.

Grimshaw, Anna, and Amanda Ravetz. 2005. "Introduction: Visualizing Anthropology." In *Visualizing Anthropology*, edited by Anna Grimshaw and Amanda Ravetz, 1–16. Bristol: Intellect Books.

Hertz, Garnet. 2012. "Conversations in Critical Making." *ctheory*. www.ctheory.net/articles.aspx?id=760.

Kester, Grant H. 2009. "Questionnaire on 'The Contemporary.'" *October* 130:3–124.

———. 2011. *The One and the Many: Contemporary Collaborative Art in a Global Context*. Durham, NC: Duke University Press.

Marcus, George E., ed. 1998. *Para-Sites: A Casebook against Cynical Reason*. Late Editions: Cultural Studies for the End of the Century, vol. 7. Chicago: University of Chicago Press.

Mol, Annemarie, Ingunn Moser, and Jeannette Pols. 2010. "Care: Putting Practice into Theory." In *Care in Practice: On Tinkering in Clinics, Homes and Farms*, edited by Annemarie Mol, Ingunn Moser, and Jeannette Pols, 7–26. Perspectives from Empirical Science Studies. Bielefeld: transcript Verlag.

Molesworth, Helen. 2010. "How to Install Art as a Feminist." In *Women Artists at the Museum of Modern Art*, edited by Cornelia Butler and Alexandra Schwartz, 449–513. New York: Museum of Modern Art.

Schneider, Arnd, and Christopher Wright. 2006. "The Challenge of Practice." In *Contemporary Art and Anthropology*, edited by Arnd Schneider and Christopher Wright, 1–27. Oxford: Berg.

———. 2010. *Between Art and Anthropology*. London: Bloomsbury Press.

———. 2013. *Anthropology and Art Practice*. London: Bloomsbury Press.

Scott, Monique. 2014. "White Walls, 'Black City': Reflections on 'Exhibition as Residency—Art, Anthropology, Collaboration.'" *Visual Anthropology Review* 30(2): 190–98.

Smith, Trudi Lynn. 2014. "Anthropology of Historical Photography in a Protected Area: Life and Death in Waterton Lakes National Park, Alberta." *Anthropologica* 56:117–53.

Taussig, Michael. 2011. *I Swear I Saw This*. Chicago: University of Chicago Press.

Vélez, Humberto. 2011. Humberto Vélez website. Accessed April 25, 2017. http://humbertovelez.com/projects/toronto/.

6

LIMN

Experimenting with Collaboration

Stephen J. Collier, Martin Høyem,
Christopher Kelty, and Andrew Lakoff

Limn is a scholarly magazine that focuses on tensions arising at the intersection of politics, expertise, and collective life. It is also an experiment in scholarly publishing in the interpretive human sciences that aims to make possible new kinds of communication and collective work. *Limn* is available both in an open access web format version and in print. Each issue of the print magazine is custom designed by Martin Høyem with a range of imagery and graphic material related to the contributions, including, in some issues, a featured graphic that links diverse contributions in a common conceptual problem-space.

The results of this small-scale, outsider experiment in publishing short, timely, and conceptually engaged work have exceeded our expectations. While it is, of course, hard to measure success, there are some helpful indicators. As of this writing, we have published ten issues. We have published over 1,500 pages of writing by more 120 contributors. Over 1,000 subscribers are on our mailing list and our Twitter account has more than 1,000 followers. Anecdotally, our colleagues seem to appreciate *Limn* as a welcome alternative to existing venues of scholarly publishing. Despite the fact that *Limn* offers none of the professional rewards of publication in standard academic journals, nearly everyone we invite to write for *Limn* agrees to do so.

From the outset, we have seen *Limn* as a vehicle for exploring new forms of collaboration in the interpretive human sciences. Our interest in this challenge emerged against a shared background in the rapidly changing field of American anthropology during the 1990s and 2000s. At the time, the discipline encouraged individualized work on particular sites or across sites and valorized virtuosic

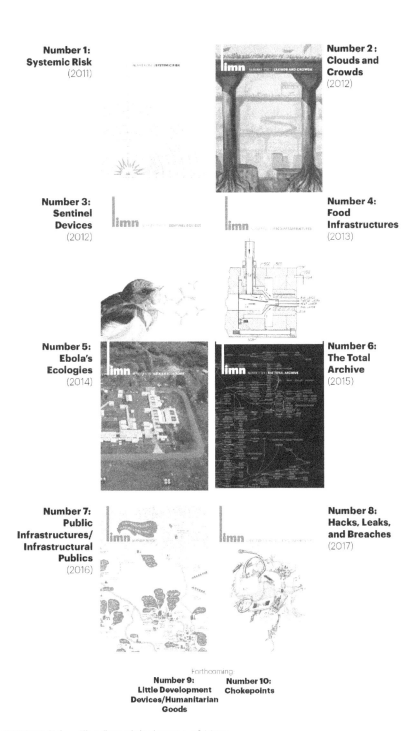

Number 1:
Systemic Risk
(2011)

Number 2:
Clouds and
Crowds
(2012)

Number 3:
Sentinel
Devices
(2012)

Number 4:
Food
Infrastructures
(2013)

Number 5:
Ebola's
Ecologies
(2014)

Number 6:
The Total
Archive
(2015)

Number 7:
Public
Infrastructures/
Infrastructural
Publics
(2016)

Number 8:
Hacks, Leaks,
and Breaches
(2017)

Forthcoming:
Number 9:
Little Development
Devices/Humanitarian
Goods

Number 10:
Chokepoints

FIGURE 6.1. The first eight issues of *Limn*

interpretation and writing, with little space for collaborative inquiry or concept work beyond highly abstract discussions of theory. However appropriate (or inappropriate) these orientations were for anthropology as traditionally conceived, it seemed a different approach was needed for studying the kinds of issues that interested us, and that were in fact moving to the center of the discipline at the time, relating to science, technology, global health, bureaucratic rationality, and planning. Yet then-dominant discussions of method continued to emphasize a familiar model of ethnographic fieldwork leading to the discovery of difference. Given this background, we were all interested in exploring how work in specific sites could be brought into communication, and what alternative models of inquiry, writing, and publication might foster collaboration.

We had pursued this concern with collaboration—in various combinations—in a range of prior projects that employed well-established vehicles of collective work: the conference panel, the workshop, the collected volume, and the like.[1] We first began to pursue alternative venues for collaboration in the Anthropology of the Contemporary Research Collaboratory (ARC). In launching *Limn* as a separate initiative, we were particularly concerned with exploring various aspects of collaboration: What kind of collective work did we want to accomplish? How to expand the network of collaborators? How to establish a distinctive approach to the anthropology of the contemporary while remaining open to cross-fertilization with other approaches? How to reimagine what scholarly work and publication could be in light of the internet and new models of open access publication? And how might collaboration provide a way to respond in a timely manner to contemporary problems?

Two early experiments in collaboration shaped our approach to *Limn*. The first was based on a conference (organized by Alberto Corsìn in Madrid on "Prototyping") for which we asked participants to do something unusual: produce (i.e., "prototype") short pieces before the conference unencumbered by theory or methodological reflection, that would be collected and published (issue no. 0, "Prototyping Prototyping") before the conference was held. That model of solicitation carried over into later issues.

The second experiment in collaboration that shaped our approach to *Limn* arose from our interest in generating some kind of response to the 2009 Deepwater Horizon disaster. We knew that thinkers from a range of disciplines might have something to say about it, and we intuited that if we tapped into a network of knowledgeable scholars, and juxtaposed their perspectives, something novel would emerge—a vantage point distinct from the more first-order perspectives that were publicly circulating in the immediate aftermath of the event. But there was no venue for rapid response or short, accessible articles that situated this event and the issues it raised on this broader canvas. We settled on the idea not to convoke an issue focused directly on Deepwater Horizon but rather to try to illuminate the event by placing it in the context of other events that raised similar problems, and alongside a range of genealogical framings. This is what we meant by the title "Limn": to illuminate the space around the event, to understand how it became intelligible in a certain way, rather than simply reporting on it. The issue that eventually emerged out of these discussions was centered on the problem of systemic risk, as well as the norms, such as resilience and preparedness, that are invoked in response.

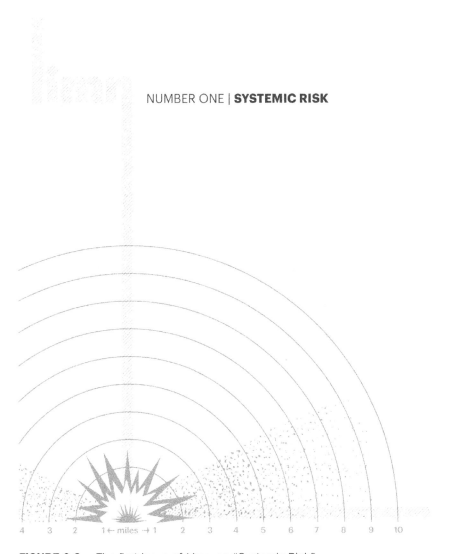

NUMBER ONE | **SYSTEMIC RISK**

FIGURE 6.2.   The first issue of *Limn*, on "Systemic Risk"

In the process of work on *Limn*, issue no. 1, we took note of a highly productive dynamic. The essays broadened our frame of reference for a problem that we had been working on more narrowly to think about how a concept from a particular domain (systemic risk was a term of art in financial regulation) might illuminate a broader problematization of contemporary life. At the same time, the contributors to this issue found that their own work was reframed by this connection with a diverse set of cases and a broadened conceptual field. The initial success of this experiment triggered a discussion about the mix of online and offline platforms available to us, about design and imagery, about audience, and about the research networks that might be constituted or extended by this practice. We never envisioned the magazine as an end in itself, but rather we saw it as a tool for sparking conversation among participants interested in exploring a carefully articulated problem: each issue aimed to produce both genealogical framings and concept work that would illuminate, or limn, a range of contemporary events and problems. We were inspired by the notion of curation as opposed to theorization: that is, conceptually motivated selection and juxtaposition of articles on specific sites and topics in order to bring them into conversation in the hope of generating surprise for readers and contributors and for ourselves. At the same time, *Limn*, issue no. 1, pointed to a model that did not involve simply assembling preexisting work. Rather, it involved circulating a prompt that invited contributors to rethink existing work in light of a particular problem.

What does this experiment tell us about collaboration in the contemporary human sciences? Two vectors of collaboration in *Limn* are relevant to this volume and broader discussions in anthropology: (1) the nature of our work together as three editors and one designer of these ten issues in various configurations, which has had its own vibrant and ongoing intellectual draw for each of us; and (2) the nature of the collaboration we have tried to instigate in each of the issues, among the authors and issue editors. The first vector includes our own intellectual interest in problems and concepts: an experiment in a particular kind of inquiry in the interpretive human and social sciences. The second includes our practice of soliciting contributions (rather than accepting submissions), extensively revising the prompts for each issue to clarify the central problems that might drive a particular issue, and attempting to work with authors to "*Limn*-ify" their work by encouraging engagement with the prompt and the work of other contributors. By this we mean: attention to the shared problem that frames the issue; an emphasis on the elaboration of a striking empirical case; avoidance of disciplinary jargon or internal academic references; and brevity (we ask that contributions be 2,500 words or less).

Collaboration as Editors: Concept Work and Its Challenges

From the first issue ("Systemic Risk") forward, the three of us have reflected on our role as editors of *Limn*. Given our aspiration to bring scholars from a range of traditions and fields together to work on shared concepts, across divergent approaches and topics, our editorial work has been integral to the collaborative process. For every issue we have explored with each other, and with our issue editors, the core concept or problems that should be at the center of the issue, and the historical framing that would bring it to life. A great deal of this work takes place in the crafting, revising, and narrowing of prompts which we use to identify and then invite particular people to participate in an issue. These prompts are not published, and the work that goes into them is not directly visible in the journal itself though they often provide a first outline for the introduction or preface to each issue. The prompts are meant to provoke the collaborative inquiry of a set of authors, and they have worked differently in the different issues.[2]

Concept work has also been a persistent goal of our collaboration in *Limn*, whose meaning we have deliberated on as editors (see, for instance, Rabinow et al. 2008). At times, it has meant crafting and testing pragmatic concepts that can make novel sense of salient public problems, or proposing a way to revise dominant or conventional ways of framing problems in order to better understand new developments. In other cases, it has involved identifying concepts that experts, policy makers, and advocates are actively defining and contesting in the domains we examine: public infrastructure or systemic risk, for example. A complementary sense of concept work is as a practice of grouping problems that brings certain things to light (e.g., the pervasive importance of systemic risk across many domains) and also clarifies their stakes. The process of honing a key concept in relation to varied empirical soundings is at the heart of our model of collaboration. In every case, we have urged authors to use their own work to engage with the concepts and problems staged in the prompt, and to take advantage of the short form and relatively quick process in order to try out alternative ways of putting their work into dialogue with others.

Substantively, it has also become clear that the three of us have steered *Limn* into particular domains of investigation that we care about, largely having to do with issues like global health, infrastructure, information technology, data and algorithms, catastrophe and disaster, risk and planning. If there is a triad that has emerged—from time to time—as a slogan for the magazine, it might be "Politics, Expertise, Collectives," indicating an interest in how new collectivities are both called into being and governed through a combination of political and technical means (or in a Foucauldian frame that we share, how "political technologies" and "governmental rationalities" are being rethought in the face of changing actualities).

In the years since 2011, we have gotten many different proposals for issues—far more than we could publish. One of the most interesting and rewarding aspects of this collaborative work has been the process of thinking about which proposals would make good issues, and for those we accept, working to turn a topic into a problem. What is especially interesting to track, as this process unfolds, is that our own sense of the problem changes as—in conversation with our issue editors— we put together lists of potential contributors and begin to think about how other domains relate to the problem as originally formulated.

A related challenge has been the technical complexity of our topics. We are interested in inquiry that takes this complexity seriously, but not for its own sake. Often the challenge of concept work is to simply identify the places in a topic (or an individual contribution) where a deep familiarity with some technical issue can be connected to a shared set of concepts in play. This practice draws from our joint commitments (in different ways) to science studies, history of science and medicine, and anthropology to render the actual details and history of a problem clearly—but to do so in a way that is not driven by any particular disciplinary or theoretical frame.

Forms of Collaborative Inquiry: Different Issues and Different Results

The attempt to provoke collaborative inquiry via prompts and invited contributors has had different effects across the issues we have produced so far. Some issues are called into being by very specific events (the 2014 Ebola epidemic). Others, meanwhile, are serendipitously addressed to, or outpaced by, ill-defined but urgent issues (hackers, hacking, and leaking during and after the 2016 presidential campaign). Our insistence on building issues around problems of public concern can sometimes focus the issue and sometimes permit it to spread out in various directions. In some cases, there is some vague thing that is focusing public attention diffusely (issue no. 2 on cloud computing/crowdsourcing), in others there is a precise actors' concept (issue no. 1 on systemic risk), and in still others a problem that remained unsettled throughout the collaboration (issue no. 4 on food infrastructures in one case, and perhaps also issue no. 8 on hacking).

Event-Precipitated Collaborations (Issue No. 1, "Systemic Risk," and No. 5 "Ebola's Ecologies")

Two of the issues have been directly precipitated by events. "Systemic Risk" followed the BP Deepwater Oil Spill, and placed the event in relationship to the broader emergence of systemic risk as a central problem of governmental rationality in the late twentieth and early twenty-first centuries. As we revised the prompt for that issue, it became apparent that the concept of systemic risk, because it had origins in the economics of finance and was being used to talk about an environmental disaster, would be usefully approached from a variety of angles: defense, information technology, disaster preparedness, ecology, and so on. *Limn*, issue no. 1 still stands out for us as a model of an issue with a clear concept with obvious public significance, and a set of contributions that, taken together, illuminate the concept in provocative ways.

Similarly, the 2014 Ebola epidemic catalyzed a number of academic communities (the blog *Somatosphere* also ran a series) to respond, to test ideas and concepts as the event unfolded. It was an event that brought a particular range of elements into relation—and, in a sense, rendered them problematic—in a way that we could only capture through articles that looked at it at a number of scales, from various sites, centers of expert knowledge and political decision. Our particular contribution involved querying how the global health preparedness apparatus—which has been a subject of inquiry outside of *Limn* (esp. Lakoff and Collier 2008; Lakoff 2017)—responded at different scales to this singular event.

Issues That Intervene in a Scholarly Debate (Issue No. 2, "Crowds and Clouds," and No. 7, "Public Infrastructures/Infrastructural Publics")

Two of the issues ended up doing a different kind of work. Both "Clouds and Crowds" and "Public Infrastructures/Infrastructural Publics" tried to loosen up, or work around, some rigid assumptions about widely acknowledged and discussed topics. In the case of "Crowds and Clouds," broad attention has been paid to new information technologies like cloud computing and crowdsourcing, without there being a real conceptual core to the kinds of work and analysis being done. Most writing on these topics has consisted of punditry about the utopian and dystopian aspects, and has often simply conjugated technology and collectivity (networked publics, virtual communities, etc.). "Clouds and Crowds" asked authors to focus on the notion of "representing and intervening in collectivities" of various sorts, and contributors rose to the challenge of thinking through (in contemporary and historical cases) the way collectivities are called into being by new technologies (from software to new statistical tools). The result was an excellent example of concept work in the way that it gave rise to a notion of collective kinds as a tool for thinking about the relationship of new IT and old collectivities.

"Public Infrastructures" did a similar kind of work through collaboration. The purpose was to loosen some rigid assumptions about new relationships among

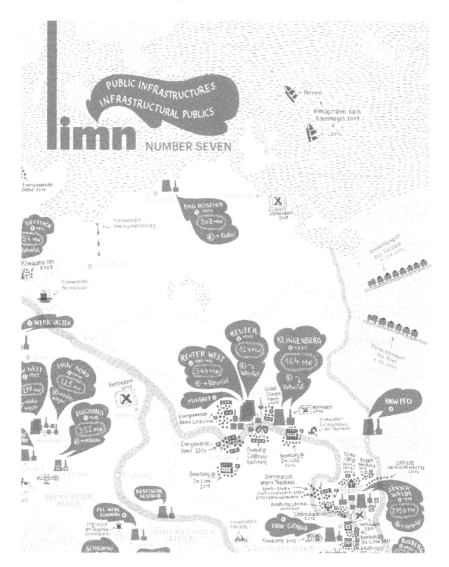

FIGURES 6.3A and **B.**   *Limn*, issue no. 7, (left) print version, (right) online version

infrastructure, publics, and experts that have emerged from a particular diagnosis of the present—related to neoliberalized infrastructure—and to encourage authors to reorient their work about both publics and infrastructures. The collaboration did not exactly serve to illustrate a coherent counterstory. Rather, it served to generate reflection on the varieties of these relationships, to place these elements in motion by showing their diverse combinations, and thus to open up a space of thought.

About Us   Issues   Researchers   Collaborate   **Search:**

Issue 7: Public Infrastructures/Infrastructural Publics

Editors: **STEPHEN J. COLLIER, JAMES CHRISTOPHER MIZES**, and **ANTINA VON SCHNITZLER**

Buy paper   Buy PDF

Infrastructure has always had a privileged relationship to both expertise and the public in modern government. But in the early 21st century, this relationship is inflected in novel ways. The purposes public infrastructure was meant to serve—welfare, quality of life, economic development, and so on—persist. But they are often conceptualized differently, promoted by different agencies, and articulated through novel technological and collective relations. This issue of *Limn* explores new formations of infrastructure, publicness, and expertise.The contributions examine how new forms of expertise conceive the public and make claims in its name, how publics are making novel claims on experts (and claims to expertise), and how earlier norms and techniques of infra-structure provisioning are being adapted in the process.

FEATURING WORK BY
Stephen J. Collier,
James Christopher Mizes,
Antina von Schnitzler, Soe Lin Aung,
Sven Opitz, Ute Tellmann,
Jonathan Bach, Alan Wiig,
Andrea Ballestero, Penny Harvey,
Hannah Knox, Gökçe Günel,
Emma Park, Kevin P. Donovan,
Ashley Carse, Andrew Lakoff,
Andreas Folkers, Nikhil Anand,
Savannah Cox, Kevin Grove,
Andrew Barry,
Canay Özden-Schilling,
Cymene Howe, Dominic Boyer, and
Catherine Fennell

Published July 2016

IN THIS ISSUE:

Preface: Public Infrastructures / Infrastructural Publics

Stephen J. Collier, James Christopher Mizes, and Antina von Schnitzler ask how infrastructures and their publics are taking shape today.

The Thick and Thin of the Zone

Soe Lin Aung examines the Thilawa special economic zone to shed light on infrastructure's changing publics in contemporary Myanmar.

Who Owns Africa's Infrastructure?

James Christopher Mizes examines how an emerging style of African infrastructure planning and finance is inflecting an old political collectivity with "new" values.

Europe's Materialism: Infrastructures and Political Space

Sven Opitz and Ute Tellmann explore energy infrastructure and the construction of a European commons.

China's Infrastructural Fix

How is modernity being reclaimed as a Chinese project? Jonathan Bach investigates the politics of infra-structure in today's most ambitious developmental state.

Crafting a Digital Public

What makes a city smart? Alan Wiig examines a project to promote urban development through information infrastructure in Philadelphia.

Spongy Aquifers, Messy Publics

Is an aquifer a tank or a sponge? Andrea Ballestero investigates how publics navigate the scientific indeterminacy of the underground in Costa Rica.

Infrastructural Incursions

What does it take to flood a highway? Penny Harvey and Hannah Knox examine how old infrastructure projects—and old infrastructural publics—get submerged by new ones in Peru.

FIGURES 6.3A and **B.**   (Continued)

Issues Precipitated by Conferences and Other Collaborations (Issue No. 3, "Sentinel Devices," and No. 6, "The Total Archive")

Two issues of *Limn* have emerged out of other forms of collaboration, confer-ences, or ongoing projects. The issue on "Sentinel Devices" arose from a joint US-French workshop that took place in France, and included a series of articles that were first presented there and then workshopped into an issue. The issue had a clear concept at the center (sentinel devices) around which, once again, a variety of different cases and scales were brought to bear. And it built on the insights that had arisen—about vulnerability, technological interdependence, and the problem of anticipating the uncertain—in the "Systemic Risk" issue. As with many such cases, in-person discussion allowed us to keep the focus on the concept and its usefulness across the cases.

The "Total Archive" issue came out of a conference that had been organized independently of any of us and then was pitched subsequently as an issue; it expanded to include people who were not at the conference, and incorporated ideas and concepts that were not originally central to the design of the conference—but the issue managed to amplify the historical and genealogical concern into something new. It built on the current obsession with "big data"—and the presentism that surrounds such discussions—and put it in a much longer historical frame of attempts to catalog "all the information in the world." In conversation and in planning, this issue also built on the earlier work of "Crowds and Clouds"—on collective kinds and the politics of new technological forms—seeking to draw these conversations together in ways that were neither strictly topical nor disciplinary, but engaged with the problems and concepts that have animated the other issues of *Limn*.

A Problem in Motion

In issue no. 8, "Hacks, Leaks, and Breaches," the problem at the heart of the issue remained constantly in motion. Every day—and especially as we put together the issue—cases of hacking emerged, from the leaks and hacks of the 2016 election in the United States, to breaches at Equifax or Verizon. But rather than focus the issue, these new cases often pulled it in new directions. There are essays focused on the definition of the hacker, some on the meaning of leaks and journalism today, and others that connect better to the systemic risk and infrastructure discussions in other issues. What seemed at first to be a coherent problem turned out to actually be several problems rolled into one. This issue is also the first example in which we achieved something we had long thought would be part of the project: incorporating nonacademic voices, including three journalists, one hacker, and a lawyer who defends hackers. In addition, the issue produced the elusive collaborative conversation—an essay by an activist/journalist (Naomi Colvin of the Courage Foundation) responding to two of the originally solicited essays (by Molly Sauter, and by Adam Fish and Luca Follis). Unlike our other issues, few of the solicited articles responded directly to the original prompt that we wrote about the political threshold of hacking—perhaps because the topic has its own momentum and force, and many people just have something to say about it.

The timeliness we seek to produce around these issues can be a double-edged sword: on the one hand, we have sought to accelerate the often painfully slow academic publishing process; on the other hand, the 72-hour attention cycle of mainstream and social media clearly foils attempts to think collaboratively. Each issue allows us to explore the space in between these two temporalities with respect to contemporary problems.

Making *Limn* Now and in the Future

Making *Limn* has also been an experiment in scholarly publishing in a time of rapid and significant change in that world. *Limn* has built on various experiences: Kelty's experience with the success of the blog *Savage Minds*, the collaboration around ARC, the rise and spread of open access, and the rapid change in the availability and suitability of technical tools for the job. Publishing *Limn* is also a reaction to the increasing standardization and normalization of academic journals and article forms, a renewed sense of disciplinary gatekeeping in the academic publishing world, and the slow publication process and public inaccessibility of most disciplinary journals. These possibilities and challenges structure (and limit) what *Limn* has done or can be. Despite what might have been a desire to radically break with existing forms or to go all digital, we also recognized early on that the print magazine still commands a large degree of respect and authority among our audience and confers a sense that the endeavor is more than a blog or a kind of online confab. Our commitment to producing a bespoke, beautiful object is both a tribute to the history of the small magazine (and a desire to preserve that form and practice in the face of digital dissolution), and an attempt to think about design, juxtaposition, layout, format and collaboration in ways that are no longer possible in most scholarly publications.

Limn has remained a labor of love; it is not a formal organization at this stage, but only a collective of individuals working to create the website and magazine. It is also a going concern in which many people contribute labor and are remunerated in different ways. The general editors also serve as managing editors and contribute time and labor "in kind" as fully employed and salaried academics. For each issue, different editors (Ashley Carse, Biella Coleman, Jason Cons, Xaq Frohlich, Lilly Irani, Boris Jardine, Mikko Jauho, Frederic Keck, Townsend Middleton, James Chris Mizes, Bart Penders, Peter Redfield, David Schleifer, Antina von Schnitzler, Nick Seaver, and Alice Street), read, edit, and respond to each article and conduct some of the managerial work of keeping up to twenty authors on task. Our copyeditors, *Limn*'s main designer (Høyem), and any artists or nonacademic contributors are paid going rates for their freelance work. These costs are drawn from research grants or funds of any available, appropriate sort. The print version makes no profits, and any royalties are folded back into each subsequent issue. There is no advertising in *Limn*, and we do not make use of data on readers or website visitors for any purposes. There is no marketing or promotion, and no involvement from any professional press or journal, no managing editor or interns; all the production and distribution for the journal relies on other infrastructures (tools like Amazon's CreateSpace or MailChimp) which are both liberating and, at the same time, unstable because of their own constantly shifting business models. Whatever success we have had has, no doubt, been due to the scholarship of our authors and the promotional efforts of our readers and colleagues who support the project.

Limn has, since its origins, been committed to being an open access publication. All the online articles are free to view, print, download, circulate, and republish (under a CC By-SA-NC license), including PDF versions of the print version. We do not charge "article processing fees" to publish, though we also do not accept unsolicited submissions, meaning that while we are open access to read, we are not open access to publish in, and could no doubt do a much better job of diversifying and expanding our audience of readers and writers alike in the future.

Lastly, we continue to think of *Limn* as if it were more than a journal: as an umbrella, a network, or a platform, "*Limn* 2.0"—but not a movement, or a school. What remains at the heart of the endeavor is the desire to find places of thought and inquiry that escape the more stultifying aspects of university life, and that sustain the pleasure of intellectual engagement without disappearing from the view (of our colleagues, and to some extent the university as well) entirely.

NOTES

1. One widely read effort was the collected volume *Global Assemblages* (Ong and Collier 2004).

2. Prompts for past issues are available on our website at http://limn.it/wp-content/uploads/Limn-Invites-All.pdf.

REFERENCES

Lakoff, Andrew. 2017. *Unprepared: Global Health in a Time of Emergency*. Berkeley: University of California Press.

Lakoff, Andrew, and Stephen J. Collier. 2008. "The Problem of Securing Health." In *Biosecurity Interventions: Global Health and Security in Question*. New York: Columbia University Press.

Ong, Aihwa, and Stephen J. Collier, eds. 2004. *Global Assemblages: Technology, Politics, and Ethics as Anthropological Problems*. Oxford: Wiley-Blackwell.

Rabinow, Paul, George E. Marcus, James D. Faubion, and Tobias Rees. 2008. *Designs for an Anthropology of the Contemporary*. Durham, NC: Duke University Press.

7

WHAT'S SO FUNNY 'BOUT PECE, TAF, AND DATA SHARING?

*Mike Fortun, Lindsay Poirier, Alli Morgan, Brian Callahan, and Kim Fortun**

Here we discuss four different ways we are involved in and with collaborative projects. They share in many ways a form, shape, or style, and may be imagined as nested within each other, like *matryoshka* dolls—if *matryoshka* could be rendered hyperdimensional, so that there were no smaller and larger "scales" but each could suddenly shift places and relationships. Each of our collaborative projects is in conversation with, informed by, or at least rubs up against each of the others, sometimes the framing form, at other times the framed content. Their differences are less a matter of scale (smaller to larger collaborations) or temporal development (early to later collaborations), and more a matter of any given collaborative project being both inside and outside of another, a flickering switch of figure and ground, an exchange in which one form becomes content for another, whose content in turn (in)forms the next, setting in motion chains of demands and possibilities that animate the collaborations and set the stage for new lines of experiment, growth, and change.

The first one we discuss (but not logically, organizationally, or historically first) is PECE, the Platform for Experimental Collaborative Ethnography, the digital infrastructure we have been developing for several years to support new

* With Vinay Baindur, Brandon Costelloe-Kuehn, Thomas Depree, Sam Elrahman, Erica Fletcher, Govind Gopakumar, Rodolfo Hernandez, Jason Baird Jackson, Madhura Joglekar, Scott Kellogg, Ali Kenner, Aalok Khandekar, Jobby Kunjachen, John Mathew, Maria Michails, Rohit Negi, Angela Okune, Dan Price, Deepa Reddy, Surajit Sarkar, Pankaj Sekhsaria, Prerna Srigyan, Sharon Traweek et al. (aka The World-PECE.org Network of Networks).

FIGURE 7.1.   Matryoshka dolls, courtesy of Wikimedia under a Creative Commons license (CC BY-SA 3.0), https://commons.wikimedia.org/wiki/File:Matryoshka_transparent.png

collaborative projects in anthropology. The next collaborative project presented here is the much longer-standing collaboration of The Asthma Files (TAF), an experimental ethnographic research project that eventually led to the conceptualization and development of PECE. TAF is now in large part realized through our 6+ Cities Research project on air quality science and governance in comparative cultural context, the third project discussed here. All of these can be thought of as taking shape within another looser, larger, more dispersed, and more sporadically collaborative (for us) layer, the Digital Practices in History and Ethnography Interest Group (DPHE-IG) we organized within the Research Data Alliance (RDA), a global collaboration of individuals and institutions working to make data more easily and openly shareable.

We present each of these through a primarily descriptive style, for several reasons. The first iteration of this chapter was written to share with participants in the workshop on collaboration held at the Center for Ethnography at the University of California, Irvine, and for this assignment, an empirical dimension was explicitly troped as more important than the theoretical. As George Marcus wrote to us in an email: "It is fine if you would like to include broader conceptual or methodological reflections on collaboration, but what is most important is that we get a detailed sense of what your collaboration has involved so far so that we are all familiar with each other's projects by the time we gather." But beyond that, we also tend to be somewhat matter-of-fact about collaboration, collaborative projects, and the collaborative form. We, of course, have our reasons for and a commitment to collaboration, many of which we learned from or had reinforced by our fieldwork experiences among scientists and engineers, for whom interdisciplinary collaboration is definitely "a thing"—a thing difficult to define and delineate, let alone actually pull off, but also a much desired and culturally supported "thing." But collaboration is also in some ways just something that we do. We recognize that it's not for everyone, and that it's not right for every project. It has its virtues, but those do not make collaboration any more virtuous than other ethnographic forms. Collaboration is vital to future ethnography, but it is hardly the only way to do that futuring. Our commitments to collaboration are best described as thoroughly experimental: *trying* collaboration is crucial, to build and multiply collaborative projects, so as to better understand what they can and cannot do.

In that sense, the collaborative form, for us, is also the experimental form analyzed by Hans-Jorg Rheinberger as essential to a modern scientific style, in which the limits (of knowledge as a system of signs, of laboratory equipment as a system of material devices) are the active site of a double movement: work *and* play, closure *and* openness, structure *and* de-structure, reliable technical reproduction of phenomena *and* the generation of unanticipated, surprising events and objects. These double movements of experimental systems are, for Rheinberger, how sciences grow and even progress in the sense of becoming more encompassing, more productive, more competent in more situations. Each of our projects is experimental in this sense as we've learned it through Rheinberger's analysis of scientific work and change, and not simply in the sense of doing something new and avante-garde. We experiment by working the structures and infrastructures (technical, organizational, interpersonal) that provide the stable grounds for producing, saving, and sharing our individual and collective data, and by playing the inevitable movements, insufficiencies, and open edges of these (infra)structures to keep things lively, interesting, and new.

In keeping with these dual matter-of-fact and experimental commitments, in which what we call "light structure" enables both stability and change, and in which dazzling theorization is at least partly deferred as one pursues more mundane outcomes, we decided to adopt for this chapter a well-known and productive light structure, a rhetorical convention or prompt that formed the basis of the journalists' "Five W" questions—in an older version, the "seven circumstances" ascribed to Hermagoras of Temnos: *who, what, when, where, why, in what way, by what means* (in Latin, *quis, quid, quando, ubi, cur, quem ad modum, quibus adminiculis*)?[1] As we will elaborate later on, in the PECE platform and in the collaborative projects it supports we rely extensively on such light structures:

minimal, open-ended forms that, when instantiated in different technologies or media, help facilitate collaboration and comparative analysis. Responding to them is always an interpretive act (*what does "when is the collaboration?" ask for?*), but one whose differences are always in contact with shared continuities and connections.

PECE: Platform for Comparative Experimental Ethnography

Who

A small collaborative "Design Team," initially centered at Rensselaer Polytechnic Institute (now more geographically dispersed), has been at the core of PECE development for the past several years (https://worldpece.org/content/pece-design-team#). Mike Fortun and Kim Fortun initiated and led the project, which has depended on (collaborations depend on dependencies) two of their graduate students in the Department of Science and Technology Studies who are also highly technically skilled, Lindsay Poirier (who has earned the title lead platform architect) and Brian Callahan (our lead open knowledge developer). Both Lindsay and Brian have utilized their work with PECE and their engagement with digital/technical worlds more generally as part of their fieldwork for different, broader PhD dissertation projects. Other current and former graduate students at Rensselaer Polytechnic Institute (RPI) also contributed to PECE's design and implementation, including Alli Morgan, Ali Kenner, Brandon Costelloe-Kuehn, and Erik Bigras. The Rensselaer computer science PhD student Dominic DiFranzo and the UCLA anthropology graduate student Luis Felipe Murillo also circulated through our group for a period of time and made important contributions to the platform. After a brief (failed) experiment with a Plone developer (Plone is a content management system, or CMS, that we explored in an earlier collaboration with Dan Price at the University of Houston), the actual coding/building of PECE was accomplished in a Drupal by contracting in 2015 with Taller, a Brazilian "digital business studio that turns ideas into innovative business" (http://taller.net.br/en/#section-members). Renato Vasconcellos Gomes (http://revax.com.br/) was our main developer at Taller, and he has continued to work independently (and enthusiastically!) with us since then. Another Boston-based Drupal development company, the "worker-owned cooperative" Agaric (http://agaric.com/), has made more limited contributions.

What

From our most recent (collaboratively produced) project statement:

The Platform for Experimental, Collaborative Ethnography: History and Current Capabilities

PECE (worldpece.org) is an open-source, Drupal-based platform designed to support a wide range of collaborative humanities projects. PECE provides a space for geographically dispersed researchers to share primary materials (such as field notes, grey matter, photographs, and recorded interviews), provides tools supporting analysis and interpretation of these materials, and allows researchers to experiment with new ways of publishing their results, addressing diverse audiences. A core goal is to support greater collaboration among empirical humanities researchers, and between these researchers and researchers in other fields. The project is working to theorize, methodologically enact, and technically support "collaborative hermeneutics."

PECE is shaped by the empirical demands and theoretical tenets of experimental ethnography, but is designed to be used by an array of research groups, helping build out a rich ecology of interoperable digital projects that link researchers in different fields, and with diverse stakeholders. The platform design emerges from concrete ethnographic practices and (newly invented) collaborative work flows, inflected by poststructural understandings of language, meaning and knowledge. PECE's "design logics" are meant to stay on the surface, open to debate and revision. This effort is sustained by the PECE design group, on PECE's own platform, and platform users are encouraged to continually help develop them.

A signature feature of PECE is the way it supports the archiving, sharing, and collaborative use of a diverse (and ever growing) set of "structured analytics"—sets of questions researchers use to identify, generate, and interpret empirical humanities data. Archiving and sharing these structured analytics exposes a work flow and intellectual process often invisible and tacit in humanities research. Digital research infrastructure in the natural and social sciences often exposes such workflows, aiming for increased reproducibility of research results; digital humanists face a related but somewhat different challenge and goal. In the humanities, fine-grained exposure of workflows and intellectual processes can convey the depth and rigor of humanist analysis—what John Dewey would have called not its reproducibility, but its warrantability—while also supporting new forms of peer review and collaboration early in the research process. With capacity to share "structured analytics," researchers can 1) better examine why and how data was created, 2) analyze data using multiple frameworks, from diverse traditions of thought (open to juxtaposition), and 3) analyze data collaboratively, leveraging robust interpretive pluralism among researchers rather than simple reproducibility. This is supported with a tool that allows researchers to integrate multiple annotations produced by different researchers using PECE's shared structured analytics, allowing easy visualization of multiple researchers' analyses and interpretations at all stages of the research process.

When

For the better part of 2015–16, the PECE design team had weekly two-hour face-to-face meetings, with regular email and Skype contact happening around that. Even if that tempo has since abated, PECE is, out of all our collaborations, the one that is the most constant even if not the most active presence in our attention-scape. For most of 2016, Lindsay always had a Skype chat window open with Taller during each of our six "legs" of development. You can see the record of code additions and deletions in figure 7.2. Lindsay was the central figure in the technosocial work of this collaboration (again, earning her the title lead platform

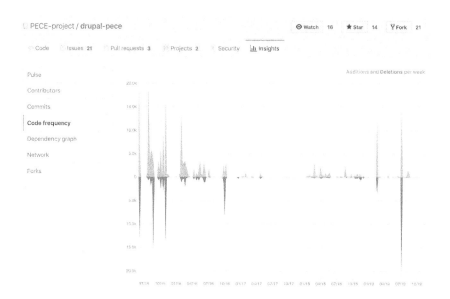

FIGURE 7.2.   Screenshot of GitHub page for PECE, https://github.com/ revagomes/drupal-pece/graphs/code-frequency, data forked from PECE, accessed May 16, 2020

architect in many of our documents); between cajoling Taller to keep to schedule, testing new features as they were developed and either approving them or identifying bugs, and writing the user stories that would define the next leg of development work, she logged the most hours of any of us. And she continues, as lead platform architect, to supervise all new software development, still keeping a Skype window onto Brazil to stay in touch with Renato.

Platform development never went as quickly as we or our collaborators wanted, and we consider PECE to be in permanent beta mode: it works well, but it could always work better, and we are always planning and writing grants for that. The constant drone of software development was punctuated by other events in time; milestones like the first public release of PECE (May 2016) on GitHub became important markers that quickened the collaboration's pace.

The best short answer, then, to the light structure question "When is PECE?" is "More or less always."

Where

Aside from the Brazilian Drupal developers, this collaboration ran almost entirely at RPI among its faculty and graduate students. Members of Rensselaer's "Tetherless World" constellation of computer, web, and data scientists supported us with occasional feedback and advice, web hosting, and a bit of funding. It is also where we convened several design- and user-feedback workshops where we involved other scholars, like Jason Baird Jackson and Sharon Traweek, with professional or research interests and commitments to digital developments.

Another answer to the "Where?" analytic is "GitHub." The PECE collaboration resulted in writing code into GitHub where, in the time of permanent beta, it quietly awaits further forks that will develop it anew. And in a slightly different instantiation, PECE's current code is zipped up into a "distro," for anyone to download, install on a server, and open into a new project.

Why

PECE is part of what we have thought of as "an infrastructural moment in the human sciences" (Fortun and Fortun 2015). A differential continuation of anthropology's "experimental moment" of the 1980s described by Marcus and Fischer (1986), we described the 2000s as an "infrastructural moment" characterized by new (digital) technological demands and possibilities, with issues of open access publication central to them. If ethnography was to continue to be experimental and grow to be more collaborative, those collaborative experiments needed digital infrastructure designed (and not simply adopted from elsewhere) to support them.

We became great admirers of recent infrastructure projects in cultural anthropology with similar intent, like Open Folklore (https://openfolklore.org), Digital Himalaya (https://digitalhimalaya.com), and Mukurtu CMS (https://mukurtu.org). There may be many collaborative projects in anthropology, but only a few of those have tried to design and provide new digital scaffolding to multiply the attempts.

PECE can also be thought of as an experiment in collective curation, one that provides the digital infrastructure to distribute collaboratively the work of compiling, documenting, characterizing, archiving, interpreting, and making public an agglomeration of ethnographic data bearing on complex, heterogeneous, cultural phenomena. Why? Not because we were fueled by some dream of exhaustive totality (Lemov 2015), nor because we thought every ethnographer needed to make all their data about everything and everyone completely open and accessible. But there are many ethnographers, we reckoned, in projects like ours where issues of privacy and research ethics were manageable (we "study up," for the most part), and simply making *more* of our newly created or otherwise singular data *more* accessible to *more* researchers would just be good, or at least a good experiment to try, even though it would not lead us all into a state of anthro*parousia*. Just as "raw data" is at least somewhat oxymoronic (Gitelman 2013), so too is "private data": the more public data can be made to be, the more it can be data. We wanted PECE to provide a means, in a limited number of cases, to render into data that which might otherwise remain as ephemera, gray matter, or just one of the dozens of interviews conducted every day, surely, by an ethnographer somewhere that would end up—either for reasons of research ethics, or the outdated expectations of funding agencies, or a culture of proprietary individualized scholarship—locked away in a file drawer.

In What Way

Although the mantra of "more hack, less yack" was never a particularly productive or apt one in the field of digital humanities writ large, the two terms nevertheless sum up much of the collaborative labor and its division: Kim and Mike worked almost exclusively through talk, while Lindsay, Brian, and others did the typing/ coding/hacking—but much yacking too. Yacking includes reading: we collaboratively read, analyzed, and discussed a wide and varied scholarly literature in digital humanities (see, e.g., Gold 2012), especially those dealing with the archival form (Derrida 1998; Brown, Clements, and Grundy 2006; Klein 2013; Turin 2011).

By What Means

While yacking has been a more or less ongoing feature of the collaboration, the hack came in waves, as funding allowed (again, see figure 7.2). The development of the data model and practical policies (how permissions are handled on the platform, backups, data expiration, etc.) was done with RDA funding, which also paid for some of the Drupal development work. Funding for all the rest of the Drupal programming was pieced together through the NSF grant that supported the 6+ Cities Project (described in a later section), and two RPI internal program grants. Brian mostly gifted his time, knowledge, and skills to PECE; Lindsay has been supported through a research assistantship not through the Department of Science and Technology Studies at RPI but through the Tetherless World Constellation (information, web, and computer science). Consistent with the dominant cultural logics of collaborative labor, each of them has committed more to PECE than what they have been remunerated for.

The Asthma Files (TAF)

Who

This collaboration started as a collaborative research project between Kim and Mike Fortun, stemming from their research as anthropologists of the environmental sciences and genomics, respectively, responding to new initiatives in those fields involving asthma as a place where new methods for collaborative "gene-environment interaction" research could be worked out. At the start, it involved the Fortuns and their graduate students, former graduate students, and undergraduate students at both RPI and other universities, working on an array of projects, some more independent, some more intricately entangled, all collaborative at some level. Undergraduates have played a significant role in this collaboration; easing their involvement was one of the explicit motivations for building PECE. TAF is open-ended, designed to accommodate and welcome any short- or long-term contributors, on any existing topic or any new ones generally related to breathing, air, respiratory disorders, and the many sciences thereof. A graduate student in the RPI STS department at the time, Alli Morgan was responsible for much of the topical, substantive, and administrative developments, including organizing RPI undergraduate researchers to contribute to the project. A former graduate student, Ali Kenner, whose doctoral dissertation spun off from an earlier (pre-PECE) form of TAF, has provided much content to the current project/platform, both through her own energetic research (Kenner 2018), and through a rotating cast of undergraduate and graduate students in her classes at Drexel University. We know most of these Drexel collaborators only through their work on the platform. As of mid-2017, much of the activity at TAF occured through the 6+ Cities Project described in the next section.

What

From The Asthma Files (https://theasthmafiles.org) website:

> The Asthma Files (TAF) is a collaborative ethnographic research project designed to advance understanding and efforts to address environmental public health challenges around the world.
>
> Focusing on dramatic global incidence of asthma and other respiratory illnesses as a starting point, the project spirals out to address growing concern about the health impact of air pollution and associated need to build scientific, clinical and public health capacity to address environmental determinants of human health. Through ethnographic interviews and analysis of scientific publications, policy debates, and media coverage, the project draws together many different ways of approaching environmental public health, aiming to enhance comparative and collaborative perspective.
>
> A key aim is to develop comparative understanding of different styles of both environmental health research and environmental health governance, in different urban and national settings. The project will result in a theoretically robust, empirically grounded conception of (environmental health) research and governance styles, detailing and categorizing different ways of developing environmental health data, advancing the sciences of environment and health, and directing these toward governance of complex problems. The project thus builds on work in the history and anthropology of science on how "thought styles" shape scientific research, and extends it to sociocultural analysis of "governance styles."

When

TAF has a longer history than PECE, and for many years was the collaborative research project that eventually gave rise first to the conceptualization and then to the design and building of PECE. TAF has existed on different platforms, beginning in 2001 as a PowerPoint file that we (Kim Fortun and Mike Fortun) built, beginning as a collaboration of two, where each slide was a file presenting a concept, institution, researcher, or other such entity drawn from our research illustrating different "asthma knowledges." The intent was to privilege difference and epistemological pluralism over the consensus-driven, monopolistic approaches favored in dominant scientific discourses. By 2007 TAF had become a wiki to which our students could make their own contributions, diversifying the topics and expanding the scope of TAF.[2] We started a Zotero group library in 2009 to store the collaboratively compiled bibliographical references; in 2020 it had 44 members and over 3,000 references. By early 2012, we had begun migrating to a platform built with the Plone CMS, in collaboration with Dan Price and the Texas Learning and Computing Center at the University of Houston. Throughout this history, TAF also had weekly meetings, mostly with its RPI members but often including other participants by Skype. Those weekly meetings led eventually to the weekly PECE meetings, and the developments in and on Drupal described earlier, and the eventual migration of TAF to the PECE platform in 2016. (We can only quickly reemphasize here the importance that the development in the 2000s of increasingly stable and available digital technologies like Skype, Google Docs, Drupal, and Zotero have had on our ability (and desire) to collaborate across geographic and other differences.)

Where

For the first several years of its development (pre-PECE), TAF was a collaboration entirely within the RPI STS faculty and graduate students (and a limited number of undergraduates). As the number of collaborators grew, TAF began to develop a focus on specific "asthmatic spaces," where the emergent geospatial unit was the city: Houston first, then Knoxville, Tehran, Philadelphia, New York City. "Asthmatic spaces" was one of six thematic "cabinets" into which asthma "files" were organized (the others were "accounting for asthma," "knowing asthma," "experiencing asthma," "caring for asthma," and "communicating asthma"). This city-centric orientation eventually led to the even more expansive collaboration of the 6+ Cities Project.

Why

Asthma represents the kind of complex condition—chronic, multicausal, confoundingly variable, researched by numerous different expert communities—that demands collaborative methods and approaches. That statement is true for the scientists who research asthma, for whom interdisciplinarity or transdisciplinarity or team science are valued and ubiquitous (and poorly defined and elusive) terms, and it is as true for us as ethnographers: an anthropology of asthma cannot not be collaborative. The PECE platform was designed to configure the collaboration among different researchers and their contributions to produce what we called "kaleidoscopic perspective." The intent again was to privilege or foreground explanatory pluralism and difference by juxtaposing varied materials and analyses in ways that might displace or disrupt the drives toward consensus, harmonization, and totalization that characterize the dominant styles not only in the natural sciences but in the human sciences as well.

In What Way

Although almost everything about TAF is collaborative, or depends on collaboration, we highlight two collaborative dimensions here that PECE *infrastructures* (to be read as a verb) into the TAF project as core innovations: (1) the annotation module, built around what we called "collaborative analytics"; and (2) what we at first referred to metonymically as "the asthma file" and now call (to differentiate it from the TAF project and generalize it) "the PECE essay."

1. The PECE annotation module is an instance of light structure that encourages and leverages explanatory pluralism and collaborative hermeneutics: documents, images, audio and video interviews, and any other artefact contributed by a researcher can be collaboratively and interpretively analyzed by *n* other researchers who respond to an open-ended series of shared, open-ended questions. The PECE project statement describes what collaborative analytics look like in practice:

   In this stage, researchers analyse artefacts, oriented by a set of shared questions. A researcher does not have to respond to every question, but each response becomes its own "object" within PECE, making it available for later comparison and combination with other responses to the same question addressed in the analysis of other artefacts. Researchers can also add questions to the shared set of questions. . . . Many annotations, especially early in the work of a project, are of relevant published material, but any object can be annotated: an image, an interview or interview excerpt, a *Nature* article. The annotations are structured to ease sharing and comparing of "notes," and to pull analysis back to a project's "shared questions." As a researcher writes an annotation, the entry window presents her with a series of these questions, to which all other project collaborators are also responding. A researcher may ignore some questions and write extensively on others, but each response becomes . . . available in a structured way for recombination with other annotations on other materials.

The TAF site, for example, has these kinds of collaborative analytics structured for "Profiling a Data Policy," "Reading Digital Infrastructure," "Profiling an Organization," and "Annotating a Scientific Study" (to name only a few). The latter presents researchers with questions such as "How was the study funded?"; "Describe how this study has traveled. Has it been used in news reports, cited by health officials, or used as the basis of other studies?"; and "How, if at all, does the study address vulnerable populations?" Any user can add a new question to any collaborative analytic; PECE's digital infrastructure was designed to credit such collaborative contributions of questions, so the system values and credits the authorship of questions and analytics as much as it credits the authorship of data and interpretative analysis.

Indeed, every component of these collaborative analytics was *infrastructured* and designed (this consumed a lot of time and money) to be, in effect, its own data object, digitally outfitted with enough appropriate metadata to make it creditable, archivable, searchable, and reiterable—that is, any part of a collaborative analytic can be reorganized and restructured around any other part. If you searched in TAF on "ozone," for example, it would have returned (in July 2018) 302 results that could then be filtered out according to type; 179 bibliographic references imported from our collaborative Zotero group library, 65 annotations, 27 PDFs that uploaded directly to the site, and one question that was part of a collaborative analytic. Clicking on one of the 65 annotations takes you to a particular response from a particular researcher to a particular artefact pertaining somehow to ozone (perhaps its effect on lungs); clicking from there on the collaborative question that annotation was written in response to, opens a page listing all the other responses to that analytic concerning ozone, by all other researchers, for all other artefacts (perhaps concerning its status in EPA regulatory policy, or the environmental group that developed an app to provide near–real-time ozone data to Houstonians, or new satellite technologies for monitoring it). It is through such infrastructural design and developments that ethnographic collaboration on asthma (expansively understood), we hope, can be leveraged, multiplied, diversified—reorganized and rewritten experimentally, again and again.

2. The PECE essay is a digital-literary form also designed to instantiate and/ or leverage such disjunctive, juxtapositional, collage-ish aesthetics and practices likened to surrealism by James Clifford (Clifford 1981). So, taking any of those 302 search results for ozone, say, a TAF researcher can juxtapose on a single screen multiple images, documents, audio-video artefacts, or annotations authored by multiple collaborators, putting them into lightly structured relation (more or less loosely) to any chosen topic or subject area such as ozone. The PECE essay pursues those "kaleidoscopic logics" that are demanded by complex conditions such as asthma, and the other similarly disseminated, dissensus-riddled phenomena that demand collaborative work and involvement from ethnographers—but presented in ways that keep the differences and "suturings" (Clifford's term) visible.

We thought this would be easy to code as digital infrastructure. It was not. We have invested extensively in software development for the PECE essay to make continual improvements: to allow multiple authors, for example, to allow annotations to be added to the essay, and to allow the overall essay itself to be annotated. Even after much time and money, we are already dreaming of and pining for PECE Essay Version 2.0, and already know that we will then be wanting Version 3.0, which we can't as yet afford.

You can see an early example of Version 1.n here: https://theasthmafiles.org/content/mobilizing-asthma-research/essay. A new collaboration which began after we first wrote this piece, STS Across Borders, makes extensive use of the PECE essay to document and present the extensive research in science and technology studies and related activities occurring globally; a UC Irvine anthropology graduate student Angela Okune, for example, curates and presents a wide range of materials pertaining to science, data, and science and technology studies in a number of African nations (Okune and Chaudhury 2018).

By What Means

Collaboration, to reiterate, requires infrastructure, media, a platform. When The Asthma Files project began fifteen years ago, it manifested publicly as a PowerPoint file and slideshow, but only on the occasion of a public talk by one or both of us ("public" in the sense of a small academic audience in a university classroom or auditorium). As the project and number of collaborators grew, that format quickly became unmanageable and insufficient for documenting data provenance, for preserving and sharing data, and for similar "data life cycle" issues to which we were becoming more attuned through our involvement in the Research Data Alliance (see the section on the RDA's Digital Practices in History and Ethnography Interest Group). This led to the conceptualization, design, and development of PECE, with one of its aims being a more expansive public for the collaboration and collaborative research to address.

The Asthma Files research itself was for the most part squeezed into and out of our spare time for many years. Some of the undergraduate students who contributed research were paid as work-study students, but most did it for academic credit. The first time that dedicated funding and time for TAF-specific research was secured was for our Six Cities project, described next.

6+ Cities

Who

The core TAF collaboration (Kim and Mike; then Ali Kenner with her dissertation research) organized a research/teaching event on asthma and air pollution with Dan Price, a philosopher turned environmental studies scholar teaching at the University of Houston. This built up the TAF research thread on "asthmatic spaces," which began to develop comparative studies of New York, Houston, and Tehran (through Tahereh Saheb's dissertation research). That thread of work has grown into our current 6+ Cities project, also characterized by a research scope that has expanded from asthma (albeit asthma writ large) to become a comparative ethnographic study of environmental health governance in Phila-delphia (where our lead collaborator remains Ali Kenner), Houston (Dan Price), Albany (Scott Kellogg), New York City (Sam Elrahman, Thomas Depree), Beijing (Rodolfo Hernandez), and Bangalore (Govind Gopakumar, Vinay Baindur). That collaborative project has continued to expand even more into the open-ended 6+ Cities project that now includes the additional Indian cities of New Delhi (Surajit Sarkar, Rohit Negi, Prerna Srigyan), Hyderabad (Pankaj Sekhsaria, Aalok Khandekar), Chennai (Deepa Reddy), and Pune (John Mathew). This collabora-tion is anchored in an academic kinship network of our current and former stu-dents. A former graduate student (now an assistant professor of anthropology/ sociology at the Indian Institute of Technology in Hyderabad) Aalok Khandekar leads the 6+ Cities research in India, and Alli Morgan works on the group coor-dination and administration.

What

The collaborative research focus here shifted from TAF's main concerns of asthma sciences and asthma care, to environmental health governance styles and how air pollution, in particular, is monitored, analyzed, and remediated (in the multiple senses of that term) in varied cultural/political contexts. Cities emerged as the chosen ethnographic object or level of analysis in part as an effect of a growing literature on data in "smart cities," and its intersection with an increas-ing focus on cities in scholarship on governance. Our initial choice of six cities was intended to echo a landmark scientific collaboration of the 1980s that came to be called The Six Cities Study, one of many collaborative research projects in the sciences that we admire, and that have fueled our own collaborative drives. Most closely identified with the Harvard School of Public Health, the original Six Cities Study researchers (working in a different set of cities than ours) were the first to analyze large and diverse data sets to demonstrate conclusively that air pollution seriously harmed public health (Dockery et al. 1993).

When and Where

As with the other collaborations described earlier, we have tried to plan regular weekly two-hour meetings with the local Rensselaer-based members, sometimes joined by others via Skype. Beginning in 2017, we have tried to hold Skype conference calls about every two or three weeks with most of the researchers in the Indian cities that were added. We have ourselves done a few two-week concentrated fieldwork stints of interviewing and research with our collaborator in Beijing, Rodolfo Hernandez (Kim and Mike, November 2016), and some of our collaborators in India (Kim, March 2017), and similar briefer research stints with our US-based collaborators. So this research, too, is regular and distributed over time, throughout the collaboration, coordinated largely through the TAF instance of the PECE platform.

Why

Cities were chosen less by logic or through some research algorithm, and more by a kind of collaborative opportunism: Where did we know someone, or know someone who knew someone, who had appropriate ethnographic interests or expertise? This in part explains the initial omission of seemingly obvious cities such as Los Angeles (now that we have moved to the University of California at Irvine, we are adding in Los Angeles and its neighboring areas). We are trying to say something about cities as a middle level or unit of governance, where air is understood through actions styled by multiple actors distributed across lower (city inhabitants, neighborhood groups, and NGOs) and higher (regional, national, international bodies and regulations) levels.

In What Way

Much of the research effort has been fluid and open-ended, a kind of operationalization of the "+" in the project's title. As the TAF collaboration has grown into the 6+ Cities collaboration, though, there has been a need for more light structure to organize the research and its administration. Especially in the case of the Indian cities, our collaborators have become in effect paid consultants, for whom we have tried to specify expectations and deliverables (e.g., 30 interviews, 100 entries added to a collective Zotero library, 20 article annotations, etc.). We have budgeted for 300 hours of work from each consultant, but as we state in our agreement with consultants: "We realize that research is never quite so straightforward . . . and will require more than 300 hours. The RPI group will help make up the difference. We also hope to create synergies that will help us accomplish more collaboratively than we could have individually. All project participants are free and encouraged to use material collected for the project in their own projects."[3]

By What Means

Our initial Six Cities research was funded through a two-year NSF research grant; a small percentage of this went to PECE platform development. The research in Indian cities that is part of the 6+ Cities project was funded through a grant from the Azim Premji Foundation in India.

Research Data Alliance's Digital Practices in History and Ethnography Interest Group (DPHE-IG RDA)

Who

Kim Fortun, Mike Fortun, and Jason Jackson (Indiana University, Mathers Museum of World Cultures, and openfolklore.org) have, since 2013, been cochairs and cofounders of the Research Data Alliance's Digital Practices in History and Ethnography Interest Group, which is one of many and indeed a growing number of interest and working groups (e.g., a Metadata IG, a Wheat Data Interoperability IG, a Linguistics Data IG, a Structural Biology IG) that make up the Research Data Alliance.[4] There are about 120 listed members of the DPHE-IG. At most, about one-quarter of those are researchers we know personally who joined RDA through our interest group; the other three-fourths are drawn from the broader RDA membership who have also subscribed to the DPHE-IG. Our graduate student and PECE platform architect, Lindsay Poirier, is now an RDA Fellow, a recognition previously held by our former graduate student, Brandon Costelloe-Kuehn, and now also held by one of our newest collaborators, Vivian Wong (UCLA). RDA Fellows work with an IG and are remunerated with travel funds to the semiannual plenary conferences held in cities like San Diego, Dublin, Amsterdam, Tokyo, and Barcelona. Our working sessions at RDA plenary conferences are usually attended by around twenty to thirty people; our call-in webinars in which researchers present their projects or discuss data sharing issues (these were organized most regularly in 2015–16 and more sporadically since) usually have five to ten participants.

What

From the DPHE-IG description on the RDA website:

> RDA's Digital Practices in History and Ethnography Interest Group (DPHP-IG) works to advance data standards, practices and infrastructure

for historical and ethnographic research, contributing to broader efforts in the digital humanities and social sciences.

Goals
- Advance development of digital infrastructure for historical and ethnographic research through engagement with concrete scholarly practice and projects (such as Open Folklore, the Nunaliit Atlas Framework, the Platform for Experimental and Collaborative Ethnography and Indiana University's Mathers Museum of World Cultures).
- Advance conceptualization of the special characteristics and digital potential of humanities and qualitative social science data, including conceptualization of ethnographic and historical research data as "big data."
- Advance capacity to share, integrate, visualize and act with different kinds of data and analyses, including qualitative data and the kinds of analyses produced through historical and ethnographic research.

Planned Outcomes and Benefits
- Build a global network of people involved in the development of data infrastructure for historical and ethnographic research, providing opportunities to share digital tools and project development experience. Monthly, call-in "project shares" since summer 2013 contribute to this.
- Link people involved in development of data infrastructure for historical and ethnographic research to data scientists and technologists, and to people in other research domains involved in data infrastructure development (leveraging the connections provided by RDA).
- Characterize and recommend best-practice meta-data standards for researcher-created primary data (field notes, recorded interviews, etc.) in history and ethnography. This will be the focus of the first Working Group spun out of this Interest Group.
- Characterize and recommend user agreements, citation practices, digital exhibition protocols, and other mechanisms that will facilitate sharing and public availability of historical and ethnographic data (recognizing the need to customize access according to data type and context).
- Develop an ethnographic project to document and analyze data practices and culture in different research communities, especially

as represented in the RDA. The comparative knowledge created by the project can undergird deep research collaboration across diverse fields.

When

The Research Data Alliance was established in 2013, and our interest group was one of the early IGs formed that year—the same year that the United States formalized its Federal Open Data Policy requiring government data to be made available in open, machine-readable formats. It was developments like these in both government and scientific data landscapes that reinforced our sense that infrastructure was vital to support; we found ourselves both studying the "open data" wave as researchers, and simultaneously riding it as open data practitioners.

This more distributed, looser collaboration runs mostly in the background for us, but makes productive sporadic foregroundings in the forms of the virtual "project share" GoToMeetings (for a while about once every few weeks, now less frequent), and when one or two of the cochairs or our RDA Fellows attend an RDA plenary conference for face-to-face working sessions.

Where

The DPHE-IG originated at RPI when we worked there; it is not completely coincidental that key RDA leadership figures (in computer and web sciences) are also at RPI. RDA styles itself as global (5,400 members in 123 countries), although there are three main divisions: RDA-US, RDA-EU, and RDA-AU. The biannual plenary conferences have been held almost entirely in major cities in the United States and the European Union: Dublin, Amsterdam, San Diego, Paris, Berlin, and Washington, DC. Asia and Africa are acknowledged as places where outreach and greater inclusion need to occur; Tokyo was the site of one of the plenary meetings in 2016, and Gabarone, Botswana, was the site of a 2018 plenary meeting.

Although most of our collaborative work with RDA occurs virtually, as is true of RDA generally, our group meetings at the plenary conferences have been important not only for keeping abreast of new data developments but also for making new contacts and beginning new collaborations; Ilya Zaslavsky, a computer scientist at the University of California, San Diego, for example, attended our IG session at the Berlin conference in March 2018, leading to a conversation that has grown into a new collaboration that will try to make the more qualitative methods and tools of PECE interoperable with the more statistical quantitative methods and tools he has designed called SuAVE (Survey Analysis via Visual Exploration, http://suave.sdsc.edu/).

Why

The DPHE-IG adopts the presumptive promise of RDA itself: that data sharing is inherently good, and furthering the freer and more open sharing of more (and better) data is part of a researcher's ethico-political responsibility. A primary way through which that responsibility is manifested is through the construction of and care for digital infrastructure (including cultural protocols) for the creation, archiving, maintenance, and sharing of data. Of course, matters of privacy and the ethics and regulation of data flows and use are subjects of RDA interest and work, but openness, sharing, and borderlessness are the dominant tropes:

> The Research Data Alliance (RDA) was launched as a community-driven organization in 2013 by the European Commission, the United States National Science Foundation and National Institute of Standards and Technology, and the Australian Government's Department of Innovation with the goal of building the social and technical infrastructure to enable open sharing of data.
>
> With over 7000 members from 137 countries (June 2018), RDA provides a neutral space where its members can come together through focused global Working and Interest Groups to develop and adopt infrastructure that promotes data-sharing and data-driven research, and accelerate the growth of a cohesive data community that integrates contributors across domain, research, national, geographical and generational boundaries. (https://www.rd-alliance.org/about-rda)

In What Way

RDA supplied crucial funding for the development of PECE data infrastructure; we were awarded a grant to adopt the outcomes of RDA's Practical Policies Working Group by coding them into the data model, data handling, and permissions systems of PECE. RDA has also been a constant source of comparative insights and ideas from "data wranglers" in numerous fields, from neutron physics and genomics to library and information sciences.

By What Means

The DPHE-IG collaboration works mostly virtually (GoTo Meeting, Skype conferencing, Google Docs). When we first started, we hosted biweekly project shares where we invited researchers with noteworthy experience in data sharing efforts in any domain (e.g., Scalar and Project Bamboo in the digital humanities, the National Snow and Ice Data Center and DataONE in the sciences). These have become less frequent, and our work has in large part shifted toward a spin-off working group (the Empirical Humanities Metadata WG) that will survey, summarize, and distill preferred metadata models and practices in what we call the "empirical humanities": ethnographic and historical research that has as a primary goal the generation of new data, which will be further enhanced through "collaborative hermeneutics" and shared widely for continued reinterpretation and redatafication. The WG Case Statement (which had to go through multiple rounds of editing and review before the group was approved) lays out the rationale:

> Given the cultural and social complexity (as well as technical, ecological and economic complexity) of many global problems today, collaborative empirical humanities research has renewed urgency. For decades, research in these fields has been an almost entirely individual-centric enterprise. Field notes, found documents, found or researcher-created photographs or recordings and other data used in cultural analysis are very rarely shared, except when reduced or rendered into some form of publication or museum display.
>
> One of the primary barriers to sharing data within the empirical humanities is a lack of agreed-upon protocols for metadata standards for user-created primary research data. While there has been a great deal of work in the cultural heritage arena, especially within museums and libraries, and the dilemmas of qualitative data re-use are well documented (see Holstein and Gubrium 2003), the issues associated with preparing data for later use by third parties are yet to be thoroughly conceptualized. . . . Many researchers find themselves caught in the confusing space between the dizzying proliferation of standards and a one-size-fits-all approach that can miss out on the diversity of data practices within disciplines. Working closely with existing metadata-focused RDA groups . . . we will produce a simple list of recommended metadata fields for a delimited set of artifact types, analytics and use cases. Once endorsed by the RDA, and taken up by early adopters, these best practices will be a go-to resource for researchers that may then choose to modify (add or subtract) the fields we suggest for their own purposes. Development and uptake of shared metadata practices and tools will make user-created research data more findable and usable within these research traditions. The work of this WG could also contribute to the development of mechanisms providing greater credit and incentives for sharing data.[5]

The Depositivist (Feverishly Archival, Experimental, Infrastructural) Style of Collaboration

In our 6+ Cities Project, we have come to summarize a key goal of our collaborative efforts as explicating the "environmental health governance style" of each city: how a city's diverse actors (agencies, experts, citizens) come to know and try to improve the composition of the air over time in that region. How could we characterize the mixes of democratic, bureaucratic, and technocratic patterns and movements peculiar to each place, with its variable nestings in local, regional, national, and global institutions, regulatory regimes, and histories? How do citizens get involved (or not), how do sciences get understood and referenced (or not), how are technical and socioeconomic resources invested (or not)?

There were several reasons we chose style as a kind of governing concept for our research: for one, we found long-standing efforts by historians, sociologists, and philosophers of science (and scientists themselves) to characterize styles of thinking, reasoning, or doing science to be interesting and worth extending. Ludwik Fleck's concept of the thought-style is perhaps most familiar, as is Ian Hacking's extensive work characterizing different styles of scientific reason (summarized in Hacking 2012). Like culture, style connoted for us something subtle and subsurface yet also substantial, elusive yet omnipresent, and enduring yet inviting of change and play. The experimental style, speculative style, deductive style, or statistical style of doing science, to name but a few of the styles that have been traced, have been fruitful designations to differentiate and qualify a science otherwise prone to unification, idealization, or reification, while not avoiding the science category altogether—strategic essentialism by stylization, if you will, or writing science under (styled) erasure.

And that was another reason for adopting style as a sign of something that, no matter how subtle or elusive or shape-shifting, is always somehow written (with a stylus). To be styled—and only science (at least a certain version of it) dreams of itself, or its future self, as unstyled—is to be impressed in or into a material or medium: a piece of paper, a body, a cityscape, a distributed digital network. Each of our collaborations was, in this sense, a project of writing/styling—not just writing about, and not just involving writing as one of the activities that collaborators did, but itself written/styled.

Collaboration too, like science, might be fruitfully approached and analyzed through the concept of style, then, rather than along its more conventionally codified axes (cooperative/competitive, social/solitary, gift/commodity, etc.). How would we characterize the style of our collaboration? We start by naming it the depositivist style, and go on to elaborate its feverishly archival, experimental, and infrastructural qualities that together compose our style of collaboration.

Our depositivist style of collaboration is marked by the trace of a positivist style of science, but one with its ground mined under by the play and work of deconstruction. To name only one sign of this aspect of the depositivist style: our comfort with and even embrace of the term "data," which raises more than a few hackles among more than a few anthropologists. (The title of our chapter is a wry reference to these kinds of responses, which find our affinities to the sciences and their ideals somewhat funny, odd, or otherwise out of the anthropological mainstream.) The depositivist style also embraces the experimentalist style, as described earlier in this chapter, that characterizes even the most positivist of sciences. Depositivism thus aligns our collaborative work in anthropology with a broader conception and history of the human (i.e., styled) sciences.

As is true of so many contemporary sciences, our depositivist style of collaboration is also one that privileges the deposition or archiving of data as much as, and in many cases more than, its use. Depositivism is a style of deferral, then, another trace of its broader deconstructivist legacy. It is a sedimentary style of collaborative anthropology, similar to scientific styles of work and thought in many other domains such as genomics and neuroscience: data accretes constantly, collected as much for future analytic capacities as it is for present purposes.

> The metaphor of sedimentation comes from Husserl's Crisis (1970), but is used in a way opposite to his. In caricature, Husserl thought it was the philosophical task of his time of European crisis to clear away the sediment. That was a specific response to the 1930s. We should, he thought, try to recover the original experiences underlying fundamental events, such as the discovery of mathematical proof (the *Ursprung* of geometry) and Galileo's mathematization of nature. He wanted to remove the sediment, to reach, perhaps, a pre-Galilean state. In our contrary perspective, the sediment, hardened over a long time by great pressures into rock, is a collection of achievements founded on human ingenuity, innate propensities, and interaction with everything. Like any sedimentary deposit, it may undergo radical change in the future, but it cannot be undone. (Hacking 2012, 600)

The depositivist style of archiving is a feverish one, however, a heated and ill-at-ease one that differs from the calmer assurances of positivist archives. Jacques Derrida's *Archive Fever*, a short book styled as a long essay that has impressed itself upon our collaborations in many ways, elucidates this aspect of our style. Like nearly all Derrida's writings, this essay tracks back and forth through a tight series of tangles concerning psychoanalysis, its history, history and memory more broadly, science and technoscience, and the question of whether psycho-analysis could or should be named—*tagged*, we might say today, in our new tele-technological landscape—a "Jewish science." Derrida too refuses the dream of an unstyled science, sciences unimpressed by the conditions of their production, affirming psychoanalysis's status as a science (contra Karl Popper), but a styled, "Jewish"(-ish) one. In the process, he raises the question of archives, and the feverish, troubled uneasiness (*mal d'archive*) of their authority and status:

> The question of the archive is not, we repeat, a question of the past. It is not a question of a concept dealing with the past that might *already* be at our disposal or not at our disposal, an archivable concept of the archive. It is a question of the future, the question of the future itself, the question of a response, of a promise and of a responsibility for tomor-row. The archive: if we want to know what that will have meant, we will only know in times to come. Perhaps. Not tomorrow but in times to come, later on or perhaps never. A spectral messianicity is at work in the concept of the archive and ties it, like religion, like history, like science itself, to a very singular experience of the promise. (Derrida 1998, 36)

For us, then, the depositivist style is only partly about what a collaboration has actually achieved or archived—although we are not lacking or disinterested in such deliverables. The depositivist style is even more about what the experimen-tal, archival collaboration is becoming, or will have become, and what infrastruc-tures can keep that archive becoming, keep it troubled and feverishly excited and excitable, and experimentally open to unplanned futures. Depositivist collabora-tion is collaboration for the sake of building (infrastructure for) further, more robust collaboration. The depositivist style is a collaborative style directed only in part by a defined collective end product, tangible result, culminating exhibition, or project; it is even more attentive to organizing the ongoing work of a collec-tive toward continually reiterating itself, extending itself into new collaborations.

A depositivist (archival, experimental, infrastructural) style is a promising style, requiring trust from its collaborators, and commitments of care—always putting the labor back into collaboration. It is patient and feverish, oscillating between satisfied and dissatisfied with the interminable work of building col-laborative infrastructure for future collaborations that might and might not be there. A depositivist style is an uneasy and responsive style, a style of stay-with-us and stay-with-it, a style of impatient deferral that keeps on keeping promises.

NOTES

1. We cite the collaborative entry at https://en.wikipedia.org/wiki/Five_Ws. Wikipedia notes the many variations of this device (now widely regarded as old-fashioned), includ-ing Rudyard Kipling's rendition in "The Elephant's Child" from *The Just-So Stories*:

I keep six honest serving-men
(They taught me all I knew);
Their names are What and Why and When
And How and Where and Who.

2. TAF, http://theasthmafiles.wikispaces.com/The+Asthma+Files+Wiki (site discontinued).

3. See TAF 6+ Cities Workplan for Project Consultants, accessed May 16, 2020, http://theasthmafiles.org/content/taf-6-cities-work-plan-project-consultants.

4. See Digital Practices in History and Ethnography Interest Group, accessed May 16, 2020, https://www.rd-alliance.org/groups/digital-practices-history-and-ethnography-ig.html.

5. See Empirical Humanities Metadata Working Group, accessed May 16, 2020, https://rd-alliance.org/group/empirical-humanities-metadata-working-group/case-statement/empirical-humanities-metadata.

REFERENCES

Brown, Susan, Patricia Clements, and Isobel Grundy. 2006. "Sorting Things In: Feminist Knowledge Representation and Changing Modes of Scholarly Production." *Women's Studies International Forum*, Feminisms and Print Culture, 1830–1930s, in the Digital Age 29 (3): 317–25. https://doi.org/10.1016/j.wsif.2006.04.010.

Clifford, James. 1981. "On Ethnographic Surrealism." *Comparative Studies in Society and History* 23 (4): 539–64. https://www.jstor.org/stable/178393.

Derrida, Jacques. 1998. *Archive Fever: A Freudian Impression.* Chicago: University of Chicago Press.

Dockery, Douglas W., C. Arden Pope, Xiping Xu, John D. Spengler, James H. Ware, Martha E. Fay, Benjamin G. Ferris, and Frank E. Speizer. 1993. "An Association between Air Pollution and Mortality in Six U.S. Cities." *New England Journal of Medicine* 329 (24): 1753–59. https://doi.org/10.1056/NEJM199312093292401.

Fortun, Kim, and Mike Fortun. 2015. "An Infrastructural Moment in the Human Sciences." *Cultural Anthropology* 30 (3): 359–67. https://doi.org/10.14506/ca30.3.01.

Fortun, Mike, Kim Fortun, and George Marcus. 2016. "Computers in/and Anthropology: The Poetics and Politics of Digitization." In *Routledge Companion to Digital Ethnography*, edited by Larissa Hjorth, Heather Horst, Anne Galloway, and Genevieve Bell, 11–20. New York: Routledge.

Gitelman, Lisa, ed. 2013. *Raw Data Is an Oxymoron.* Cambridge, MA: MIT Press.

Gold, Matthew K. 2012. *Debates in the Digital Humanities.* Minneapolis: University of Minnesota Press.

Hacking, Ian. 2012. "'Language, Truth and Reason' 30 Years Later." "Styles of Thinking." Special issue, *Studies in History and Philosophy of Science Part A* 43 (4): 599–609.

Holstein, James A., and Jaber F. Gubrium, eds. 2003. *Inside Interviewing: New Lenses, New Concerns.* Thousand Oaks, CA: Sage.

Kenner, Alison. 2018. *Breathtaking: Asthma Care in a Time of Climate Change.* Minneapolis: University of Minnesota Press.

Klein, Lauren F. 2013. "The Image of Absence: Archival Silence, Data Visualization, and James Hemings." *American Literature* 85 (4): 661–88. https://doi.org/10.1215/00029831-2367310.

Lemov, Rebecca. 2015. *Databases of Dreams: The Lost Quest to Catalog Humanity.* New Haven, CT: Yale University Press.

Marcus, George E., and Michael M. J. Fischer. 1986. *Anthropology as Cultural Critique: An Experimental Moment in the Human Sciences.* Chicago: University of Chicago Press.

Okune, Angela, and Aadita Chaudhury. 2018. "STS in 'Africa' in Formation." In STS Across Borders Digital Exhibit, curated by Aalok Khandekar and Kim Fortun. Society for Social Studies of Science. https://stsinfrastructures.org/content/sts-africa-formation-1/essay.

Turin, Mark. 2011. "Born Archival: The Ebb and Flow of Digital Documents from the Field." *History and Anthropology* 22 (4): 445–60. https://doi.org/10.1080/02757 206.2011.626776.

8

A COLLABORATIVE ETHNOGRAPHY OF TRANSNATIONAL CAPITALISM

Sylvia Yanagisako and Lisa Rofel

Since the 1980s, Italian textile and clothing firms have been outsourcing manufacturing to China and, more recently, China has become the most promising market for Italian fashion brands. This has led to the development of a variety of forms of collaboration between Italian and Chinese firms and entrepreneurs. For the past twelve years, we have pursued our own collaboration—a collaborative ethnography of the transnational capitalism being forged by the Italians and Chinese engaged in textile and garment production and distribution in China. The result has been a coauthored monograph, *Fabricating Transnational Capitalism: A Collaborative Ethnography of Italian-Chinese Global Fashion*. A project such as ours is perforce multisited, as it includes people, social relations, and institutions that inhabit and cut across national boundaries and places, even though the majority of the encounters and interactions take place primarily in one space— China. It is also multiperspectival, as it necessitates a deep understanding of the different historically informed goals, concerns, and sentiments that the Italians and Chinese engaged in these collaborations bring to them.

Our main goal in this project has been twofold. The first has been to understand how the Chinese and Italians engaged in these transnational relations of production are reformulating their ideas and practices of capitalist enterprise, including investment and management strategies, labor, value, and inequality. In doing so, we aim to redress the paucity of ethnographic studies of the cross-border relations of finance, production, and distribution on which transnational capitalism and global commodity supply chains rely, and refine our notions of transnational capitalism which is too often portrayed as a monolithic and purely economic force.

Our second goal has been to develop a new methodology for studying transnational capitalism in this global era. We argue that collaborative research of the sort we have pursued generates important analytical insights and, consequently, a reconceptualization of transnational capitalism. What we advocate is not merely a method for the collection of data, but a methodology for the study of transnational cultural production that entails both methods and concepts. Crucial to this methodology is the ethnographic capacity to listen to and understand the multiple parties engaged in transnational relations of production and distribution. Until now, almost all anthropological research on transnationalism, whether focused on capitalism, religion, or media, has been conducted by a single ethnographer. In these studies, a lone ethnographer focuses primarily on one of the parties in the encounter, thus overlooking (or even misconstruing) the goals, commitments, and historical legacies of the other parties. Few researchers, after all, have the area expertise to understand the historical legacies that multiple participants in transnational encounters who do not share their own background bring to the encounter, let alone the linguistic skills to engage in deep dialogue and participant observation with them. Collaborative research by two or more anthropologists with complementary linguistic skills and area expertise provides a more robust way to investigate such transnational encounters. In our case, Rofel's area expertise and past research in China (1999, 2007) and Yanagisako's area expertise and past research in Italy (2002, 2012) provided us with knowledge of the legacies of capital, labor, kinship, gender, politics, and the state crucial to a comprehensive ethnographic analysis of Italian-Chinese ventures. Understanding both the Italian and Chinese actors and their histories in these partnerships has enabled us to forge a more comprehensive, interactional analysis of the actions and reactions, interpretations and misinterpretations, understandings and misunderstandings through which the Italians and Chinese in these transnational business collaborations reformulate their goals, strategies, values, and identities.

Our study offers an alternative to the conventional comparative method in anthropology—one that we think is better suited to the modes of cultural production and transformation prevalent in the world today. Rather than engage in a comparative study of essentialized, abstract models of Italian capitalism and Chinese capitalism, we have pursued a study of the coproduction of Italian-Chinese transnational capitalism. This enables us to go beyond asserting that the core features of capitalism are instantiated in culturally diverse ways. Rather than emphasize capitalism's unity or how it reproduces itself—an analytical approach that assumes capitalism has a stable core—we focus on the specific core dynamics of capitalism that are key to transformations in a particular historical moment.

Our analysis highlights the ways in which capitalist practices emerge in relation to nationalism, gender, kinship, politics, the state, and social inequality.

While this point has been made by others, these supposedly noneconomic relations and practices generally tend to be treated as either historical backdrop or as determined by capitalism reified as a social actor. We do not hew to a classic dialectical materialist approach (e.g., Harvey 2005) in which history plays an important role but then is overcome in a new era of capitalism. We contend, instead, that historical legacies play a crucial role as Chinese and Italians bring reinterpretations of their pasts—including past social inequalities and transnational histories—into their formulations of capitalist action. We do not, moreover, merely demonstrate how the distinctive histories of Italians and Chinese form an assemblage or are articulated in these transnational collaborations. Our collaborative research enables us to show how their interactions also produce the significance and meaning of these histories.

For more than a decade, we have engaged in this collaborative ethnographic research, following Italian firm owners, Chinese and Italian production and distribution managers, and Chinese entrepreneurs, officials, factory workers, retail clerks, and consumers engaged in these ventures. During this time, much has changed, including the field of power in which Chinese and Italians are situated. As a result, we have been especially interested in how relations between the Italians and Chinese have been shaped by the shifting asymmetries of power between them. Transnational capitalism, after all, is a historically situated form of unequal social interdependence in which people produce forms of labor, value, inequality, and identities, along with commodities. All of these are mediated by the form of their social interdependence. We ask rather than assume which processes of social mediation are key to the forms being constituted in these transnational relations of production and how they are both being structured by and restructuring people's historical legacies, worldviews, and understandings of themselves and the world. As we view capitalism as a cultural practice, we are interested in the ways in which human capacities and orientations—including beliefs, sentiments, values, knowledge, and skills—operate as material and cultural forces of production to incite, enable, and shape processes of production and distribution. We are interested, in turn, in how cultural practices of capitalism forged in particular historical encounters reshape the orientations, sentiments, and values of human actors.

Collaborative Ethnographic Research

Our collaborative project arose through the convergences of our respective previous research. Rofel began her research in Hangzhou's silk industry in 1984, just as economic reform was taking off in China's urban centers. She witnessed the devolution of central planning, the ability of state-run silk factories to pursue profits, the beginnings of hiring migrant labor, and the desire of some of the young urban factory workers to leave the factory and become entrepreneurs (Rofel 1999). These silk factories sold their silk garments and silk quilt covers to a domestic market that was just beginning to develop. They also surreptitiously sold goods through Hong Kong, but otherwise had no direct contact with foreign businesses. The city of Shenzhen, on the border with Hong Kong, had just been invented to be the sole, cordoned-off location in China to experiment with direct foreign investment. By coincidence, in the same year, Yanagisako began her research in Como, Italy, on family firms in the silk industry. Like all textile industries in Italy, Como's silk industry had been composed almost entirely of family firms throughout both its preindustrial and industrial history.[1] Although the industry was thriving in this period, anxieties about competition from China were already pervasive—so much so that some firm owners initially harbored suspicions that Yanagisako was a spy for the Chinese silk industry.

By the late 1980s, Rofel began to find foreigners investing in the Lower Yangzi River region but always in joint ventures with some counterpart of the Chinese government, whether municipal, provincial, or central. Foreign trade was overwhelmingly controlled by state-owned import-export bureaus. The silk factories where Rofel had done research were finding themselves flourishing through foreign trade but also pinched by competition from rural-based silk factories, with their significantly lower wages, that had sprung up around the more loosely controlled rural industrialization efforts. Only in the 1990s were foreigners allowed to make direct arrangements with textile factories. By the late 1990s, Chinese factories were vigorously searching for foreign production and trade partners. At the same time, silk manufacturing began a precipitous decline. Together with foreign companies, Chinese factories began to combine silk with other fabrics. By the turn of the century, most of the fifteen main silk factories Rofel had researched in the mid-1980s had closed, merged, privatized, become joint ventures with foreign firms, or produced almost solely for export.

Meanwhile, the Italian silk industry suffered a significant decline in the 1990s, much of which the Italian manufacturers in Como blamed on unfair competition from China. They accused China of having intentionally flooded the global market with cheap silk garments, undercutting the prestige of silk, although they also acknowledged that lifestyle changes in Europe and the United States had contributed to the decline of silk consumption. The increase in women's employment meant that women no longer had the time or the interest in caring for silk clothing, including silk lingerie, and the shift toward more casual fashion meant that fewer men were wearing silk ties on a daily basis. Throughout the 1990s and in the first years of the next decade, Como's leading firms experimented with a variety of strategies, including new fabric mixtures and outsourcing manufacturing to Romania, India, and China. None of these efforts were successful in turning around the decline of Como's silk industry.

The collaborations between Italian and Chinese in silk production thus led to our own collaboration in research. In 2002 we began preliminary research in the Shanghai area, tracking those Como silk firms and other textile producers that were outsourcing manufacturing or forging joint ventures with Chinese firms. We were joined in this by Simona Segre Reinach, an anthropologist and fashion studies scholar, who had worked before with Sylvia Yanagisako and who helped us understand how these transnational collaborations fit into the history of Italian and Chinese fashion. As our research proceeded, so did the numbers of Italian textile and clothing firms outsourcing production in China, actively seeking joint ventures, and opening retail stores. Having discovered that Como's silk firms made up only a small part of the Italian-Chinese collaborations in fashion, we broadened our study to include the transnational manufacture and distribution of a range of Italian textiles and fashion brands.

We pursued ethnographic research in China both together and separately among firms in the greater Shanghai area, including Hangzhou and Jiaxing, and in Wenzhou. Lisa Rofel also conducted interviews and participant observation among workers in the factory she wrote about in her first book, in a silk yarn factory, and in a business that has textile, dyeing, and garment factories, as well as following the networks of entrepreneurs connected to one another in the export of fashion clothing. We did a small amount of research together in Italy—in particular, on the *pronta moda* (fast fashion) industry in women's clothing in Prato, which had been developed by the largest Chinese community in Italy. Finally, Sylvia Yanagisako followed the Italian firms back to their headquarters and production sites in Como, Milan, and Rome and also interviewed industry representatives and government officials.

There were some clear benefits of going together to visit firms and factories. The obvious one was that we each brought different cultural knowledge, in addition to linguistic competence, to these interactions and interviews. Our respective knowledge of where the Chinese and Italians were coming from was crucial to interpreting their comments, actions, and practices. For example, when Italian firm owners and managers praised the technical efficiency and work ethic of Chinese workers, it was clear to Yanagisako that their comments had to be understood in the context of the past struggles between capital and labor in Italy and their perspective on fiscal crisis, politics, and debt.

We also found it very useful to have two sets of eyes and ears to record observations in field notes and to respond to the questions each of us raised about the actions, discourse, and attitudes of the "other." This meant that each of us was constantly having to make explicit our interpretations of informants' statements and actions and the basis for them. Having an interlocutor in the field proved to be an excellent challenge, as well as being quite humbling when each of us became aware of what we had missed that the other had picked up. Indeed, this raised some serious questions about the accuracy and reliability of the observations of the lone ethnographer in the field. This is not to say that two ethnographers together in the field is always the ideal solution, as we will see in the next section.

On a more humorous note, we should add that another benefit of our research collaboration was the amusement and bemusement we generated for our informants in both Italy and China. Most Italians and Chinese perceive Sylvia Yanagisako to be Chinese, even after discovering that she neither speaks Chinese nor has Chinese ancestors. Indeed, we often explained that she was born and raised in Hawaii, to underplay her Japanese ancestry. Lisa Rofel, on the other hand, can easily be mistaken as Italian, even though she does not have Italian ancestors, nor does she speak Italian. On several occasions, Chinese entrepreneurs, managers, and workers continued to address their responses to Yanagisako, even after Rofel asked the questions in Mandarin and translated answers into English for Yanagisako.

Challenges of Collaborative Fieldwork

Our collaborative fieldwork was not without its challenges and problems. Perhaps the greatest was the difficulty of working in a multilinguistic setting in which various informants had different linguistic competencies. When we interviewed Chinese together, Rofel had to translate into English for Yanagisako, who does not speak Mandarin. When we interviewed Italians together, Yanagisako had to translate into English for Rofel, who does not speak Italian. Pausing for translation impeded the flow of conversation and the intimacy of one-on-one interactions. Listening to the translation, moreover, even as they did not understand it or only partially understood it, brought on a kind of verbal mirroring effect that made informants' more self-conscious of what they were saying and of the potential distortions of translation. In addition, the presence of a non-Chinese or non-Italian speaker sometimes led people to switch to English which—given their limited English speaking abilities—made for much less informative, stilted, and sometimes downright confusing speech.

These confusions, along with the way in which translation impeded the flow and intimacy of conversations, eventually led us to cut down on conducting interviews and participant observation together. Instead, we increasingly pursued separate, although coordinated, research activities. Yet our experience in the joint interviews and events were invaluable in providing us with a familiarity and insight into the people and settings each other worked with.

Another challenge of our collaborative fieldwork was the difficulty of getting access to both parties in specific business collaborations and joint ventures. Yanagisako's initial contacts were with Italian family firm owners and managers, Rofel's was with Chinese manager/entrepreneurs and workers. The differential power relations and tensions between Italian and Chinese in joint ventures and other collaborations meant that it was often difficult to get access to all the parties involved. Chinese manager/entrepreneurs were often uneasy about introducing us to their Italian partners or speaking with us when we had gotten in touch with them through their Italian partners. The reasons for this uneasiness became clear over time as we began to understand the complex relations of cooperation and competition, trust and betrayal that characterized these partnerships.

Collaborative Writing

In cowriting our ethnography we did not seek to present a single narrative voice. While we worked together on the theoretical framework and methodology presented in the introduction to the book and coauthored part 1 on the negotiation of labor value, we purposely retained our different narrative styles in writing separate chapters in parts 2 and 3. This may have resulted in some unevenness in narrative and representation, as for example, in our description of Italian and Chinese informants. One of the readers for Duke University Press mentioned that Rofel's descriptions of the Chinese included their fashion style, while Yanagisako's did not. This was somewhat ironic, given the Italian's sense of their superior knowledge of fashion, and reflected Yanagisako's decision not to reinforce stereotypes of Italians. Rofel's descriptions of the Chinese, on the other hand, illustrated their self-presentation as cosmopolitan urban citizens. In the end, we decided that the differences in our representational and narrative styles of writing made our respective analytic strategies more transparent than if we had tried to write in one voice.

An issue and point of tension that we became aware of both in fieldwork and in writing the monograph was our tendency to advocate and defend the views of those informants with whom each of us was linguistically more aligned. Rofel sometimes found the Italians more patronizing and arrogant in their views of the Chinese than Yanagisako did. Conversely, Yanagisako at times thought the Chinese were more offended by the Italians than was warranted. The productive tensions of coauthoring a multiperspectival ethnography raised important questions about how the convention of the ethnographer as empathetic listener leads toward an identification with her informants, making it difficult to be an empathetic listener of those who are critical of them (i.e., the views of the other's other).

Three core themes that emerged through our collaborative research and analysis provide the framework for our analysis of transnational capitalist processes and the organizational structure of our book. Part 1, which we coauthored, addresses the negotiations over value between Italian firm owners and managers and Chinese entrepreneurs, the asymmetries in their relations that shape these negotiations, and how they justify or hope to transform them. We analyze the various emphases that Italian owners and managers and Chinese entrepreneurs and managers place on their respective national and cultural identities, historical legacies, relationship to fashion, and place both within China and beyond it. In this first part, we argue that the production of the value of labor and labor power is always a process of negotiation within historically specific fields of power. The interactive character of this process both enabled and called for an integrated analysis of the Chinese and Italians engaged in it, even as their perspectives, legacies, and identities differ.

In part 2, we trace the historical legacies and revisionist histories through which various Chinese and Italian social actors established their collaborations, as well as how they interpret their respective individual, family, class, and cultural-national histories to explain their current situation and their hopes and concerns for the future. We examine the importance of these legacies and revisionist histories for the way in which their transnational capitalist projects are forged. In contrast to part 1, part 2 includes a coauthored introduction, a chapter by Yanagisako on the Italians, and a chapter by Rofel on the Chinese. This format allows us to trace the ways in which transnational collaborations are formed without fragmenting our analysis of how they are shaped by the respective historical legacies of the Italians and the Chinese. A deep understanding of these respective historical legacies is crucial to understanding the different ideas about labor, inequality, commodities, nation, state, and family they bring to their collaborations.

Segre Reinach's chapter, coming between parts 2 and 3, interrogates Italian fashion as simultaneously a discourse, a product, and a national brand. As an anthropologist and fashion studies scholar, she examines the evolution of the relations between Italians and Chinese in fashion production through three forms of collaboration: sourcing, in which Italians procured both raw materials and labor in China; fashion production, in both its material (manufacturing) and immaterial aspects; and branding, the distribution of fashion products through the signifier of the brand. She elaborates on the changing tensions in their relations as the Italians and Chinese negotiate the transformations in both China's economy and Italy's global fashion industry. The latter, Segre Reinach argues, has been undergoing an identity crisis as the globalization of *Made in Italy* has dismantled the original fashion-production model rooted in the alliance between *stilismo* and large-scale industrial manufacturing which was responsible for its success.

Part 3 of our book focuses on the kinship and gender relations that are critical to, but have different valences for, the Italians and Chinese and the manner in which they develop collaborative relationships. While the Italians tout the family-based nature of their firms, Chinese entrepreneurs often have a more ambivalent and ambiguous relationship to claiming they are a family firm, in large part due to the way public discourse about corruption pinpoints family favoritism. Given the different historical legacies that shape Chinese and Italian ideas about the nexus of family, business, and state, part 3, like part 2, includes a coauthored introduction, a chapter by Yanagisako on the Italians, and a chapter by Rofel on the Chinese. This enables our respective chapters to focus on key kinship and gender sentiments, concerns, and aspirations of the Italians and Chinese without being constrained by a conventional comparative analysis. For example, in her chapter, Rofel asserts that, for the Chinese, corruption is a key frame through which family business is construed, and she shows how this shapes and constrains their approach to family business. Corruption, however, is not a salient issue for Italian family firms because the link between family and business has been normalized and normative in Italian capitalism. Consequently, any attempt to pursue a parallel analysis of corruption and Italian family firms would distort our understanding of the concerns and issues that Italians bring with them to their transnational collaborations and encounters. Instead, in her chapter, Yanagisako analyzes two distinct processes of generation that are crucial to understanding Italian family firms, both their historical persistence and the generation of new ones. She shows how the transnational expansion of the Italian textile and clothing industry has had different consequences for these two crucial processes of generation and, consequently, for Italian family firms in both Italy and China.

Does a multiperspectival ethnography generate a different kind of dialogue than the usual one between ethnographer and informants? In other words, are our informants engaged in a dialogue not only with us as ethnographers but also with the cultural others they are engaged in collaborations with? Hence, rather than stories people tell themselves about themselves through their dialogue with the anthropologist, are these stories people tell anthropologists about themselves in their relations with their others? Given the disparate views our informants have of both their and other people's motives, orientations, and actions, should a collaborative ethnography produce an account that not only incorporates multiple perspectives but also analytically resolves them?

We anthropologists have only begun to explore these questions.

NOTE

1. In 1985, out of the approximately four hundred firms in the province of Como, which employed about thirteen thousand workers, there was only one joint-stock company that was owned by investors from outside Como.

REFERENCES

Harvey, David. 2005. *A Brief History of Neoliberalism*. Oxford: Oxford University Press.

Rofel, Lisa. 1999. *Other Modernities: Gendered Yearnings in China after Socialism*. Berkeley: University of California Press.

——. 2007. *Desiring China: Experiments in Neoliberalism, Sexuality and Public Culture*. Durham, NC: Duke University Press.

Rofel, Lisa, and Sylvia Yanagisako. 2019. *Fabricating Transnational Capitalism: A Collaborative Ethnography of Italian-Chinese Global Fashion*. Durham, NC: Duke University Press.

Yanagisako, Sylvia. 2002. *Producing Culture and Capital: Family Firms in Italy*. Princeton, NJ: Princeton University Press.

——. 2012. "Immaterial and Industrial Labor: On False Binaries in Hardt and Negri's Trilogy." *Focaal*, no. 64: 16–23.

9

HYPERNORMALIZATION, COLLABORATIVE ANALYTICS, AND THE MAKING OF "AMERICAN STIOB"

Alexei Yurchak and Dominic Boyer

In this chapter we revisit a collaboration that produced an article that was a significant moment in both of our careers. We tell the story in two parts. The first is a chronicle of how the article project came into being (as told by Dominic). The second part is an analysis of how our collaborative process impacted the conceptual tools and analytical process we developed (as told by Alexei).

Chronicle of the Making of an Article (Dominic Boyer)

Like Tom Waits once said of his songs, anthropological insight often has meager beginnings—a hunch, a slight puzzling, an observation or moment of recognition that happens to ramify. In the case of "American stiob," Dominic was reading Alexei's *Everything Was Forever until It Was No More: The Last Soviet Generation*, in preparation for a graduate seminar he was teaching at Cornell University in spring 2006. In chapter 7, Alexei wrote:

> We will use the slang term *stiob* to refer to the ironic aesthetic practiced by groups such as the Mit'ki and necrorealists. *Stiob* was a peculiar form of irony that differed from sarcasm, cynicism, derision or any of the more familiar genres of absurd humor. It required such a degree of *overidentification* with the object, person, or idea at which this *stiob* was directed that it was often impossible to tell whether it was a form

151

of sincere support, subtle ridicule, or a peculiar mixture of the two. The practitioners of *stiob* themselves refused to draw a line between these sentiments, producing an incredible combination of seriousness and irony, with no suggestive signs of whether it should be interpreted as the former or the latter, refusing the very dichotomy between the two. (2006, 249–50)

Katie Stewart writes about those affective moments when something "snaps into place" (2007, 5) and this was one of them. But to understand why this passage was so affectively resonant, it is worth recalling that early 2006 was something of a golden era for ironic aesthetic practice in popular culture in the United States. The country was halfway into the second presidential term of George W. Bush, dispirited by twenty-five years of neoliberal (post)political consensus, mired in unending conflicts in Afghanistan and Iraq, and governed by a political regime that routinely lifted pages from the playbook of authoritarian propaganda machines with the eager assistance of its unofficial Department of Agitation, Fox News. Meanwhile, Jon Stewart's *The Daily Show* had emerged as a rare channel of political insight and sincerity despite being broadcast on the Comedy Central channel and was becoming a go-to news source, especially for many younger Americans. In late 2005, the architects of *The Daily Show* had spun off *The Colbert Report*, in which Stephen Colbert inhabited the role of a Fox News–style populist opinionator and made terms like "truthiness" part of American political discourse. What we often forget today is that, in those early years of *The Colbert Report*, Colbert rarely broke character. He never sought to explain what the purpose or message of his performance might be. It worked because his audience already knew the caricature he was climbing into four nights a week; we had an unspoken understanding of the form of political performance he was ironizing and many of us shared the sense that that form was already to some degree self-caricaturing. Colbert's concentration on political form helped to bridge ideological differences; indeed, early academic scholarship on *The Colbert Report* revealed that viewers from across the political spectrum found the show funny and thought that Colbert's political sympathies, deep down, corresponded to their own (LaMarre, Landreville, and Beam 2009).

We in the audience may have felt we recognized what Colbert was doing but there still wasn't really a term for the kind of ironic-satiric practice he was pursuing. Through its character/caricature work alone—let's call it "charicature"—it was something beyond normal deadpan humor. *Everything Was Forever* contained precisely the analytic language Dominic was looking for to capture the kinds of performative occupations of US authoritative political discourse that were taking place in 2004, 2005, and 2006. Dominic was not actively researching this discourse but perhaps recognized parallels between what was happening in US political communication and the media system of the German Democratic Republic that had been a focus of his dissertation research (Boyer 2005). We didn't know each other at that time but we met not long after in 2006 when Alexei visited Cornell University to give a colloquium talk.

For the 2006 American Anthropological Association meetings in November, Dominic wrote a paper that built upon Alexei's discussion of "hegemony of form" and stiob to help analyze the former East German satire magazine, *Eulenspiegel*, that had gone on to create an interesting satirical profile for itself in the unified German public sphere. The paper focused in particular on *Eulenspiegel*'s "faking actions." In one action, at the height of the Mad Cow panic in Europe in early 1997, *Eulenspiegel* dispatched a team to travel from farm to farm in northern Germany pretending to represent an international group of experts on "Mad Chicken disease." Remaining in character for hours or days in some cases, they interviewed farmers as to whether their chickens were exhibiting any "irrational behavior." Dominic was struck by the testimony of *Eulenspiegel* journalists he had interviewed that this satirical method was something that had occurred to them before 1989 but which state surveillance had prevented them from achieving. At the conclusion of my paper, Dominic turned to Alexei's work and wrote: "Yurchak argues that *stiob* overidentification plays precisely on the overidentification with form already present within the public culture of the gerontocratic party-state. Yet it is not so unlike a subgenre of *stiob*-esque satires that have recently become very popular, for example, in U.S. television from *The Colbert Report* on cable news journalism to *South Park* on children's cartoons to *Da Ali G Show* on hip-hop, fashion, and postsocialist alterity. In this respect, I'm tempted to say that *Eulenspiegel*'s early 1990s satire anticipated something in late capitalist public culture rather than simply imitating it."

In an e-mail to Alexei sent shortly after the conference, Dominic attached a copy of the paper, explaining that "it contains a little homage to your work on satire as well as an idea (contained at the end) about how your analysis of socialist hegemony of form could be refunctioned to analyze nonsocialist contexts as well. . . . I'll pitch this idea to you again when we talk later this week." By early June 2007, we were already referring to "our project," an effort to transport the analytics of Alexei's work on late Soviet socialism to the contemporary American context. By September 2007, we had resolved to write up a short version of the argument for *Anthropology News* and to produce an essay-length version of the project as a keynote for the 2008 Soyuz meetings at the University of California, Berkeley. Alexei had already written up the "Lenin was a mushroom material" earlier in the year. In October, on Halloween no less, Dominic suggested the title of "American Stiob," a play on "American Gothic" but also to capture our sense that, while the ironic/satiric practices we were finding in the US media bore some family resemblance to late Soviet stiob, we could not claim that it was exactly the same phenomenon.

We debuted an informal version of our project at the Council for European Studies meetings in March 2008, which was titled "The Hypernormal Kinship of Late Socialist and Late Capitalist Media" and then we presented the first full version of "American Stiob" as the keynote at Soyuz in April. The subtitle at that point was "On the Hypernormal Kinship of Ironic Aesthetics in 'Late Socialist' and 'Late Capitalist' Media," but most of the major analytic moves in the later article were already in place. We glossed the argument of the lecture as follows:

> In this talk, we expose and discuss a certain uncanny kinship between the modes of parody and political detachment which flourished in socialist public culture in the 1970s and 1980s and those sentiments which appear to be becoming increasingly mainstream in the United States today. What we hope to illustrate is not a one-to-one correspondence between these modes as though there were some kind of modern path dependency encompassing both socialism and capitalism. Rather our argument lives more at the level of institutional and ideological formations. What we argue is that the highly monopolized and normalized media institutions and circulatory channels of late socialist public culture anticipated, in remarkable and perhaps unexpected ways, contemporary trends in American media and public culture as well. Thus, it is perhaps unsurprising that analogues to the ironic modalities normally associated with late socialism have recently become highly intuitive and popular in the United States as well. We call these analogues "American *stiob*" to accentuate our sense of their family resemblance and common origins.

Rereading the Soyuz talk now, it seems that we had worked out the ideological and media analysis in rough form—indeed, we had stitched together our already existing paradigms, which was expeditious but also reflected our balance of contributions to the project. It is also clear from the lecture that we had essentially worked out the case study material we would need to anchor the argument, even though we had not developed our ethnographic perspective in much detail. The major difference between the Soyuz edition and the later published article was that we framed the project very much as a stock-taking of postsocialist studies a decade and a half after the collapse of Soviet socialism and as an effort to imagine what lessons socialism could still teach a world now evidently wholly in the throes of (neo)liberalism.

This was also, in essence, the intervention we proposed in our short article for the August issue of the *Anthropology Newsletter* (Boyer and Yurchak 2008).

The postsocialist studies framing perhaps feels a bit parochial now given the article's subsequent uptake but it was quite meaningful to us. Both of us had invested substantial energy in understanding the logics and lifeworlds of late socialism—and Alexei, of course, had lived it!—and we were concerned that this area of scholarship not gradually drift toward becoming of purely historical interest rather than retaining its robust anthropological and comparative significance. This was a crucial motivation in the design of the project. The warm reception of the keynote address and subsequent discussions with colleagues made us think that we should develop the paper further and try to publish it. We spent much of the summer of 2008 sending drafts back and forth as we sought to elaborate various elements of the project all the while reacting to new stiob material that began to appear, especially in the context of the 2008 US presidential election campaign.

By August most of the individual elements were in place but we needed to stitch everything together smoothly, to make sure that the argument was firmly tied to the ethnography and to make sure we had the argument articulated in the way we wanted it to be. Through a happy coincidence, we were both living in Washington, DC, during fall semester, 2008. So we were able to meet for several long writing sessions in which we worked to finalize our article manuscript. We always met at a cafe/bar/bookstore called Busboys and Poets at Fourteenth and V Streets. Our conversations were quite detailed and patient. Beyond the work of assemblage and smoothing, we actually ended up debating particular sentences and phrasings for long periods of time. The conversations also absorbed the terroir of our environment, the powerful energy and sense of purpose which inhabited that place and time, magnified by the fact that Busboys had already become something of an epicenter for progressive political action and performance in DC. Just a block from the thriving and diverse U Street Corridor, on a street richly decorated with iconic Obama Hope murals and posters, it felt like a particularly anticipatory space. Change of some kind was coming after the long, hard grind of the Bush-Cheney regime and its wars and authoritarianism.

The first draft of the full article was completed only a few days before the presidential election on November 4. The next day, in the exhausted delight at our object of analysis's collapse, we sent the manuscript for "American Stiob" in to the journal *Cultural Anthropology*. Their reviewers were generally quite supportive of the project but they also offered insightful criticism, which led us to refine and clarify the argument in several places. One point of dissatisfaction for one reviewer was the causality we attributed to the media's role in late liberal hypernormalization:

> I also wasn't fully satisfied by the "news media have become less diverse" answer to the question why. There have been so many changes

> to the news media and how we get news that I'm not sure that a sin-
> gle cause-effect relationship suffices. I'm also still craving a political
> explanation.... My own personal take on what Colbert and Stewart are
> doing is mocking Republican speech, which is so rife with oxymorons
> (compassionate conservativism), nonsensical neologisms (remember
> affirmative access?), false claims (Mission Accomplished!) that it invites
> parody. [OK, OK, the Democrats do this too, but I'm not sure they do it
> to the extent of the Republicans.]

We couldn't deny, of course, that the rightist political establishment was both a
vivid example of, and obvious target for, the kind of performances we were term-
ing "American stiob." But our argument was ultimately that hypernormalization
and performative shift were evident across the political spectrum for a combination of ideological and institutional reasons. Still, the ideological dimension
of the argument had clearly become too muted in the mix. So, in the revision
process, we sought to build its signal strength.

The other main concern raised in the peer review was more difficult to address.
Two of the three reviewers had problems with the term "stiob" as the gloss for the
phenomenon under investigation. One wrote:

> My main issue with this paper is probably not fixable: I don't love the
> word stiob. It's obscure in Russian; it is not a word in wide use, and when
> it is used (on Russian internet humor sites, for example) it rarely seems
> to be employed in its 'correct' original meaning as a parody involving
> super-straight caricature. It is of course totally obscure in English; . . .
> Because of this, I fear that the concept won't have a great deal of "trav-
> eling power." I find myself wishing there were some other word that
> would capture this phenomenon, more memorably, to give it more
> long-term traction. Try as I might, though, I can't come up with such a
> word, and I recognize that the whole structure of their argument may
> make it critical to use this terminology.

We had a serious discussion about this criticism but decided, in the end, that
"stiob" was too central to the analytic apparatus of the essay not to forefront it.
Alexei was quite critical of the idea that stiob was obscure in Russia and con-
vinced that it was a term that would travel well at least in former socialist countries. Of course, there is no way to know now whether a different title would have
generated a larger or broader readership for the essay. But it seems to have been
read and appreciated by some outside postsocialist studies as well. There is now a
"stiob international" page on Facebook with several hundred participants.

Today "American stiob" resonates tragically well with the global crisis of legiti-
macy for late liberalism and with the rise of populist authoritarianism in Europe,

the United States, and elsewhere. The last paragraph of the *Cultural Anthropology* article is particularly haunting:

> There are contexts when pure opposition may be inefficient, counterproductive, or impossible; and when another politics takes center stage. As we described at the outset, the parodic genre of stiob—based on overidentification with the dominant form of discourse and its performances—is an example of an alternative aesthetics and practice of political critique. And now it is drawing attention to important trends in the media and political cultures of late liberalism. We do not know yet whether American stiob will produce significant political effects let alone whether it could ever become the basis of a new, more familiar politics of opposition. But, we do know that it retains remarkable family resemblance to the stiob interventions that originated during late socialism in Eastern Europe; and, we also know that in that context the aesthetics and politics of stiob contributed significantly to the disenchantment of the dominant discourse and thus to socialism's sudden and spectacular end.

One thing we had perhaps not fully considered in the heady days of 2008 was that the disenchantment and decay of late liberalism would open the door to virulent authoritarian populism instead of the progressive alt-global populism we had hoped for. Douglas Holmes's brilliant work (2000) on the rise of European integralism was out there but a great many of us underestimated its prescience. At the time of this writing (mid-2017), the world is facing questions about the resilience and viability of liberalism in what Andrea Muehlebach has so aptly termed "the time of monsters" (2016). In the end, although it does seem that "American Stiob" was very much a product of its historical moment, it does seem like an apt and perhaps even urgent time to return to investigating the hypernormalization of late liberal political communication and what might emerge from its ruins. So there will be an eventual sequel to "American Stiob" even if its tone will likely be more tragic than comic as befits our times.

How the Collaborative Approach Changed Our Analytical Tools (Alexei Yurchak)

One of the most interesting and productive aspects of our collaborative writing is how it affected several key analytical concepts we used. In the process of writing, these concepts developed, becoming broader, more autonomous, and more flexible. In this section, we will account for this conceptual development. But first we have to introduce some parameters of the collaborative project.

Comparative Framework

In this collaboration, we brought our different types of expertise and focus to the table—for example, Dominic's work on East German socialism, Western German liberalism, German reunification, and journalistic media; and Alexei's focus on the former Soviet Union, the Soviet collapse, post-Soviet transformation, and ideological discourse. This difference in perspectives enabled a broad comparative analysis, where even contexts and objects that may appear incompatible could be brought together under one analytical framework. For example, the political discourse in the Soviet Union and socialist Eastern Europe could be compared with the political and media discourse in contemporary liberal contexts, particularly the United States.

The collaborative approach also allowed us to consider late socialism and late capitalism not only comparatively but also as two parts of one unified system that mutually enabled one another. In this view, not only Russia and Eastern Europe, but also the United States and the West more broadly, are considered to be equally postcommunist and post–Cold War. As Susan Buck-Morss remarked after the Soviet collapse, "We are all post-Soviet now." Instead of, or in addition to, focusing on differences between late socialism and late capitalism, this perspective shifted our focus to commonalities in the development of their political and media languages.

Multidimensional View of Discourse

The collaborative nature of this project also implied another difference in emphasis and expertise—Alexei's focus on forms, repetition, and imitation (in language and other semiotic forms) and Dominic's focus on mediation and circulation. Bringing these different foci together provided a kind of stereo vision of discourse, allowing us to create a multidimensional analysis of discursive change—from linguistic forms and structures, to conditions of their production, repetition, imitation, mediation, and circulation, to forms of their ironic subversion—that is more nuanced than is usually the case in linguistic anthropology and discourse analysis approaches. Using this method, and the comparative framework just mentioned, we were able to identify similarities in the political and media discourses in late socialism and late capitalism. We demonstrated that, despite tremendous differences between the conditions under which these political discourses exist in their contexts (e.g., in the former case political discourse is subjected to centralized constraints imposed by the party-state, while in the latter case it is subjected to the constraints of market democracy), some mutations that they go through are remarkably similar.

Further Development of Analytical Tools

In his book that traces the genealogy of political discourse in the Soviet period, Alexei developed several concepts that proved useful for our analysis of the US political and media discourse. These concepts included "hypernormalization," "performative shift," "overidentification," and several others. Dominic's analysis of the transformations of media in the context of late capitalism and online digital platforms proved compatible with these concepts. Our collaborative synthesis of these analytical tools meant that they became broader in their application (capable of analyzing not only the socialist, but also capitalist and newly emerging contexts), more autonomous (less rooted in concrete conditions and periods), and more flexible (capable of tracing new emerging forms that differ from how these concepts have been so far). In the rest of this discussion, we will elaborate on how these analytical concepts transformed as a result of collaborative writing and how they may continue transforming in our ongoing research.

Emerging Political Forms and Conceptual Tools for Their Analysis

First, let us briefly introduce the analytical concepts just mentioned. The first two—hypernormalization and performative shift—describe not just a fixed condition of discourse, but a process of its ongoing mutation.

They were first introduced in Alexei's book about the unexpected collapse of the Soviet system in the late 1980s. In the book, they describe a mutation that took place in the Soviet political discourse during late socialism (the post-Stalin period, between the mid-1950s and mid-1980s). This mutation was twofold. First, it amounted to a progressive ossification of the forms of political discourse (linguistic, visual, ritualistic). This shift was precipitated by a constant repetition of these forms under specific conditions, when a shared canon of what constituted a politically correct form of the party language was no longer available (it disappeared after Stalin's death), and the only guarantee of remaining within the parameters of politically correct language was to imitate previous texts and speeches that had already been in circulation. The production of new political texts had shifted heavily toward the repetition and recombination of prior texts. As a result, the linguistic form of political language (and other semiotic forms) had become more predictable and repeatable, while at the same time becoming more inflated and cumbersome. Ideological language had gone through not just normalization (becoming organized around one ossified norm) but hypernormalization—frozen forms of this language were progressively undergoing a snowballing effect, becoming more and more unwieldy. In other words, the form of political language was drifting toward increasing predictability and, at the same time, unwieldiness. In the ironic popular speech of the 1970s, this unique, hypernormalized language of the Soviet political texts and speeches was known as wooden language.

Second, this mutation at the level of form in political language had a concomitant effect at the level of meaning. In most cases, it had become more meaningful to reproduce verbatim these hypernormalized linguistic formulas than to attend closely to the referential meanings they supposedly communicated. Contrary to a common misconception, this did not mean that the political language in the Soviet Union became meaningless—rather, its meaning had shifted from the constantive dimension of language (how truthfully linguistic formulations represent reality) to the performative dimension (how successfully these formulations are reproduced). Discourse became treated for its performative meaning: the role it now played was akin to that of a ritual, when uttering precise linguistic formulas was not necessarily expected to describe reality accurately, but rather was seen as a means of reproducing institutional contexts, one's social status, and so on. Alexei's concept of performative shift captured this mutation of political discourse.

When we looked more closely at the political and media discourse in the contemporary United States, both concepts—hypernormalization and performative shift—proved quite useful; at the same time, they themselves underwent considerable transformation. To illustrate this point, let us focus on hypernormalization.

The political and media discourse in the United States, we observed, had long displayed a tendency toward becoming hypernormalized—full of sound-bites, talking points, predictable formulas, whose sheer repetition (in the speeches of politicians and rhetoric of media pundits) was often more important than critical attention to how truthfully they described reality. This feature of discourse was readily observed, for example, during the presidential primaries around 2008, when we started writing our collaborative project. We recognized that the growing popularity of Jon Stewart's *Daily Show*—which provided ironic commentaries on the formulaic nature of political and media discourse—was a symptom of ongoing changes in discourse that were akin to hypernormalization. In our collaborative article, "American Stiob" (2010), we wrote: "During the 2008 election year broadcasts, for example, Stewart assembled multiple clips from different TV channels to demonstrate that instead of scrutinizing the complex meanings of social and political issues at stake in the elections, media channels focused all their efforts and ingenuity on representing the elections in hypernormalized form—in endless figures, numbers, charts, soundbites, talking points— which are repeated from network to network and from one context to the next."

The reasons for this hypernormalized mutation of discourse in the US context were clearly quite different. In the Soviet case, hypernormalization occurred when two conditions coincided: first, all political producers worked under immense pressure to remain true to the norm of politically correct party language; second, what this norm in fact amounted to was no longer explicitly explained and discussed. As a result of these two conditions, excessive imitation and copying of previous instances of discourse led to its hypernormalization. In the US context, hypernormalization occurred under a different but comparable kind of pressure: the pressure to remain newsworthy in the market of news and commentaries that was becoming increasingly fast-paced and immediate, which meant that what constituted newsworthiness in any concrete case was becoming increasingly unclear and open-ended. This shift resulted in the growing practices of quoting, copying, cutting-and-pasting, and imitating linguistic formulas and descriptions across media channels and platforms.

The collaborative framework led to a further development of our analytical concepts, including that of hypernormalization—this concept could now encompass processes that seemed to be incompatible with each other but which led to similar results. To elaborate: in Alexei's book, this concept referred to the ideological language of the party that claimed to be controlled from the center and to describe reality accurately, while in fact it was no longer centrally controlled and no longer interpreted by anyone as a truthful description of reality. In our analysis of the United States, political and media language seemed to be the opposite of the Soviet one—it had no ideological center, was democratic and multivocal, and it too claimed to represent reality accurately. In fact, however, this language was also increasingly focused on repeating and imitating predictable formulas and sound-bites. In these two different contexts, political discourse went through comparable transformations, but the reasons for them were different.

To summarize: The concept of hypernormalization has transformed in our collaborative project. It broadened and became more autonomous from concrete contexts and more flexible, without losing its original meaning and analytical power. It continued to describe spontaneous mutations of discourse toward greater predictability, but no longer had to refer to the language of a singular ideology (e.g., communism) and could now refer to broad discursive formations with multiple ideological positions, voices, and origins.

In our current collaborative project, which continues the analysis that was started in the American stiob article, the concept of hypernormalization will be developed further. Today—in the era of ubiquitous social media and WikiLeaks, online news sites that lack clear sources, hackers, and internet trolls—Putin's control of massive media channels in Russia, and Trump's uninformed rhetoric in the United States—hypernormalization continues to be one of the aspects of the ongoing mutation of political and media discourse (of course, there are many new forms of mutation that are waiting to be analyzed).

For example, hypernormalization today seems relevant to the widespread claim that political and media languages are populated with invented facts and fake news and are confronted with the regime of post-truth. In these contexts, linguistic form is decoupled from referential meaning in multiple new ways. For example, in Putin's Russia this development is exemplified by the emergence of state-supported federal TV channels and online troll factories that manipulate accounts of events more directly than before, mixing real facts and fake facts in their news coverage, political talk shows, and online discussions. The main effect of this practice is not necessarily to fool the audience into believing every fake story and invented fact, but rather to get the audience used to the idea that "news" and "facts" should be read *not* for how true or false they are, but for how effective or ineffective, patriotic or unpatriotic, pro-Russian or pro-Western they are. In this model, once again discourse is read not at the level of its constative dimension (how truthfully it represents), but its performative dimension (how successfully it represents). Audiences may consider some facts to be true, but still insist that it is more important (for considerations of practicality, security, patriotism, or sovereignty, etc.) to conceal or misrepresent these facts.

This approach to truth is becoming increasingly common in the US media and politics too—for example, when the facts published by WikiLeaks are considered not for how true they are but for how desirable or threatening they are. One may also compare it with the claim that Putin's interference affected the outcome of the US elections. At the moment, it is far from clear what aspects of this interference are true and whether and to what extent they have been consequential. However, such considerations seem to be of secondary importance. At least in many cases, the discourse on interference is more important not for how truthfully it represents reality, but for how successfully it renders the unexpected outcome of the elections as alien, illegitimate, not representing who we are, and therefore in need of being reverted. Once again, the political rhetoric is produced and interpreted not for how accurately it represents reality, but for how effectively it does so.

It seems clear that the concept of hypernormalization, and the related concept of performative shift, will continue being relevant for this analysis. However, new conceptual tools will also be needed. Interestingly, one proof that hypernormalization has a considerable analytical import is a 2016 documentary by the British filmmaker Adam Curtis called *HyperNormalization* (the term he borrowed from Alexei's book). In this documentary, Curtis offers an analysis of the political transformations in the West after the crisis of communism that brought about a change in the conceptions of democracy and in the links between political language and its representations of truth.

REFERENCES

Boyer, Dominic. 2005. *Spirit and System: Media, Intellectuals and the Dialectic in Modern German Culture*. Chicago: University of Chicago Press.

Boyer, Dominic, and Alexei Yurchak. 2008. "Postsocialist Studies, Cultures of Parody and American *Stiob*." *Anthropology News* (November): 8–9.

——. 2010. "American Stiob: Or, What Late Socialist Aesthetics of Parody Reveal about Contemporary Political Culture in the West." *Cultural Anthropology* 25 (2): 179–221.

Holmes, Douglas R. 2000. *Integral Europe: Fast Capitalism, Multiculturalism, Neofascism*. Princeton, NJ: Princeton University Press.

LaMarre, Heather L., Kristen D. Landreville, and Michael A. Beam. 2009. "The Irony of Satire: Political Ideology and the Motivation to See What You Want to See in *The Colbert Report*." *International Journal of Press/Politics* 14 (2): 212–31.

Muehlebach, Andrea. 2016. "Time of Monsters." Cultural Anthropology website, Fieldsights, Theorizing the Contemporary. October 27, 2016. https://culanth.org/fieldsights/979-time-of-monsters.

Stewart, Kathleen. 2007. *Ordinary Affects*. Durham, NC: Duke University Press.

Yurchak, Alexei. 2006. *Everything Was Forever until It Was No More: The Last Soviet Generation*. Princeton, NJ: Princeton University Press.

10

AN ACCOUNT OF THE *CULTURES OF ENERGY* PODCAST AS COLLABORATION—OFFERED IN PODCAST FORM, OF COURSE

Dominic Boyer and Cymene Howe

CYMENE: So, Dominic, why did we decide to start a podcast?

DOMINIC: What an interesting question! It was a little over a year ago and, in the first instance, the idea emerged from just wanting to listen to something other than music on my long walks to and from public transportation in Houston. I guess I had some ambient awareness that podcasts existed but I had never really listened to them. But then I stumbled onto this website called Grantland, which has subsequently been shuttered, which tried to do a kind of more intellectual pop culture and media coverage. They sponsored a couple of podcasts that I found interesting and from there I started discovering other podcasts like Maron's WTF, the X Files Files, and Harmontown. I was definitely gravitating toward culture and comedy at first.

Anyway, as I got deeper into the podcast world, the aspect of the listener experience that interested me was realizing how much expert knowledge and trade talk I was willing to absorb and familiarize myself with because of having become invested in the people who were speaking. It's like listening to an entertaining serialized conversation and the ante is a willingness to learn something about their social world so you can get the jokes and so on. Remember that, at this point, most of the stuff that I'm listening to is frankly more pop culture oriented, as an escape from academic life. At the same time, I came to feel that there was maybe an opportunity in this podcast medium to expose folks to academic scholarship so long as you could keep it lively and engaging. Because in the end the real pleasure of a podcast is imagining oneself as part of an interesting conversation among voices you like. The content of the conversation can be anything.

So that was the idea at the start. Then, as an experiment, I thought well maybe we should try to have our center [Center for Energy and Environmental Research in the Human Sciences (CENHS) at Rice University] do a podcast on energy/environment issues—because it didn't seem as though there was much podcast activity in that domain—and maybe I should ask Cymene Howe to help. Because it turns out that Cymene Howe is an entertaining character with a background in radio, which I guess is something we should disclose, that our background in radio in some ways maybe prepared us to do this a little bit.

CYMENE: I wanted to point out, following what you just said, that getting to know the hosts and the people who they (or we) are interviewing and listening to how they think or how they speak, how they interact, is a really important aspect of what makes the podcast, as a form, special. It reminds me of the fact that when I have met academic authors I'm actually more invested in their written work.

The in-person connection is really compelling, it is a way of knowing the voice or the pen beyond the page, and beyond the text that one reads. It may not be fully "personal" and in the case of the podcast can hardly be said to be "in person" but, nonetheless, it is a human encounter that doesn't require the page or written text as a mediational device.

DOMINIC: Let me just add that my sense—and maybe this is in part because we're anthropologists and anthropologists are people who literally have to get off university campuses to lead their lives and who often go to very interesting places and have adventures there—has always been that academics get this terrible rap for being so boring and so buttoned up and so unable to converse with people who are not their own kind. My experience is that we know a lot of really wonderfully interesting people who happen to work in academia who would be interesting people no matter what they were doing. That does not always come across on the written page though, like you were saying.

CYMENE: Yes. Most people speak differently than they write, right? It is a different intellectual and synaptic process. Natural speech is just that, "natural" because it is not usually overwrought, carefully crafted speech of the kind that we put to paper. Speaking, especially in its more extemporaneous forms, is a very distinct medium in that sense.

In part, what makes the podcast collaborative are its formal properties of being both spoken and heard. The collaborative project between you and me as hosts happens live on the air, but also in thinking about who to invite and how to talk with them in the moment. There is the consideration of how to form and follow up with questions. I suppose there is an extensional collaboration with our audience too, who in many ways may be largely anonymous until bit by bit we have been able to meet people.

In meeting our listeners, I have been struck by the obvious: here are people whom I've never met and yet they know these rather random things about my life and your life, our anecdotal musings. Because of the contextual, quotidian ways that these musings unfold, especially in the introductory segment of the podcast, they have a banal charm that listeners seem to enjoy and that may even be therapeutic, in some cases, for us. Here, of course, I am thinking of the utterly grisly toy I imagined for Donald Trump's head, but also thinking of our occasional Freudian dream analysis or reading aloud some of our choice spam emails. These tales and reflections are connective tissue, I think, between the sometimes heavy intellectual conversations that take place on the podcast. The podcast, as a medium, encourages an intimacy with our audience in ways that many written forms (at least academic written forms) do not. It is strange because, again, we are unseen as are our audiences and yet there is a proximity and intimacy in the form that feels unique.

DOMINIC: A podcast represents a public of a certain kind.

CYMENE: Yes. And our listeners have a little podcast canon among themselves. I've heard listeners talking about episodes and sharing that experience not just with us as hosts but between themselves as listeners. One of my undergraduate students, for example, told me that as he listens he is always generating his own questions for the guests which sometimes correspond to ours and other times don't. In either case, he found himself doing some intellectual push-ups that he enjoyed.

There are scholarly podcasts where authors are interviewed about their new books. In our podcast we do talk about authors' books, sometimes multiple books or articles, but we also try and extend it to think about ideas, and more broadly methodological questions about teaching as well as their general thoughts and reflections on the moment.

This is another important piece of how the podcast is formed: it is contemporary. We really do bring in the tweet of the moment or the headlines. It has a conscious historicity to it that many written texts try to erase in order to make their messages more timeless and relevant beyond the short time horizon of publishing. In the podcast we have a clear attention to reflecting on the present—both ourselves and our guests—but without having it be journalism of the "just the facts ma'am" variety.

DOMINIC: Being present and in the moment for the conversation is a crucial aspect of podcasting to be sure. At the same time, the recordings also constitute an archive. This podcast is probably the closest thing that I've ever had to a diary. For example, with the 2016 election, you could listen back to those episodes and reconstruct in real time our emotional breakdown and reconstitution.

CYMENE: It is an audio diary in some sense.

DOMINIC: An archive that was unintended but still important. The other thing I wanted to second is this idea that the podcast is also a collaboration with the audience. I think we've taken pretty much every note that we've received from listeners including technical advice, like "You need to jack up the volume a little bit for European smartphones."

CYMENE: Right, or sometimes turn it down!

DOMINIC: Yeah, or "Try to turn down the electric sounds a little bit because they startle me."

CYMENE: Craig Campbell said he almost ran over an old woman when he was listening in his car and it deafened him to the point of nearly swerving into some unsuspecting soul!

DOMINIC: The thing about podcasting is that it's a medium very tolerant of amateurs, in that you can begin with very little knowledge and basic equipment and still do a pretty good job. But what I was going to say about the collaboration with our guests is that it's a very different dynamic from how we would engage somebody who had, say, given a paper in our department or at a conference. The game there is always to elevate the discourse, not to stump somebody exactly, but to show that you have this great expertise and mastery and maybe you pull some quote from some theorist out of your back pocket. You ask, "But have you thought about this or this book?"

CYMENE: I would never do that. That's just showing off.

DOMINIC: We've all done it [*chuckling*] and it is what we all do.

CYMENE: I'm teasing. [*Chuckles*] It's what every academic does seemingly all the time. It's almost embarrassing.

DOMINIC: I don't actually believe that back-and-forth is a bad thing. You go give a talk. You give your audience some challenging things to think about. Then they perform their art and craft and skills by reacting on the fly by talking back with their own takes. It's improvisational.

CYMENE: It is improvisational to be sure. When we tune into the naked performance of it is where I become disillusioned, but that is OK.

DOMINIC: And it's political—

CYMENE: Sometimes—

DOMINIC: —and it's informative.

CYMENE: Sometimes it is generative.

DOMINIC: On the podcast, meanwhile, it's much more about keeping the conversation going. It really is about trying to help somebody to articulate their work, to elicit what's interesting about it, to promote it in a way.

CYMENE: Yes. We're here to make you look good or sound good anyway.

DOMINIC: We do work to make people sound good, which goes all the way down into the editing. I spend a lot of time editing people's ums and ers out, removing awkward pauses, all of that.

CYMENE: I think that is hard for some academics that we interview to understand: that this conversation is not about destabilizing them or putting them on guard.

DOMINIC: At least a couple of folks have commented that they like what we're doing as an alternative mode of engagement. They like that it's primarily an affirmational conversation where our job is to recognize the value of someone's work and to set them up to sound really good. And not to engage in the usual type of critical competitive warfare that's part of academic life.

CYMENE: Right. And that's a switch. Yet it's not that we don't ask questions. It is inquiry, but the purpose is not to undermine and critique, unlike so much of the academic universe.

DOMINIC: There aren't gotcha questions in what we do. And I do think that is also particularly appropriate given that our thematic focus is on energy and the environment. The work of the center in general has been to try to create networks of like-minded people who want to work constructively and collaboratively on big issues like climate change or the Anthropocene. It's hard to do that if you spend the whole time fighting over who's got the better concepts.

CYMENE: Yes. Exactly.

DOMINIC: It's not like head-to-head Capitalocene versus Anthropocene on today's podcast. [*Laughter*] Two concepts enter, only one will emerge victorious!

CYMENE: Although that could be a good double episode. But only if Neologocene wins the battle in the end.

I would also add, and this is following on what you said earlier about the medium, that there's something really nice about being off-screen. When I write, I'm on my laptop and I'm hunkered over, and I'm destroying my back slowly but surely with every keystroke. We spend so much time on computer screens, phone screens, whatever, that it's exhausting. I like moving out of that visual domain. Not just for corporeal reasons but also as a way into a different aesthetic.

Being off-screen and in-voice makes me think about the quality and vividness of voice. We had a good podcast with a sound artist named Lawrence English. What he does is an epistemology of listening. Hearing is not the same thing as listening, he says. Listening is a different kind of engagement and a different kind of act. It's akin to training. You have to attune your mind to certain kinds of sounds in order to be able to listen to the messages embedded within those sounds, as well as the affective dimensions embodied in those sounds. The audio, or aural, medium of the podcast is fundamental to its shape and its epistemic space. As hosts, we are sounds in someone's head, which is an interesting anthropological place to be I suppose.

It's not like we are reading to people exactly, but I wonder if there is a comfort in being talked to or with? Instead of reading text and absorbing information through symbols on a screen or on a page, you hear a human voice, several human voices. As children, we love to be read to.

And there are real differences in the aural form. When we read a text, we are in some ways reading aloud to ourselves; we take those symbols and process them to create imaginaries. Reading is fully creative in that way. Whereas when you take an image, let's say a photograph or a picture, that image is worth a thousand words and the creative imagining has been done in part by the image itself.

When we read symbols on a page, we make the picture in our brains. When we look at an image of, say, a fantastical sci-fi world that an artist has rendered, then some of our imaginary is taken away, now fixed in space and time and shape and color. The aural dimension is a nice mediation between the two because it allows something akin to an audio painting.

It's a creative rendering that's both symbolic and sensorial. Cognitively, it allows a different scope and engagement that is distinct, not better, just different from what we can find in the symbolic world of letters and the visual register of image.

DOMINIC: I agree. I mean there's a music to language. There's a discursive aspect to the storytelling aspect of it that can be quite charismatic. And that is a nice antidote to all the handwringing about how academics only know how to talk to other academics. But usually the ideas for communicating with broader publics end up being more advocacy for the textual. Like, we should blog more.

CYMENE: Make it shorter.

DOMINIC: Sure, make it shorter. And nothing against blogs, but what I'm arguing—and I think this expresses the philosophy of the podcast pretty well—is if somebody wants to get on and talk about Heidegger for an hour they can do that. It's totally OK to do a deep dive into some difficult work; we'll do our best to hang in there with you. Thus some of our episodes are very challenging to listen to as a result. I'm thinking of Beth Povinelli's, which is actually also our most downloaded episode. You need to listen attentively to that episode because she's getting into some really dense philosophical territory with her book.

But Beth is also really funny when she's not being serious. And we try to hit that balance with other episodes, to bring out the breezy and fun—for example, the one we did recently with Lisa Messeri. It's not that there's not some deep thinking in it and serious issues at hand, but the conversation itself is playful and more what you would expect from a conversation than a text. Having that range is important because we're not advocating sacrificing our specialized concepts and insights.

What we want to do instead is to create an environment in which there is polyphony. And alongside different voices, also different registers. If listeners are having fun with one episode, they may give a more technical episode a try because they like being in our circle. Maybe this is a way some of our more challenging ideas, which I still think have a lot of value, can leak out of our biosphere and get out into the broader discourse.

CYMENE: Right. We don't know exactly who is listening. We have an idea of who many of our listeners are, but we have a lot of conjecture and speculation too. If they keep on downloading then they must be getting something out of it. Some acts of translation are happening. And this is sort of obvious, but we have a really accessible forum here. This is really low tech.

DOMINIC: It's free and easy and there's no paywall. You just go to our website or iTunes and download or stream it.

CYMENE: It is just simple audio-recording equipment that is needed to engineer the podcast. It's inexpensive. You can do it anywhere really. That too gives it a broader appeal in the sense that it can be anywhere, done by anyone. All the democratizing of information that the internet promises—this is another piece of that. As you said before, it's like the return of precorporate radio.

DOMINIC: Local radio, college radio, all that good stuff we grew up with. Why don't we talk a bit about the podcast as part of our longer-term collaborative relationship because obviously this isn't our first collaboration. Do you think that this podcast collaboration would have been possible without our earlier collaborations, let's say on research projects? Is it a different kind of collaboration?

CYMENE: I don't know. That is a challenging one because we have this other life collaboration that makes it pretty hard to untangle all the rest of them.

DOMINIC: What are you talking about? I literally just met you. [*Laughter*] But, qualitatively, how do you think this podcast collaboration has differed from the others or what aspects of it do you think are singular or interesting as compared with other kinds of collaborations you've done, either with me or with other people?

CYMENE: Well. My first thought was that it's more fun.

DOMINIC: Agreed.

CYMENE: We get to go and read really interesting texts that we may not have read before. That's stimulating and a good learning exercise. Then we are on and live and we need to just jump into it. Like we've said a few times to people on the podcast: it's like attending a smart dinner party and being part of the really good conversation at the end of the table. I liked Saskia Sassen's response to that: "I love to do dinner parties!"

DOMINIC: I would underscore that the ludic aspect of podcasting is one of its more distinctive features. Again, it's not that we didn't find things to joke about and laugh about during fieldwork. But in some sense, when you're recording these episodes, you're very aware of the fact that you are at some level also trying to entertain people. At least a little. You're trying to keep people's attention, which means you might err on the side of joking or throw in a little shtick. For us, it's pretty spontaneous, we don't really do scripted content, funny or otherwise. We might write up questions, but even then I mean it's mostly flying by the seat of our pants. That, too, is qualitatively different from much of our normal intellectual practice.

CYMENE: Right. Although without making any claims to being a stand-up comedian.

DOMINIC: We'll get there. Give us time.

CYMENE: The podcast does give us some space to be more natural, like you would be around friends—including the playful element of friendship.

DOMINIC: Any final thoughts?

CYMENE: Maybe we can end with an origin story. During one of our episodes, the podcast summit, we tossed around a question about the derivation of the term "podcast." We decided it came from iPod, because you would listen to them on an iPod.

DOMINIC: Right.

CYMENE: Then we started riffing on what other elements of podness there could be. We came up with a seedpod, for example: sprouting new ideas out of these generative little seeds that are encapsulated in the husk.

DOMINIC: I liked that one.

CYMENE: The introduction to the conversation is the husk and then you get to the seeds, the juicy, nutritional tidbits shared by our guests.

We were also thinking about a pod as a space pod, like the containers they hurl out into outer space that have the Elvis Presley record or the picture of Marilyn Monroe or whatever. They're like a time capsule that gets tossed out into space. Maybe that's another way to think about the podcasts. We already mentioned the diary archive and the historicity of the conversation. We are talking about contemporary phenomena and this means there is a time-encapsulation element to the podcast too.

And finally, as we always say, everyone who's been on the pod is a friend of the pod. But (!) we could also say that we are all pod people.

11

CRAFTING *LISSA*, AN ETHNO-GRAPHIC STORY

A Collaboration in Four Parts

Sherine F. Hamdy and Coleman Nye

Lissa: A Story about Medical Promise, Friendship, and Revolution (released in November 2017) is the inaugural book of the University of Toronto Press ethno-GRAPHIC series. Based on Sherine Hamdy's ethnographic work on organ transplantation in Egypt, and Coleman Nye's research on cancer genetics in the United States, *Lissa* is a graphic work of what the groundbreaking ethnographic filmmaker Jean Rouch called "ethnofiction" (Stoller 1992, 143). *Lissa* follows two women as they grapple with difficult medical decisions in the context of the popular uprisings that began in January 2011 and unseated long-term dictator Hosni Mubarak, that we refer to as, following our Egyptian interlocutors, "the Revolution." People often ask us how and why we decided to embark on a collaborative graphic narrative of this scope and how and why we sought to bring together such different research sites. We believe that the collaborative dimension of the project is at the heart of its success in reaching a range of audiences within and beyond anthropology, while also making valuable methodological contributions to the field. *Lissa* is a unique example of the possibilities of collaborative scholarship to unsettle conventional ideas of authorship, expertise, voice, text, theory, and study.

In what follows, we offer a brief overview of the four main components of the *Lissa* project, which include (1) a graphic novel aimed toward a popular audience, (2) pedagogical appendices and two academic essays focusing on comics as ethnography, (3) a documentary film about the creation of the comic, featuring the team's research trip to Egypt, and (4) an interactive website that includes more information about the characters and context, and further links to primary and secondary research materials. We then describe the conceptual underpinnings of the project, and detail

FIGURE 11.1. Book design by Caroline Brewer and Sarula Bao. Image excerpted from *Lissa: A Story about Friendship, Medical Promise, and Revolution*. Written by Sherine Hamdy and Coleman Nye, illustrated by Caroline Brewer and Sarula Bao, and lettered by Marc Parenteau. Copyright University of Toronto Press 2017. Reprinted by permission of the publisher.

the collaborative process of crafting the novel, following *Lissa* as it changed shape through four key collaborative phases: (1) the collaboration between the authors (Hamdy and Nye) as we devised the story and drafted the original script; (2) the collaboration between the authors and the artists (Sarula Bao and Caroline Brewer) as we worked to design the characters, visually depict anthropological insights and concepts, and streamline the story; (3) the collaboration between Egyptian academics, artists, and doctors and the graphic novel team (including the authors, artists, and documentary film crew) during a trip to Cairo, as we revised the story to better reflect the realities and insights of the people who were living and working in Egypt before, during, and after the revolution; and (4) the collaboration between the authors, artists, and our visual editor, visual coach, and letterer Marc Parenteau, as we worked to translate the script into visual scenes and streamline the text.

Overview

The Graphic Novel

Anna is the daughter of an American couple working in Cairo. Layla is the Egyptian daughter of the doorman in Anna's apartment building. Together they strike up an unlikely friendship that is put to the test when both girls are faced with family health crises at home and revolutionary unrest on the streets. The graphic narrative explores how different people come to terms with illness and mortality against the backdrop of political, economic, and environmental crises. Ultimately, this form of engaged scholarship transforms the ethnographic encounter into a more accessible and visually effective form that invites readers to draw their own conclusions about how the material relates to their lives.

Coleman and Sherine wrote the book together, then worked to visually adapt it with the illustrators Sarula Bao and Caroline Brewer, and with technical guidance from Marc Parenteau. The story also changed in conversation with artists, doctors, and academics in Egypt who gave valuable feedback on the first draft.

The Pedagogical Appendices

In order to facilitate the use of *Lissa* in the classroom and to introduce the comic form to academics who may be unfamiliar with the genre, our graphic novel is supplemented with pedagogical material. The graphic novel itself is bookended by two academic essays: one by George Marcus on *Lissa* as experimental ethnography, and the other, a reflection on how comics work by the cartoonist Paul Karasik. The appendices comprise robust pedagogical material, including a time line of the Egyptian Revolution; interviews with the authors about their process; discussion questions and suggested classroom activities; and an in-depth annotated reference list for learning more about the various topics covered, including links to some of the primary materials we drew on—references about kidney failure, organ transplantation, the Egyptian Revolution, cancer and genetics, and about comics in medicine. Through the appendices, we could realize our goal of producing engaged scholarship that sheds light on global phenomena such as

FIGURE 11.2.   Film poster, designed by the Middle East Studies Center at Brown University, based on the artwork of Sarula Bao and Caroline Brewer. Reprinted by permission of Francesco Dragone.

1. the social determinants of health;
2. the consequences of commercializing both bodies and health care;
3. the ways in which we are all implicated in seemingly localized conflicts, such as the Arab Spring; and
4. the politics of knowledge making that disproportionately reward Euro-American scholars who depend on the intellectual work of people in the global South.

Documentary Film

During the process of crafting the graphic novel story and developing the characters, the two authors and two artists traveled to Cairo (a trip generously funded by the Luce Foundation). Previously, only Sherine had ever been to Egypt and the rest of the team was having a hard time placing the characters. We also wanted input from local academics and revolutionaries. The ethnographic filmmaker Francesco Dragone filmed this journey and other aspects of the process of making the academic comic. The film documents us touring the various neighborhoods and sites where the events of the novel take place and discussing our script with our Egyptian interlocutors.

This trip resulted in major revisions to the plot and characters and provided rich visual reference material for the illustrators. The film includes interviews with the two authors and two artists as we reflect on how our understanding of the characters and story changed through these encounters. It also shows

FIGURE 11.3.   Still shot from the film *The Making of Lissa* by Francesco Dragone, animation by Krissy Pelley. Reprinted by permission of Francesco Dragone.

the authors and illustrators working together on character design and aesthetic choices. In producing a film of our journey, our aim was to make our methods and process available to other scholars and artists who may wish to embark on similar illustrated forms of scholarship and to reflect on the ways in which

FIGURE 11.4.   Still shot from the film *The Making of Lissa* by Francesco Dragone, animation by Krissy Pelley. Reprinted by permission of Francesco Dragone.

FIGURE 11.5.   Still shot from the film *The Making of Lissa* by Francesco Dragone, animation by Krissy Pelley. Reprinted by permission of Francesco Dragone.

new forms of visualization allow for communicating academic research—ethnographic, scientific, medical, humanistic—to broader and more diverse audiences.

In the making of the film, Francesco contended with how to render coherent the two overlapping stories of the film—that of Layla and Anna—and that of the *Lissa* team creating their story. We brought Krissy Pelley, a Brown University–Rhode Island School of Design joint degree student working in animation, on board, and later Yasmin Orhan, also a RISD animation student, to animate Layla and Anna into Francesco's film. These animations allow viewers to see the characters, in the film, walking alongside us in the streets of Cairo.

The Website

Soon we realized we needed a website—first, to be a place where people could access the documentary film, and second, to include further primary and secondary sources related to the research, beyond what was included in the pedagogical appendices. The "Behind the Scenes" section is aimed toward academics who may be interested in learning about our process as they consider adapting their own research into graphic form. In "The Story" section, students as well as interested lay readers can examine primary and secondary sources as a way to delve deeper into some of the characters' experiences. We wanted to preserve the ethnographic complexities that we needed to cut for the sake of crafting a compelling story. We also wanted to remain faithful to the dynamics of authorship, experience, and knowledge production that are always at risk of effacement, even in a collaborative project such as this one.

In combination with the book's pedagogical appendices, further information about our process is available on the website. By centering our creative choices and bringing in other scholarly resources, we invite readers to examine alternate narrative and epistemological possibilities. The website also gives readers a chance to navigate other ideas, images, and voices at the edges of our plot.

We designed the website in collaboration with Franceso Dragone, with early input from Emma Funk (an undergraduate student at the time). The technical team creating the website consists of Darren Marinelli and John Mazza.

Concept

Collaboration between advisor and student in devising a story that brings together their different research projects in graphic form

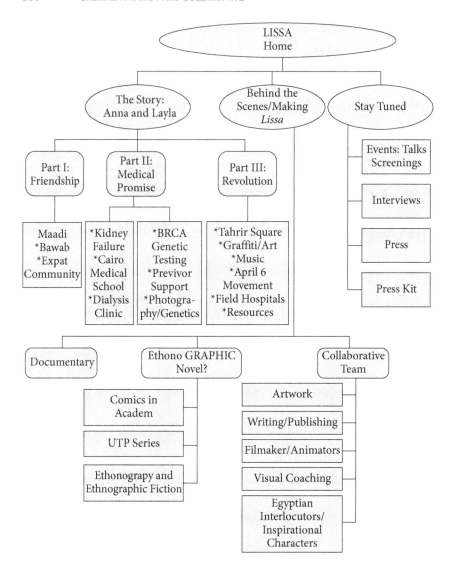

FIGURE 11.6. Early design of the website layout.

Conceptual Connections

The conceptual underpinnings of this project first emerged when Coleman was Sherine's doctoral student in anthropology at Brown University. Coleman was undertaking a project on genetic risk and cancer in the United States, and Sherine was finishing her first book on kidney failure and organ transplantation in Egypt.

In conversations about our research, we were struck by the similarities and contradictions that our two research projects exposed. Clinicians are trained to think about interventions with their patients at the scale of the individual patient's body, which of course makes sense from the medical perspective. But we see, for example, that often patients' decisions about their bodies are deeply embedded in their social relations; in both cancer genetics and organ transplantation many feel familial pressures to get surgery or not to get surgery. Often, patients seek surgical intervention to free their loved ones from the burden of their care, or from the continual expense of chronic treatment. These decisions are further socially embedded when the treatment itself—as in the case of organ donation—requires a major bodily sacrifice from a healthy family member. In the case of people who are trying to decide how to medically manage their hereditary cancer risk, family obligations also play an important role. Often a person's relationship to her own cancer risk is shaped by a history of caregiving for a parent or sibling with cancer, or through anticipating the need to protect one's (future) children from having their parent die of cancer.[1] In all medical practices, dependency on others' care is essential to medical outcome. By highlighting the inadequacy of conceiving of the patient as individualized or autonomous, we wanted to think through how patients are embedded in networks of social relations and sociopolitical contexts by reading our different field sites with and through one other.

We had drafted and presented an academic article on these themes, but never submitted it for publication. We were frustrated by the formal limitations of a standard journal article format in our attempts to convey insights that emerged from conversations about two independent projects and sites. At the time, we had just begun incorporating graphic memoirs about illness into our teaching in medical anthropology.

Comics

We began following with interest the flourishing of patient memoirs that some scholars had begun cataloging under the name "graphic medicine" (Williams 2012; Czerwiec et al. 2015) and others as "patho-graphics" (Squier 2014). Graphic illness memoirs have grown immensely popular, partly because the combination of text and image enables them to powerfully convey complex emotional states, to render the relentlessness of chronic pain, and to represent interior experiences like altered states of consciousness or invisible illness. Further, as scholars have noted (Czerwiec et al. 2015), patient memoirs decenter the authority of the medical practitioner and bring much-needed attention to the personal experiences of pain and chronic illness beyond the space of the clinic. While we were struck by how effective comics were at conveying patient experiences in our teaching, as social scientists we also wanted to find ways to situate these individual experiences within wider social patterns. We wanted to locate people's vulnerabilities to disease within their political economic context, and we wanted to shed light on the global stratification of illness that goes beyond individualized and Euro-centric accounts.

As a visually rich medium, the graphic genre presented us with the potential to convey complex anthropological insights in highly accessible ways that could also invite readers to draw their own conclusions about how the material relates to their lives. We were both finding that the visual genre opens up exciting pos-sibilities for engaging with unfamiliar contexts, the politics of representation, and the complexities of embodied experience in more tangible ways than text alone. Writer/artists like Scott McCloud, Joe Sacco, and Lynda Barry taught us how comics—far from dumbing down or simplifying concepts—could be used to add *more* complexity; through comics, we could play with layering scale, per-spective, time, and place. The spatial dimensions of the page struck us as an ideal way to bridge the contexts of the United States and Egypt. And the levity of the comic genre, we found, would make it easier to engage with difficult topics such as kidney failure, cancer, and political violence.

Ethnofiction

In order to bridge these two academic projects, we crafted a work of graphic "ethnofiction" (Jean Rouch, cited in Stoller 1992, 143). We created fictional characters to make the two different worlds intersect, crafting an absorbing character-driven narrative that allowed us to more fully examine the affinities and tensions between them. Layla and Anna, while fictional, are also in a sense composite characters, each based on scores of interviews and research. Fictional-izing them allowed us to make their worlds meaningfully converge and enabled us to make more explicit choices in conveying anthropological theory through dialogue and plot. Fictionalization also gave us the flexibility to constantly adapt the narrative in ongoing conversation with the artists and informants.

In telling a story premised on a deep friendship between two young women, one Egyptian and the other American, we sought to explore the complex con-nections between experiencing illness in the Majority and Minority Worlds.[2] Set in Cairo, the ethnographic story follows Layla and Anna as each grapples with a difficult medical decision that the other cannot fully understand, leading to a rift in their friendship. As the tension in their friendship builds, the Egyptian Revo-lution breaks out in Cairo, and each character is swept up in the turmoil. The high stakes of participating in political protest—the massive injuries and death—further highlight to Layla and Anna that people's assessments of risk and benefit will always be contextual and dependent on what else is going on in their lives.

We learn, through Layla's and Anna's stories, that making life-and-death deci-sions is not singularly determined by any static culture or by people's different personal moral codes. Determining what risk is bearable for an anticipated benefit will depend on how and why we identify the risks that we do in relation to the other risks that we have grown accustomed to bearing. Our decisions also depend on what level of trust and faith we have in medical and political institutions to deliver on their promises.

We wrote the first draft of the script together—we brainstormed the initial plot over the summer of 2015 and took turns fleshing it out in a Google Doc. We first worked to develop full characters—Anna and Layla—with flaws, motivations, and tendencies that reflected the way they would handle their medical decision making and made them complementary characters that would help one another develop and grow. In dealing with her genetic cancer risk, Anna is more focused on a solution to her own individual body, and she is deeply invested in the medical institutions to which she turns. She is also more anxious and inward-looking. Anna's love of photography was a way for us to reflect her interior world, to visually show her fraught connection to her family and genetic pasts/futures. Yet her photography also provides her with a concrete way to move beyond her individual focus on family/genes to a political interest in collective and social justice, inspired by Egypt's revolutionary action.

Meanwhile, we developed Layla as more outgoing, resolute, and rebellious. For her, medicine provides a means to care for those around her, and to engage with and change the injustices she sees every day. We see her arc from her role as a medical student, eager to attend to her ailing father, to the more political work she engages in with the April 6 Youth Movement for social justice, and as a first-aid medical responder in the field hospitals organized by Tahrir Doctors. Through Layla's growth, we see her mapping the connections between her father's illness and its "political etiologies" (Hamdy 2008)—that is, the role of a dysfunctional political state, within a complex network of global flows, in producing and neglecting disease. She comes to understand the connections between her father's kidney failure and the Egyptian state, with its utter disregard for its poor citizens. In the April 6 group, she finds like-minded youth incensed by the state's unwillingness to safeguard land from toxic dumping and its failure to provide adequate healthcare to all its citizens.

Composition

1. *Collaboration between academic authors (Hamdy and Nye) and the comic artists (Sarula Bao and Caroline Brewer), as we worked to design the characters, visually depict anthropological insights and concepts, and streamline the story.*

Neither of us are trained visual artists. After collaborating with one another to craft the story in the spring of 2015, we sought our next level of collaboration with the illustrators who would portray our script through paneled images. Clueless (in retrospect) as to how this would all work, Sherine walked down the hill from her Brown University campus office to the Illustration Department in the Rhode Island School of Design to inquire how this might be done. The department chair, Robert Brinkerhoff, put her in touch with Paul Karasik, a cartoonist and the instructor for RISD's comics class. Paul was intrigued by our idea, and patiently explained that our task was not just to find an excellent visual artist. Not all visual artists are good illustrators, he insisted; our goal was to find an illustrator who effectively tells stories through sequential art. Even if we envisioned ourselves as already having written the story, we needed artists who understood how to convey stories in image form, that is, artists with experience in drawing their own stories.

Paul had taught a comics class in the spring, and thought that his two top students, Caroline Brewer and Sarula Bao, were ready to take on such a project. Sherine obtained a small grant from Brown University's Watson Institute and worked with Coleman to complete the script over the summer. We drafted and drafted, even while life and other work projects pulled at us: Sherine presented her work on doctors in the Arab Spring at a conference in Rome that June and made a research trip to study Arab comics in Beirut; Coleman, meanwhile, moved across the country, leaving Brown University with a PhD in hand, and starting an assistant professorship at Simon Fraser University in Vancouver, British Columbia.

We mention these trips to point out the serendipity of traveling in academic networks and the opportunities that it can afford for greater collaboration and project enrichment. In Rome, Sherine met with Toby Volkman from the Luce Foundation, who was enthusiastic about the work she was doing. In Beirut, Sherine met with the well-known comics artists and scholars Lina Ghaibeh and George ("Jad") Khoury, who both insisted that it would be impossible for American student-artists to adequately depict the sites without full immersion in Egypt. Sherine wrote to Toby Volkman at the Henry Luce Foundation and submitted a grant proposal to support a research trip to Egypt for the *Lissa* coauthors and artists to visit all the sites in which the graphic novel unfolds, and for the production of an ethnographic film by Francesco Dragone to document the trip and the collaborative process.

Back in the United States, we delivered our first presentation about our script-in-progress at the Graphic Medicine Conference at Riverside in July 2015, along with Anne Brackenbury, the editor at the University of Toronto Press, who was at that point still looking to start a series combining comics and anthropology. There we also met a young illustrator, Marc Parenteau, who impressed us all with his contagious enthusiasm for comics as a powerful medium that can depict complex worlds in ways words alone cannot.

In September, buoyed by the excitement that *Lissa* generated at the conference and the possibility of a trip to Egypt, we met the artists for the first time. By then, we had brought Francesco into the project and he filmed our first meeting of Sherine, Paul, Sarula, and Caroline in Providence, and Coleman joining from Vancouver via Skype. We were thrilled that these two young artists loved the script and the story and identified strongly with the characters.

But wait, *two* artists? How would that work? We recognized that it would be far too much work for a single artist alone (we were imagining, at the time, that the graphic novel would be under 110 pages). As Sarula and Caroline talked about their ideas for the script, it made sense that each one would take on a character, just as Coleman and Sherine had in the writing. While the authors collaborated on the larger plot points, we each primarily worked on the character associated with our own research. So Coleman wrote all the parts of the original script involving Anna's character, and Sherine had written the parts involving Layla's character, and then we collaboratively hashed out all the scenes to make sure they worked together.

At first, Sarula took on Layla and Caroline adopted Anna, but as their worked progressed, they were each organically drawn to the opposite character, and they later switched. At this point, we were presented with a problem: they each have a unique style and method, and we had to figure out how to bring together the art in a coherent way in the book without asking them to sacrifice their individual aesthetics. Sarula relies wholly on digital tools, which Caroline draws traditionally with pencil and paper before scanning her work for later digital manipulation. We eventually decided to use the two artistic styles to our advantage—after all, the major conflict in the book was the characters' differing perspectives. We would see the world through Anna's lens in Sarula's art, and then in Layla's perspective through Caroline's art. When the two characters come to understand one another, the two artistic styles would merge.

So the work of producing illustrated pages had finally begun. We met to section off the elements of the plot into paneled pages—and Caroline and Sarula each marked which scenes/pages would be theirs. In the fall of 2015, Paul Karasik supervised Sarula and Caroline's progress in sketching out the plot, as an independent study project at RISD for which they were earning credit, and they continued in the Spring 2016 semester, their last year of four years of art school.

As we began to design characters and sketch scenes, we were presented with another design barrier: how to visually depict Cairo, the main setting of the novel, when only Sherine had ever actually been there. The illustrators struggled to visually place the characters in a world that was unfamiliar to them both, and the team was relying heavily on Sherine to explicate the scenic and social dimensions of Cairo that appeared in our story, but the details kept piling up. Luckily, the grant money from the Luce Foundation was approved and in December we all prepared to travel to Cairo.

It was in Cairo that Coleman met with the rest of the team in person for the first time since she had been in Vancouver since the project's inception, and we finally all got to spend time together in the same physical space, reviewing our ideas for the script and characters. It was a lot of fun for us to see it all unfold, and it also made each team (the writers and the illustrators) ask hard questions about what each scene was doing, and why it was necessary for the plot. We grappled with pacing, realizing that too much description can slow down the narrative and derail the story—and is just visually boring. We also discussed how to make the narrative more visually compelling or concise based on the artists' input and our own responses to the illustrations, and revised accordingly. For example, there was a moment when we chose to take out a violent scene because we found it too disturbing when faced with its visual representation. The graphic dimensions of the story and characters took on new visual depth and richness as we explored different parts of the city in which our characters would have lived and studied.

2. *Collaboration between Egyptian experts and interlocutors (including medical doctors and students, doctors of the revolution, comic artists, and academics) and the graphic novel team (including authors, artists, and documentary film crew) during a trip to Cairo, as we revised the story to better reflect the on-the-ground realities of people who were living and working in Egypt before, during, and after the revolution*

Sherine had packed the trip's daily schedule with meetings with Egyptian doctors, revolutionaries, and comic artists and visits to all the key sites in which *Lissa* takes place. At the Cairo University Faculty of Medicine, where Layla went to medical school in our story, we met with Dr. Dina Shokry, a prestigious faculty member who had played an important role in the revolution by training students how to keep detailed records of the protestors' injuries as a way to document the political violence. We also met with her medical students—who were, notably, all women—and told them Anna and Layla's story. The medical students were the first Egyptian audience with whom we shared the story, and we were struck that, unlike the American audiences whose reactions to our project had been great interest, curiosity, or fascination, the Egyptian students' reactions were mostly grief. The events that we depict in the story hit very close to home: they all had friends or family members who had experienced what we describe—whether late stage cancer or kidney failure or injury during the protests. The discordance in their reaction was an important lesson for us as to how stories of suffering can be consumed by distant others while remaining painful retellings for the subjects themselves. Yet, alongside their sadness, the medical students were also committed to a project that would historically record and let the rest of the world know what they had experienced. They were overall excited for our visit and the project, and happily showed us around their lecture halls, the pathology lab, and even the forensic medicine museum. Caroline and Sarula took as many photos as they could, collecting the visual references that would become so essential to their work.

Our toughest critic was Dr. Amr Shebaita, a cofounder of the nonprofit organization Tahrir Doctors, which carried out monumental work saving lives of injured protestors during the eruptions of state violence. (Sherine is working on a monograph about these doctors in collaboration with Soha Bayoumi of Harvard University). He scrapped scenes he found too melodramatic or improbable and gave us feedback on character design; for example, Anna had dark hair, he decided, as a foreigner who could also navigate Cairo's streets without drawing too much attention. Dr. Shebaita gave us wonderful ideas of how and what Layla and Anna might have done in the hectic space of the field hospitals based on his work there. He also took us on a tour, at night, of the field hospital spots around Tahrir Square. At the time of our trip, the area was heavily policed and militarized, with tanks blocking off the square to prevent any more street protests. Watchful police officers or soldiers would quickly reprimand anyone for taking out a smartphone to snap a picture. This atmosphere heightened the intensity of listening to Dr. Shebaita's stories of providing first aid in the very space that only five years earlier was a deadly conflict zone.

We wanted very much to acknowledge that narrating *Lissa* is a testament to the will, bravery, and perseverance of Egyptian revolutionary actors like Drs. Shokry and Shebaita, and we began considering how to cite them in our book. Depicting the revolutionaries brought up a host of questions for us about the ethics of representation: we were wary of falling into the trap of the Western academic tourist of the Arab Spring who drops in and extracts the knowledge being generated without having to face all the risks and distractions of political participation (Abaza 2011). At the same time, given the strong counterrevolutionary forces in the current political climate, we also worried about exposing our interlocutors to further risk by publishing their names. We maintain that there is no single right answer to this dilemma, particularly given the fact that the circumstances upon which our decision hinged are themselves quickly changing.

In the end, we decided to include the people in Egypt who contributed so much to the revolutionary action and to our story's revisions as characters in *Lissa*. We wanted to acknowledge our indebtedness to Dr. Dina Shokry and Dr. Amr Shebaita in particular: in the book, Dr. Shokry appears as Layla's university professor and Dr. Shebaita is her field hospital supervisor. Two other characters Layla encounters during the Egyptian Revolution—Reem and Alia—are also based on the revolutionaries Reem Bashery and Alia Mossallam. Through our visit to the Women and Memory Forum in Cairo, we were introduced to these women's personal stories of the revolution which were recorded and archived by Egyptian feminist researchers. Many lines of dialogue are taken directly from their narratives, and the work that Anna engages in around trying to locate missing people is based directly on Alia's experiences. For the scene where Alia meets Layla in the morgue, we drew on Alia Mossallam's firsthand account, published in an extremely powerful article in the *Egypt Independent* in 2011, which we cite and describe in the pedagogical section of the book.

Meeting with Egyptian comic artists and studying the work of Egyptian graffiti artists of the revolution was another way we sought intertextual citation and reference to what Egyptians intellectually produced during and after the revolution. If we were, in the making of *Lissa*, also making the implicit argument that visual art is a critical form of knowledge, we wanted this to be evident in the everyday visual representations that Layla and Anna would encounter in Tahrir Square. Whereas the severely militaristic and counterrevolutionary political climate during the trip depressed us, meeting with young Egyptian comic artists was the perfect antidote. We were simply floored by their creativity, adaptability, and agility in producing stunning and poignant comic art that challenged social and political taboos and forged alternate paths of representation. Based on conversations and observations from our trip, we made the decision to incorporate the work of Egyptian graffiti artists who were leveling trenchant political critiques. Throughout *Lissa*, the reader will encounter graffiti art and murals with in-text citations of the original artist. Ganzeer, one of the foremost revolutionary graffiti artists in Cairo, generously crafted the composition of the final page of our novel, and an Arabic calligrapher, Khaled Al-Saa'i, composed the visual representation for Qur'anic recitation that appears in the book. In the following pages, we include some before and after snapshots of our illustrators' incorporation of some graffiti works, as well as the image of Ganzeer's original composition.

3. *Collaboration between authors (Hamdy and Nye), artists (Bao and Brewer), and our visual editor, visual coach, and letterer Marc Parenteau*

Upon returning home from Egypt, we all had much more work to do. Sarula and Caroline had tons of visual references to organize and correlate with the pages of the story they now had to redraft, and Sherine and Coleman had major story points to revise based on the feedback we were given in Egypt. The challenge was to be flexible with the script, and open to accommodating what we had seen and heard on the trip, but at the same time to remain focused on our original story. At this point, the authors began collaboratively reworking the larger visual and narrative elements of the story and rewriting the scenes for all the characters together instead of mainly focusing on our own.

Neither of us initially knew how to write a script for a graphic novel. Our early drafts were written with tremendous detail and dialogue that, we later learned, was inappropriately heavy—and cumbersome to the demands of lettering dialogue in word balloons. We had written it like a movie script, but this doesn't work for a graphic novel. As Scott McCloud explains, film and animation are

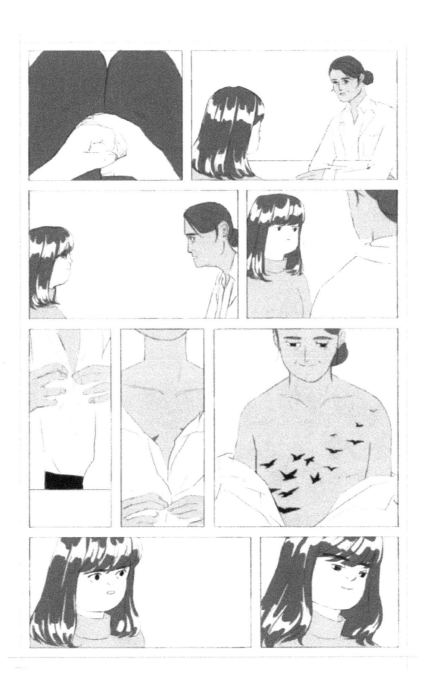

FIGURE 11.7. Page from *Lissa*, of postmastectomy tattoos, later incorporated into artwork featuring barbed wire and graffiti (figure 11.8). Image excerpted from *Lissa: A Story about Friendship, Medical Promise, and Revolution.* Written by Sherine Hamdy and Coleman Nye, illustrated by Caroline Brewer and Sarula Bao, and lettered by Marc Parenteau. Copyright University of Toronto Press 2017. Reprinted by permission of the publisher.

FIGURE 11.8. Early draft of page (left) and final draft that visually echoes graffiti by El Zeft (below left) and barbed wire from the square (below right) with the mastectomy tattoo (figure 11.7). Image excerpted from *Lissa: A Story about Friendship, Medical Promise, and Revolution.* Written by Sherine Hamdy and Coleman Nye, illustrated by Caroline Brewer and Sarula Bao, and lettered by Marc Parenteau. Copyright University of Toronto Press 2017. Reprinted by permission of the publisher.

FIGURE 11.9. Early sketch (left) and final draft (right), including graffiti artwork of Ammar Abo Bakr. Image excerpted from *Lissa: A Story about Friendship, Medical Promise, and Revolution.* Written by Sherine Hamdy and Coleman Nye, illustrated by Caroline Brewer and Sarula Bao, and lettered by Marc Parenteau. Copyright University of Toronto Press 2017. Reprinted by permission of the publisher.

time-based forms of sequential art: "Each successive frame of a movie is pro-jected on exactly the same space—the screen—while each frame of comics must occupy a different space. Space does for comics what time does for film" (1993, 7). Time, in comics, happens in the spaces between each panel—the gutter. This is actually one of the things we found most exciting about comics—it enables you to interlayer, juxtapose, and combine spaces and times—bringing multiple perspectives together in the space of a single page. However, we came to realize that we hadn't actually considered *how* this happens visually on the page when we were writing our script and had relied far too heavily on dialogue to do this work for us. So we ended up making another major and belated composition discovery: As the artists began to draw more than thumbnail sketches, we needed to make a technical shift to break the story down from the original prosaic script into numbered visual scenes or beats based on action, emotion, and language, and then break these beats into pages that corresponded with the visual scenes.

It was at this point that we all realized we were missing a bridge, someone who could better communicate the plot points, emotions, and themes of the story to the artists as they worked on designing page layout and visual scenes, and who could communicate the artists' and comics' potentials and constraints to the writ-ers. The other problem was that we were quickly depleting our funds. Remember-ing the comic artist Marc Parenteau whom we had met a year earlier at the Graphic Medicine conference, we asked if he would be willing to help us out. We were all

FIGURE 11.10A and **B.**   Original graffiti by Ammar Abo Bakr, incorporated in the *Lissa* pages. Photos taken by Soraya Morayef for the blog suzeeinthecity. wordpress.com. Reprinted by permission of the photographer.

FIGURES 11.10A and **B.**   (Continued)

incredibly lucky that he agreed—even though he was now based in Ulaanbaatar, Mongolia, researching for his own graphic novel project on global climate change.

The first thing Marc did, once granted access to our mess of a collaborative Google Doc–script, was to translate it into a less prosaic more stripped-down

FIGURE 11.11.   Early sketch (left) and final draft (right). Image excerpted from *Lissa: A Story about Friendship, Medical Promise, and Revolution.* Written by Sherine Hamdy and Coleman Nye, illustrated by Caroline Brewer and Sarula Bao, and lettered by Marc Parenteau. Copyright University of Toronto Press 2017. Reprinted by permission of the publisher.

script, massively (and painfully) cutting down our dialogue into tight 15–20 word portions that would fit in word balloons. Unsurprisingly, we had engaged in some very thick description and developed detailed dialogue to convey the complexities of social experience and medical decision making. Marc was shocked to hear that we had all calculated this to be a 110-page graphic novel and he told us it looked to him to be closer to 300. Knowing we did not have the artistic or financial capacity to produce a 300-page work, we all worked to cut out all the unnecessary scenes and dialogues, tweak the pacing, and, following Marc's lead in paring everything down, redrafting it to 219 pages. Anne Brackenbury, at the University of Toronto Press, now had to reconceive her plan and budget for publication. We were also running out of time: our student artists were close to graduation.

Marc Parenteau taught us that you have to break down the script into panels and write exactly what happens in each panel. So, if someone is running, you would write, "they run," but you have to carefully think through how many panels it takes to show they ran, and to where/from what they ran. You also have to radically reduce the text so that it can fit in a dialogue bubble in that panel—something that was a struggle for us as anthropological authors who rely heavily on text to convey nuance and progress action. Marc's rule of thumb is no more than 30–35 words per balloon, maximum. Fewer is generally better. So we

FIGURE 11.12.   Mural by Ammar Abo Bakr of the martyr Muhammad Sary, photo by Nancy Demerdash. Reprinted by permission of the photographer.

worked hard (and sometimes quite sulkily) with him to cut, cut, cut—both text and action that was unwieldy to pacing or lettering.

From Marc we also learned (belatedly) that we had to initially know, in the writing, on which side of the book each page occurs. He showed us that, at a minimum, you "have to know if what you are describing occurs on a left-hand or

FIGURE 11.13. Early sketch (left) and final draft (right). Image excerpted from *Lissa: A Story about Friendship, Medical Promise, and Revolution*. Written by Sherine Hamdy and Coleman Nye, illustrated by Caroline Brewer and Sarula Bao, and lettered by Marc Parenteau. Copyright University of Toronto Press 2017. Reprinted by permission of the publisher.

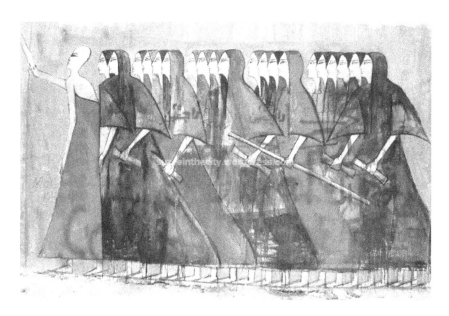

FIGURE 11.14. "Marching Women" mural by Alaa Awad. Photo taken by Soraya Morayef for the blog suzeeinthecity.wordpress.com. Reprinted with permission of photographer.

"Mural by Ganzeer. See the appendix for more information. ""Square-Script Translation (boxed letters in the center upon which the winged cat sits): "The Revolution Will Never Die"

FIGURE 11.15. Anna and Layla stand before the mural designed by Ganzeer, which cites the works of numerous other Egyptian graffiti artists and echoes themes from the book. Image excerpted from *Lissa: A Story about Friendship, Medical Promise, and Revolution.* Written by Sherine Hamdy and Coleman Nye, illustrated by Caroline Brewer and Sarula Bao, and lettered by Marc Parenteau. Original artwork on current page by Ganzeer. Copyright University of Toronto Press 2017. Reprinted by permission of the publisher and the artist.

right-hand page—the reason being that when you open a comic book, you can't help but scan the entire two-page spread. So, if Grandma dies on the right-hand page in a comic, the reader knows this before they ever start reading anything on the left. Having reveals of that sort in the wrong place can ruin the pull that you want the reader to have throughout the work" (Parenteau, quoted in Hamdy and Nye 2017, 277). Figure 11.16 is a snapshot that shows what the final script looked like. Page 1R (means page 1, right-hand side of book) and the numbered lines (1.1, 1.2, . . .) correspond to the panel. You can also see in the Google Doc where we made edits to pare the dialogue down even more. Every character counts in a comic.

In figure 11.17, you can see how this translates to an actual page. Also note how much artistic work went into translating the script prompts into visual scenes. Many conversations happened in the spaces between script and graphic page, as the authors and artists worked to set a scene and convey a feeling without words. Over the summer, we all came together in Providence for the final push, as we all worked to meet the publisher deadline.

Page 1 R

1.1   Establishing Shot: Cairo in 2005 is very smoggy.

1.2   Traffic in Cairo is maddening.

1.3   Police operate by bribes.

1.4   All men have to do military service, but the poor get the worst assignments.

1.5   Pictures of Mubarak are everywhere

Note: Possible shot arrangement can progress from wide shot of city(1:1) through mid shots of traffic/police/young country bumpkin soldiers, to detail shot of Mubarak poster (1:5) A visual device, such as say, following a bird —a swallow perhaps, if they live in Egypt— as it flies through each of the panels can help guide the reader in. I would suggest that the wall the Mubarak poster is on in 1:5 should be the wall of Anna's family's compound/apartment where the following scene takes place.

———————

Page 2 L (Main Script Lines 1-2)

2.1   Anna and Layla, 14 years old, together, are listening at the door of Sarah's room (Anna's mother), inside their 2nd floor apartment.
Mom: "Oh, I see…"

2.2   Sarah is on the phone with ~~her doctor in the U.~~a friend~~S~~., and Anna and Layla are overhearing. Anna is looking concerned and scared.
Mom: "~~Stage 4~~~~What stage is it?~~"   ":sigh:"

FIGURE 11.16.   Sample of final script.

FIGURE 11.17. Sample page that corresponds to the script. Image excerpted from *Lissa: A Story about Friendship, Medical Promise, and Revolution*. Written by Sherine Hamdy and Coleman Nye, illustrated by Caroline Brewer and Sarula Bao, and lettered by Marc Parenteau. Copyright University of Toronto Press 2017. Reprinted by permission of the publisher.

Seeing the massive amount of artwork still to be done, we asked if Marc would be willing to letter the entire text, as this required a whole new skill set for Caroline and Sarula to learn. Marc created six fonts for *Lissa* and got straight to work. He helped put us all on a schedule, and did important visual editing as the artwork came through—accounting for consistency across the panels, making sure facial expressions matched the story, that eyes were tracked so that they made sense, adding sound effects, and dealing with Arabic text and Arabic words transliterated into English as he lettered—in Mongolia. He also added the sound effects, and helped make our intertextual visual references, like the Arabic calligraphy and graffiti, cohere on the page.

Concluding Reflections

The original title for this project was *The Spaces Between*. This title, we thought, drew attention to the points of connection, overlap, and tension between our field sites, rather than reinforcing tired dichotomies between "the West" and "the Rest," the self and other, the personal and political, the individual and social. In retrospect, this old title more aptly captures the collaborative analytics at play in the gutters of our graphic work of ethnofiction. As Scott McCloud points out, in comics, the liminal space of the gutter asks the reader to be "a willing and conscious *collaborator*": it is "in the limbo of the gutter [where] human imagination takes two separate images and transforms them into a single idea" (1993, 65–66). We have worked in these gutters for much of the project, inhabiting the spaces between field sites (United States and Egypt), disciplines (anthropology and art), and genres (ethnography, fiction, comics) in our attempts to transform anthropological insights and ethnographic imaginaries into a coherent, yet complex visual narrative. What this looks like in practice is at times messy, but is also deeply pleasurable, as we have worked at the edges of what we know and how we know, and have found new ways of doing ethnography in the process.

It has been a remarkable learning experience, as we have had to translate our anthropological insights and imaginaries for the illustrators, and they have had to teach us about visual language and the technical dimensions of building comics. One of the most generative aspects of the collaborative dimensions of the theory/narrative and image/composition part of the process has been realizing how much more we can convey through the combination of text and image. Also, working with illustrators who are unfamiliar with anthropology has helped us communicate theory clearly and compellingly within the folds of a visual story. For example, one of the main medical anthropological concepts that we wanted to convey was the social and political embeddedness of the patient's body in the world. We did this in conversation with the illustrators through drafting two-page spreads for both kidney failure and cancer, talking through what we wanted to convey, mapping it, and then writing notes for how to revise. The drafts changed considerably with each conversation. These iterations are a great example of the gutter work of graphic anthropology: it is in these spaces between that the idea takes form.

NOTES

1. Angelina Jolie wrote about this in her 2013 op-ed piece in the *New York Times* entitled "My Medical Choice."

2. Majority and Minority worlds is a phrase coined by Bangladeshi photographer Shahidul Alam to stress that the majority of the world's population lives in what used to be called "the developing world"—in order to avoid the hierarchical assumptions embedded in developmentalist language and the oversimplification of the geographical terms North/South or West/East.

REFERENCES

Abaza, Mona. 2011. "Academic Tourists Sight-Seeing the Arab Spring." *Jadaliyya*, September 27, 2011. Reprinted from *Ahram Online*, September 26, 2011.

Czerwiec, M. K., Ian Williams, Susan Squier, John Gree, Kimberly Myers, and Scott Smith. 2015. *Graphic Medicine Manifesto*. University Park: Pennsylvania State University Press.

Hamdy, Sherine F. 2008. "When the State and Your Kidneys Fail." *American Ethnologist* 35 (4): 553–69.

Hamdy, Sherine F., and A. Coleman Nye. 2017. *Lissa: A Story about Medical Promise, Friendship, and Revolution*. Toronto: University of Toronto Press.

Jolie, Angelina. 2013. "My Medical Choice." *New York Times*, May 14, 2013.

McCloud, Scott. 1993. *Understanding Comics: The Invisible Art*. New York: William Morrow.

Mossallam, Alia. 2011. "Remembering the Martyrs." *Egypt Independent*, June 29, 2011.

Squier, Susan. 2014. "Comics in the Health Humanities: A New Approach to Sex and Gender Education." In *Health Humanities Reader*, edited by Therese Jones, Delese Wear, Lester D. Friedman, and Kathleen Pachucki, 226–41. New Brunswick, NJ: Rutgers University Press.

Stoller, Paul. 1992. *The Cinematic Griot: The Ethnography of Jean Rouch*. Chicago: University of Chicago Press.

Williams, Ian. 2012. "Graphic Medicine: Comics as Medical Narrative." *Medical Humanities* 38 (1): 21–27.

AFTERWORD

A Conversation on the History of Anthropological Collaboration with Rebecca Lemov

DOMINIC: So, Rebecca, you've had a chance to look at the materials, and I thought we would start with a general question that might help to contextualize your contribution to this volume. Could you discuss briefly your background and interest in collaboration in anthropology historically? That will give us a point of departure for asking some questions about how our projects here may fit within that longer tradition.

REBECCA: Sure, I was trained in anthropology in the 1990s, and although I anticipated doing a traditional ethnographic project, or I had the idea that I would do fieldwork, that didn't end up happening. And for a number of reasons I turned to the archive and found myself initially fascinated with what I thought of as the largest filing cabinet in the world, which had been created by anthropologists in the 1930s and 1940s and became known as the Human Relations Area Files. It drew me in, and I became interested in this grand effort to unify anthropology with other social sciences that seemed to go along with massive data-gathering efforts and also collaborative enterprises on a scale that was, at least if it hadn't been matched previously, indeed highly ambitious. My dissertation was in part a history of those collaborations. And you could say it was a history of big social science and big anthropology.

In a sense, it was a way of looking at the history of the dream of achieving social control or social engineering, human engineering,

through an advanced behaviorism, as a kind of advanced behavior-
ist design. And it required support in data. So the way I originally
conceived my research was that most of the projects I was looking at
had disappeared so completely from the consciousness of currently
practicing anthropologists that I found them to be almost like ruins,
but also incredibly significant ones [see Lemov 2005, 2015].

GEORGE: If I might intervene, just so people know the projects you're
referring to, could you explain what the range of those projects were?

REBECCA: One way to identify them is that they were prominent as a
bunch of acronyms, loosely speaking. The ones I wrote about in my
dissertation included the Coordinated Investigation of Micronesian
Anthropology, which was also known as CIMA. There was another,
known as the SILA, done in Latin America during World War II.
And then there was also the Harvard Department of Social Relations
(DSR) Five Cultures project, which was this massive, intensive study
of five neighboring demarcated cultures in Ramah, New Mexico,
somewhat near the site of the atomic bomb testing. It was interesting; a lot of these projects were linked to, or geographically proximal
to, nuclear testing sites. For example, in the middle of the nuclear
Pacific, on one set of islands there were the detonations at escalating
scales, and on other islands there was this uniquely intensive set of
social experiments in psychology, gauging the psyches of the different islanders and using all the latest tools of anthropology.

So you have the Micronesian studies and the New Mexican studies
that I concentrated on quite a bit. And then I found their origin in
the earlier Yale database called the HRAF, or Human Relations Area
Files, which was itself a really massive collaboration.

DOMINIC: Could you talk about what you see as some of the key similarities and differences between the norms and forms of collaborative
anthropology in that mid-twentieth-century mode, and what we're
seeing now in what we believe is kind of a resurgence of interest
in collaborative anthropological practices in the late twentieth, early
twenty-first century?

REBECCA: Off the top of my head, I think the differences are really
marked between these emergent projects you're identifying and the
midcentury collaborative efforts. But I also think it's really fascinating, and it marks a change in my thinking as well. I guess a pleasurable way of revisiting these materials is to think about them in terms
of the on-the-ground collaborations they fostered. For example, the
Harvard Ramah project. I've studied it more deeply over the years, or

more intensively, through the archives, and I wrote a later book called *Database of Dreams* (2015) that revisits some of those materials.

So I'll start with the contrasts. The most obvious ones would be that the midcentury projects were often funded by government, the military, or foundations. I guess foundations initially. They started off before World War II as projects that were munificently funded by the Rockefeller Foundation, the Carnegie Foundation, Wenner-Gren, and the other major conduits, eventually including the Ford Foundation. The idea of most prominent capitalists of the day was that they should recirculate their profits in the form of social welfare or social betterment, and these often resulted in policy programs and research programs funded through the universities. So a lot of the anthropological collaborations in the early '30s and '40s came from foundations.

And then they morphed during World War II and after into government and military money. For example, the CIMA project in Micronesia was funded by the US Navy and it was supported by the navy, so you would have things like anthropologists getting ferried to their field sites in navy vessels. I find that the relationship of the individual ethnographers to the navy was not a simple affair. That becomes really interesting to look at, and anthropologists certainly didn't conceive of what they were doing as primarily in support of US interests, necessarily, although they were required to give duplicate copies, quarterly copies of their field notes to the navy, which is also interesting.

It's certainly very much in contrast to the projects you're describing. One thing historians have done is take a follow-the-money approach. David Price's book *Cold War Anthropology* (2016) does that. You can see all the individuals, you can follow the institutions that funded them, you can follow the money trail, and it does yield significant knowledge about the projects. Yet, with the projects you're describing, I don't think that would really work. They're so heterodox. They seem much more inspired by a kind of improvisatory spirit.

Another major shift seems to be forming an alliance with science, primarily a soft conception as scientific, to a critical approach to exactly what science is, and then a turn toward a collaboration with art or artists. That seems like something very striking or fruitful in the projects you're describing.

GEORGE: This is speculative, but could you say that there was a moment in this postwar, more or less cushy relationship between what anthropologists did as research and larger projects, funded by government and perhaps corporations, when there was a loss of interest in these big postwar projects or ambitions? And that anthropological research, still in the form of specific case studies rationalized for the purpose of the academic discipline, then began to move toward this present trend of new kinds of collaboration? And in a couple of cases, they reemerge into the present interests of big finance, big science, and big government, not so much now as development projects but still as globalism?

REBECCA: Right, that would be interesting, almost full circle. You could interpret it as a kind of full-circle return to big social science and big data. Potentially, some of these projects can have that kind of sweep and scale, a potential, you could call it appropriation or use. I think your question initially was about when was the turning point or the abandonment of these large-scale comparative research programs. It really struck me in the '90s when I started studying them that they had become so invisible. They had once constituted the dominant landscape of anthropology. And then they had disappeared to such an extent that even their memory had been extirpated. People talked about Geertz, but they didn't talk about the fact that he trained within the auspices and support of these programs.

They became, I guess, epistemologically embarrassing in a certain way. And a lot of the people who worked on them themselves said it was dizzying to suddenly find yourself, your work, and decades of work suddenly become something you had to apologize for, when they had just been doing what they thought was deeply engaged fieldwork that helped, for example with the Bikini Islanders and their relocation to a new island (where they ended up living for about fifty years after their home was turned into a bomb site). Social scientists didn't feel that they were somehow these nefarious servants of empire or colonialism; they were some of the few who tried to help make conditions better for Bikinians and other nuclear expatriates. But these fieldworkers were eventually put in the position in which they felt like a lifetime of work was negated.

So there did seem to be a point at which this shifted very rapidly, and I guess the external marker would be Project Camelot in the late 1960s. And the other markers I think you talk about in your introduction quite a bit—and David Price talks about this too—is the theoretical movement to rethink what knowledge is in anthropology, and to strip away that facade of neutrality and knowledge for its own sake and this deliberate context blindness which took a really elaborate form in the midcentury. From there, the move was to become quite attentive to context and quite attentive to the proliferating effects of power dynamics. That's the change that happened in the late '60s and '70s, and that has had continuing ramifications.

DOMINIC: That's very helpful and insightful. I wanted to ask if you had any thoughts to share about the originating conditions of anthropological collaboration. In other words, we know that in the nineteenth century, a lot of anthropological research was done in the proverbial armchair, but also in the expedition form, the natural scientific model, often tied to museum collecting and the example of field sciences like biology. In the early twentieth century, at least in the United States, we had the big Boasian projects, but then also the projects that might be located on a Native American reservation with a single researcher or a team of researchers. I'm curious about how we get from there to the lone researcher model norm which has become hegemonic, it seems, in the post-mid-twentieth-century period. In other words, what caused collaborative models to originate in anthropology in the first place, and then how did they come to be displaced? Was it really just nineteenth-century empiricism at the beginning that was then troubled by decolonial and interpretive turns, or do you see other factors at play there too?

REBECCA: That's a very good question, and such an interesting one. I would take an initial pass at it by saying I think the imperative of the Torres Strait Expedition was really intensively collaborative but in a very unselfconscious "this is what one does" way. It was the model of specimen-gathering research. There's fascinating work by Riki Kuklick on the self-presentation of the data gatherers on large expeditions, for example Darwin's expeditions and those of the other nineteenth-century explorers, and the incredible amounts of material, artifacts, and often what we'd call anthropological artifacts that were being gathered up. But there was no sense that having "been there" for the gathering of a particular artifact conferred any special authority; there-ness was more something that could be delegated.

There's a big shift in the twentieth century where the feet need to be on the ground, and this is something Jim Clifford writes about in his article "On Ethnographic Authority" that there's an authority conferred by one's presence. Yet, at the same time, that doesn't seem to make collaboration impossible, at least in the way these massive, armada-style projects proceeded—for example, as in the Micronesian anthropological project, which actually had a total of forty-one investigators, including physical anthropologists, linguists, ethnographers, sociologists, and human and economic geographers. So it really wasn't just anthropology, but they called it anthropology, I guess because they were in places that were considered anthropological. In these armada-style investigations, people would separate, go off each to his or (occasionally) her own island cluster. On different islands, different disciplines could be practiced, and then you would rejoin your fellow investigators. That actually provided room for individual investigations according to one's preferred methodology, but also the sense of a shared scientific endeavor.

So when does the lone researcher emerge as the dominant paradigm? And is it simply a matter of a theoretical, a kind of hermeneutic turn? And can we lay it all at the feet of Clifford Geertz, for being such a seductive stylist? I think that one place to look might be the Six Cultures project, which was funded by Harvard University, out of John and Beatrice Whiting's laboratory of human development, in which they located six cultures around the world and sent anthropologists to each site, including one in a New England town. And they were meant to study the child-rearing practices in the most intensive, minute and micro fashion, moment by moment; how a child interacts with a twig, or a toy, or any kind of artifact was documented something like every thirty to sixty seconds. Each child was to have a filing cabinet that the anthropologist would assemble. The anthropologists wrote a very self-conscious methodological manual in which they discussed the pros and cons of this approach and how difficult it was to keep track of these miniature filing cabinets on each of their subjects, and how it became incredibly cumbersome.

By the early 1960s, the method itself and the self-consciousness about method was becoming a burden. I don't think they were really obsessive empiricists at all; I think they were obsessed about the idea of empiricism and had a kind of abstract devotion to that. That's one thing I would add to your introduction. I guess that you could say that, in a way, it was natural that the virtuosic ideal would emerge in response, kind of like "Let's leave these kinds of cumbersome methodological discussions behind and just get closer to our subjects." I guess it's a return of romanticism in a way.

GEORGE: When I went to Harvard in the early 1970s, those projects were in decline, as was Social Relations as a signature interdisciplinary graduate program which motivated them. Students could still enter those projects but you could see their vitality was less. And otherwise, you could do your own work. But this characteristic you highlighted is interesting. These projects were really driven to collect a certain sort of data and each group was different. There was the Six Cultures project (of the Whitings), and then you had the Bushmen project of Irven DeVore, you had one in Brazil directed by David Maybury-Lewis, the famous Chiapas project directed by Evon Vogt, and the late one on comparative law in the Pacific (with which I was associated) directed by Klaus Friedrich Koch. Earlier, there was the project in Indonesia directed by Douglas Oliver with which Clifford Geertz was associated. Recall also that prestigious social science at Harvard even through the 1970s was tied to the synthetic social relations program connected with Talcott Parsons.

So each one of these professorial titans had started one of these projects with very different kinds of principles. But the idea wasn't driven by a theoretical interest, a theoretical approach, a new theory of fieldwork as such; the objective was really to massively collect certain kinds of information. But in each case, the culture of the project was different. And they were intensively comparative at their base. Collaborative practice or spirit varied a good deal from project to project.

Could you say that this contrasted with the doctrine of controlled comparison that I think was very strongly portrayed at Chicago, which in turn had been influenced by British anthropology at that time? This idea that controlled comparison is ideal for doing holistic, functionalist case studies, meaning that X would study this group of Indians, and Y would study that other group of Indians, and they would be united or made collaborative by the then powerful organizing concept of area studies, in which the government had a keen interest in the name of development and defense during the Cold War. Such definitive government-supported scholarly arenas based on geography would make ethnographic projects, though fiercely individualistic as writing/analytic projects, also comparative and collaborative. But what you were actually studying was the aspirational holism in postwar anthropology, the early "big data" mentality about the purpose of all this collection through ethnography. And that was the theory, if not the mentality, of the case in anthropology.

REBECCA: Yes, it would be interesting to develop that contrast. The comparative method is very much built into all these projects, but in different ways. I think you could argue that there was a Harvard style and a Chicago style too. . . . The Chicago style, perhaps, due to the really strong influence of its Committee on Social Thought who were quite interested in developing holistic analyses or thumbprints of different cultures. So they didn't count up facts, they didn't count index cards. But at Yale and Harvard they very much did. They had a kind of audit cultural approach to facts themselves. That's what originally interested me—that it seemed so extreme. "We now have 503,000 index cards of discrete anthropological data," might be a claim someone would make.

Each project targeted particular kinds of data: like Six Cultures was interested in children's play and human development. And the Five Cultures project focused on turning questions of values in each culture into data, so that each fieldworker had to code their notes in a very particular way. I don't think you see that quite as much at Chicago, although you did have the case of David Schneider; he took part in the CIMA project, Coordinated Investigation of Micronesian Anthropology, as a grad student, and he was forced to use the Yale coding system in his field notes. There's an interesting study by Ira Bashkow (1991) of how Schneider was torn between different imperatives in the process of doing his fieldwork, and sort of resentful of having to fulfill these requirements of coding.

And then, in general, all of it was swept away in such a strikingly Ozymandian fashion in the 1990s. As many people commented, and as your introduction nicely put it, even today to collaborate is to risk sudden professional death if you want to make that your main activity.

GEORGE: When do you think the transition occurred to the situation we have today? There must have been a point, and maybe this is just my own experience and not others, when the lone ranger project, even though it maybe had origins in the earlier collaborative infrastructures for doing projects, became something of its own. So, when I was in graduate school in the 1970s, even the people who were working on the older projects were now thinking about their projects more as lone projects.

For instance, the Harvard Chiapas project. In most of the dissertations that came out of that, they were writing up ethnography according to their own purposes. They could have been, if you want, standalones. It was a controversial act then (in the 1970s) to write collective histories or accounts of that project. I'm thinking also of the controversial Yanomami project. But before the controversies, what we had was the image of the Yanomami as the fierce people and Napoleon Chagnon emerging naked from the jungle into this Yanomami community. It was the archetypical anthropologist among his people coming back to write a monograph about how his people were by their nature warlike. And it became, for undergraduates, the archetypical anthropological project in its own unique world of discovery.

And then we found out later that much of it was theater, him going upriver in a canoe, and suddenly emerging in this community with Tim Asch filming. Indeed, Chagnon was part of a University of Michigan project that was extremely controversial. This wasn't true of all projects, but could you say that a lot of the seemingly lone projects of that era were actually ideologically covering up for other conditions that had generated the possibility of doing fieldwork in many other parts of the world? In other words, nobody really worked in Malaysia, as my brother-in-law did among the Semai, without Ford Foundation Area Fellowships. And the fieldwork fellowships in that period, the '60s, were all either development or defense oriented.

There was a period when the large-scale projects in which anthropology participated as group projects—in the name of medicine, development, area studies, national defense, whatever you want—withered, or became less tightly associated with these programs. And then, after the '60s and '70s, these larger projects were orphaned. And people began to really concentrate on their individual projects again. There was a way in which they always thought of their individual projects holistically as their own in the classic postexpedition British model of "I'm off to do fieldwork among the X and come back and report holistically on them." I think that most American anthropologists were thinking about their own projects that way too. In other words, a lot of anthropology after the 1960s became independent of the collaborative context which had given origin to global fieldwork projects. The origins were forgotten or they weren't important anymore. And now, today, collaboration is reemerging in diverse ways.

REBECCA: Yeah, I think in that terrain, it's easy to see the collapse of context and at the same moment as context becomes an aspect of study, it also comes into view. It's kind of a paradox. It's easy to see what happens in the late '60s and early '70s, but I think what happens from then until the turn of the twenty-first century is a little more obscure, and it would be very interesting to think more about that, how the virtuoso ideal emerged. Geertz does seem to be a key figure for anthropology because he finds himself in that orphaned position and then becomes a virtuoso solo researcher and writer—like a rags-to-riches story. He also perfects how to demonstrate one's adeptness in certain kinds of theory. That would be interesting to think about.

In Sherry Ortner's article, "Dark Anthropology and Its Others: Theory since the Eighties," she says subjects go dark in a certain way, which she sees as a response to global conditions, neoliberalism, and also to scholarly conditions, for example the birth of the audit culture.

But it's also maybe the sense of being marooned or alone, and one thing I noticed in reading your introduction, I just love the way you end with this idea of the revelry of collaboration, even though these projects don't necessarily share a particular model. But there is a sense of this is something you do, not because you have to or not, or because someone's paying you to do it, but because it's that thing you secretly want to do. So there's a sense of casting off some of the ethos of academia which can feel like it's controlling what is acceptable, controlling what can be added up and what can be sort of mercenarily treated as intellectual capital. There's something revelatory, or freeing, or improvisatory about these projects because they spring up out of shared interests or incidental thoughts someone had or little conversations. They're less orchestrated, and in that way they have an extremely different feel from the ponderousness of some of the midcentury projects.

GEORGE: I appreciate that observation. I think it's core.

REBECCA: Because in a way it's key to say that you wouldn't follow the money there, because it's like the things you do for free, or you cobble together some way to do it. The newest generation of collaborative projects emerge from happenstance and opportunity and chance.

GEORGE: I think that captures the spirit of the projects collected here. But do you think they are simply add-ons to the lone fieldwork projects, which are actually the norm for professional qualification now? Or do you think it leads more broadly to the possibility of making ethnographic work collaborative but in a different way than in past?

REBECCA: I personally think that there's something emerging that will gain momentum. We've seen that multisite ethnography was once pretty rare, and now it's not. It's sort of accepted as, in a way, the most logical approach to fieldwork today. Although, there's still a lot of confusion, certainly in my department, about how exactly one does it, and there are certain paradoxes that are not necessarily resolvable about what will be lost if you attempt to do a multisite ethnography.

But still it's become very much mainstream. And I feel like collaboration is going to surge in that way too. And I can see it happening in other disciplines too, like in history for example. Some of it has to do with rethinking scholarship as a collective endeavor, but also rethinking the scales of scholarly attention, moving from microcosmic or overly pointillistic projects toward trying to take on broader sweeps of time and scale, sometimes engaging big data or digital methods. So it seems to me that collaboration is growing on many fronts.

In this particular set of projects that you've identified, and maybe this is particular to anthropology, I like how they have this quixotic element. They don't seem to be making claims that a new era is dawning. Their claims are more modest. Perhaps we can do this. Let's see what happens. And it's probably in the history of anthropology. Once these kinds of things gain momentum, then they do risk becoming more hegemonic.

DOMINIC: One of the themes of this volume and also of the other two volumes—the fieldwork volume, the theory volume—has been thinking about questions of graduate training, professional reproduction, how norms can change over time, in part due to teaching and training. And I wanted to ask if you had any thoughts about collaboration, how collaboration or collaborative ethics or collaborative norms could be more fully incorporated into graduate training in anthropology, or even if they should. Maybe the answer is no, they shouldn't be, it should be something that's left for later on. But I'd be very curious to know your thoughts and whether you want to connect that to your own experiences of collaboration in training during grad school.

REBECCA: When I was at Berkeley, it was before there was really much interest in collaboration. This was just before Paul Rabinow's experiment, the ARC. I was there before that. The real collaboration that's built into graduate school is through your cohort, which is potentially a wonderful collaboration. I do remember once when I was just starting grad school, we got together as a group of first- or second-year students, and we wanted to do a reading course and we asked an assistant professor if she would supervise us. We were chastised, probably with good reason, for taking the assistant professor away from her duties of getting tenure, which was sort of an extra reading based on our shared passion for a subject that we wanted to learn about.

There's a whole critique of the temporality of academia—whether too fast or too slow—that could be usefully brought to bear on graduate training, but I'm not quite sure in what ways. I'm in a history of science department, but we do have a lot of grad students who are interested in doing ethnography and are more or less confused about how to do it. And also the kinds of projects that will become acceptable, even the different media in which you can present your projects, all those issues seem to be very pressing for them. The younger you are, the more pressing those questions are, but also the more interested people often are in experimenting. It's a trade-off perhaps for having less institutional standing. It does seem silly to say, "Oh, you can do that once you have tenure. You can work with others then."

GEORGE: Ethnography isn't legitimated today as a technique for assisting in some latter-day big data project with new technology. That being the case, the relationship of an individual ethnography to any big data source has somewhat changed. Therefore, the relationship of an ethnographic project, let's say one that a typical graduate student starts, does have a relationship to dealing with collaborative relations, because they are so much a structuring principle of the terrains or subjects that any individual would want to enter into now.

I guess I'm saying that, now, the whole relation to the subject is different in that we in some way have to deal with any subject matter as being structured by collaborations. So anthropology gets pulled into a concern with collaborations by the very nature of the subjects—let's say science and technology—that it goes after.

Now, that student could come back and just use the model of the ethnographic monograph. My story of working in a lab for two years, or something like that. The celebration of ethnography in the *Writing Culture* period of the 1980s may even have prolonged the lone wolf method because it focused on the monograph as a single author writing from his or her experience. But that same period was full of efforts to write collaborative volumes; there were some interesting ones, even if they didn't catch on. So the expectations of the individualistic monograph reinforce the individualistic research that produces it. But what undermines that individualism is the idea that one's research is multisited. Multisitedness suggests you're working in an assemblage or network of collaborating subjects.

Inevitably, multisitedness draws the lone wolf project back into a workable collaborative form. And you might say that this volume is in that state of being. No one is arguing that the future is

anthropologists situated in large activist movements, or more complex, big data structures, which come to rationalize or support them.
Rather, we're tracking the emergence of collaborative fieldwork projects with more modest ambitions.

REBECCA: So there's no inevitability, rather a natural emergence. I think
that it was possibly a wrong turn taken in the '80s or '90s that the cure
for "writing culture" problems was to infinitely examine one's own
position reflectively. So then reform turns into autoethnography. It's
just all about me. I think it's much more promising and interesting
to talk about how the seeds of collaboration were already there, even
just in terms of what it means to be a fieldworker.

GEORGE: I have one more question for you about your own work on
these very ambitious 1950s projects, like George Peter Murdock's
and Burt Kaplan's. How did they end? Did they have a legacy that
affects the present situation?

REBECCA: That's a really good question. I think that, in a sense, neither of them did end. I would argue in a more obvious way that
the Murdock project continues and it's been digitized and it's on the
web, as a library resource. So basically anyone can tap into the Zuni
data that was collected. Anyone with an association with a major
library that has a subscription to the e-HRAF can access this data
now. In that sense, the project has continued to grow, even if they
don't add to the data.

What I call the database of dreams or Burt Kaplan's microcard
experiment, was in contrast an abject failure because he ran into
limitations with his chosen format. He bet on the microcard as the
most durable horse to carry these resources into the future, and
it didn't play out the way he expected. He wasn't as messianic as
Murdock. I think he just felt that these were useful data sets that
people, sometimes couples—husband/wife teams like George and
Louise Spindler—had collected in the 1930s and '40s at great pains
to themselves. Another example was Irving Hallowell, who'd given
Rorschach tests to hundreds of Ojibway Indians up and down various river systems, and Kaplan felt these had to be preserved. He had
very a preservationist mindset.

The data itself was endangered, and it was also data about the
most fragile and ephemeral aspects of human subjectivity. Kaplan
didn't know what might be made of it in the future, but just felt it
should be kept, and anthropologists weren't doing a very good job
of keeping it. It sat in dusty corners of their offices. So he really tried

to use the most technologically advanced system to organize and preserve it. And that system, what I call the pathos of the perishable format, took hold of the project in the sense that he bet on the wrong horse. The microcards soon failed, rapidly failed, spectacularly failed, in fact. Finally, Kaplan's whole system of preservation fell into a state of suspended animation, and it just sat there, neither disappearing or reappearing, in stasis for decades. Anyone could access it if they chose to but nobody actually chose to.

Murdock's and Kaplan's are twin projects in the sense that they both have an afterlife, or a continuing life, but to me, I found the database of dreams to be an almost unprecedented modernist collaborative enterprise, in the sense that it really is made of voices. It's composed of the voices of many, many people. Literally their dreams, their Rorschach tests, their life histories, or things they might have wanted to tell the anthropologist and sometimes what they didn't want to tell them. Taken under various conditions and then kind of jumbled together in a way that it's hard to reconstruct. It raises the question of how you read the database.

GEORGE: That's such a fantastic statement of its legacy. It's like an extraordinary art project rather than a fulfillment of what its scientific ideals were.

REBECCA: That's exactly how I ended up seeing it, this cacophonous, almost like a great work of literary collaboration that nobody really knows how to read, still.

DOMINIC: Is there anything we haven't covered in terms of thinking about what previous eras of collaboration in anthropology have meant for where we are today? Is there any aspect of that relationship that we haven't covered that you think is important that we do? Or any closing thoughts you might have on why we might look backward to understand our contemporary moment in collaborative anthropology?

REBECCA: I am interested in using the past not only as something I called in an earlier piece a "desperately cautionary tale," because originally I was drawn to those projects because they seemed so impossible and so much against the temper of the times, with so many epistemological and ontological assumptions that would just not be possible to hold today. But as I was saying with the database of dreams, you also discover much material that goes against the grain. So I guess I am interested in the projects themselves and also in reading their archives against the grain and respecting the way that many of them—not all of them, but some of them—were thinking of uses as yet unknown for the materials they had gathered at great effort, and often in collaborative relationships. So that's something I find worth thinking about and sometimes inspiring.

GEORGE: I just wanted to cap it by also thanking you for actually paying shrewd and accurate attention to our collection and seeing the oddness in it, in that it wasn't celebrating a new day dawning in terms of the movement from individual projects to collaborative ones, but the way that the impulse toward collaboration emerged from our current situation of institutionalized, rite-of-passage, lone wolf projects. And the way that, in each case, one finds movements toward collaboration that are also quite ambivalent about whether they can or should be generalizable.

REBECCA: I really appreciated the way that you didn't try to make it otherwise, because it becomes interesting in not knowing where they'll go.

REFERENCES AND SUGGESTIONS FOR FURTHER READING

Bashkow, Ira. 1991. "The Dynamics of Rapport in a Colonial Situation: David Schneider's Fieldwork on the Islands of Yap." In *Colonial Situations: Essays on the Contextualization of Ethnographic Knowledge*, edited by George Stocking, 170–242. Madison: University of Wisconsin Press.

Clifford, James. 1983. "On Ethnographic Authority." *Representations* 2:118–46.

Cohen-Cole, Jamie. 2014. *The Open Mind: Cold War Politics and the Sciences of Human Nature*. Chicago: University of Chicago Press.

Human Relations Area Files (ethnographic materials indexed paragraph by paragraph). Available on microfiche at many university libraries; information about accessing HRAF databases via eHRAF is found at http://hraf.yale.edu.

Isaac, Joel. 2012. *Working Knowledge: Making the Human Sciences from Parsons to Kuhn*. Cambridge, MA: Harvard University Press.

Kluckhohn, Clyde. 1951. "A Comparative Study of Values in Five Cultures." In *Navaho Veterans: A Study of Changing Values*, by Evan Z. Vogt. Cambridge, MA: Harvard University Peabody Museum), vii.

Lemov, Rebecca. 2005. *World as Laboratory: Experiments with Mice, Mazes, and Men*. New York: Hill and Wang.

———. 2010. "'Hypothetical Machines': The Science-Fiction Dreams of Cold War Social Science." "Focus: New Perspectives on Science and the Cold War," ed. David Kaiser and Hunter Heyck. Special issue, *Isis* 101:401–11.

———. 2015. *Database of Dreams: The Lost Quest to Catalog Humanity*. New Haven, CT: Yale University Press.

Ortner, Sherry. 2016. "Dark Anthropology and Its Others: Theory since the Eighties." *Hau* 6 (1): 47–73.

Powers, Willow Roberts. 2000. "The Harvard Study of Values: Mirror for Postwar Anthropology." *Journal of the History of the Behavioral Sciences* 36 (Winter): 15–29.

Price, David. 2016. *Cold War Anthropology: The CIA, the Pentagon, and the Growth of Dual Use Anthropology*. Durham, NC: Duke University Press.

Vogt, Evon Z., and Ethel M. Albert. 1966. "The 'Comparative Study of Values in Five Cultures' Project." In *People of Rimrock: A Study of Values in Five Cultures*, edited by Evon Z. Vogt and Ethel M. Albert, 1–33. Cambridge, MA: Harvard University Press.

Whiting, John, et al. *Field Guide for a Study of Socialization*. Six Cultures Series, 1. New York: Wiley, 1966. Originally published in 1954.

Contributors

Dominic Boyer is professor of anthropology at Rice University and founding director of the Center for Energy and Environmental Research in the Human Sciences (2013–19). He is currently pursuing ethnographic research with flood victims in Houston, Texas, and on electric futures across the world. His most recent book is *Energopolitics* (Duke University Press, 2019), which is part of a collaborative duograph, "Wind and Power in the Anthropocene," with Cymene Howe, which studies the politics of wind power development in southern Mexico. With Howe, he also helped make a documentary film about Iceland's first major glacier (Okjökull) lost to climate change, *Not OK: A Little Movie about a Small Glacier at the End of the World* (2018). In August 2019, together with Icelandic collaborators, they installed a memorial to Okjökull's passing, an event that attracted media attention from around the world. Boyer also produced and cohosted (with Howe) two hundred episodes of the "Cultures of Energy" podcast.

Brian Callahan is a lecturer in the Information Technology and Web Science Program at Rensselaer Polytechnic Institute. His research examines best practices for digital collaboration and cybersecurity pedagogy. He is the lead open knowledge developer for the Platform for Experimental Collaborative Ethnography (PECE).

Craig Campbell is associate professor of anthropology at the University of Texas at Austin. He is fascinated with the way that making things, curating exhibitions, and organizing workshops can function as devices for thinking and is committed to experimenting with and theorizing modes of description and evocation. Campbell's current projects include the cultural history of an unbuilt hydroelectric dam in Central Siberia, the weird time of a shadow, and the aesthetics of damaged, degraded, and manipulated photographs. He is also involved in an initiative called "Writing with Light," which explores photography and photoessays in cultural anthropology.

Luke Cantarella is a scenographer and associate professor of film and screen studies at Pace University in New York. He has designed scenery for over 140 productions across the United States and Europe and collaborates frequently with anthropologists to create design-based research engagements. Luke is a coauthor of *Ethnography by Design: Scenographic Experiments in Field Work*.

Stephen J. Collier is a faculty member in the Department of City and Regional Planning at the University of California, Berkeley. He has worked on Soviet and post-Soviet urbanism and neoliberal reform, the vital systems security in the United States, and contemporary urban resilience. He is the author of *Post-Soviet Social: Neoliberalism, Social Modernity, Biopolitics* (Princeton University Press, 2011) and coeditor (with Aihwa Ong) of *Global Assemblages: Technology, Politics, and Ethics as Anthropological Problems* (Blackwell, 2004), and (with Andrew Lakoff) *Biosecurity Interventions: Global Health and Security in Question* (Columbia University Press, 2008). He is a cofounder and coeditor of *Limn* magazine, for which he has coedited issues on system vulnerability, disease ecologies, public infrastructure, and small development devices.

Kim Fortun is professor of anthropology at the University of California, Irvine. Her research and teaching focus on environmental risk and disaster, data practices and politics, and experimental ethnographic methods and research design. Her research has examined how people in different geographic and organizational contexts understand environmental problems, uneven distributions of environmental health risks, developments in the environmental health sciences, and factors that contribute to disaster vulnerability. Currently, Fortun is working on a book titled *Late Industrialism*: *Making Environmental Sense*, on *The Asthma Files*, a collaborative project to understand how air pollution and environmental public health are dealt with in different contexts, and as research director of the Platform for Experimental and Collaborative Ethnography (PECE).

Mike Fortun is associate professor of anthropology at the University of California, Irvine. His research has centered on the history and anthropology of the life sciences, in particular the contemporary science, culture, and political economy of genomics. He is design director for the Platform for Experimental and Collaborative Ethnography (PECE), digital empirical humanities infrastructure that supports collaborative ethnographic research).

Sherine F. Hamdy is associate professor of anthropology at the University of California, Irvine. She joined the faculty there in July 2017, after serving as a professor at Brown University for eleven years. She is the author of *Our Bodies Belong to God: Organ Transplants, Islam, and the Struggle for Human Dignity in Egypt* (University of California Press, 2012) and coauthor of *Lissa: A Story of Friendship, Medical Promise, and Revolution* (University of Toronto Press, 2017). She is currently coauthoring, with Soha Bayoumi (Harvard University), a manuscript on the role of doctors in the popular uprisings that took place in Egypt from 2011 to 2013 and has a young adult graphic novel under contract with Penguin Random House, which tells the coming-of-age story of a Muslim American girl.

Christine Hegel is associate professor of anthropology at Western Connecticut State University. Her research has moved in multiple interconnecting directions, from debt relations in contemporary Egypt to the meanings and modalities of work and livelihood rights in Finland and New York City. An interest in how art and design practices can enrich ethnography runs through much of this work, and she is currently engaged in collaborative research and participatory design projects with informal recyclers in Brooklyn, New York. She is the coauthor of *Ethnography by Design: Scenographic Experiments in Fieldwork* with Luke Cantarella and George E. Marcus (Bloomsbury Press 2019).

Kate Hennessy is an associate professor specializing in media at Simon Fraser University's School of Interactive Arts and Technology, and director of the Making Culture Lab. Her research and art practice explores new memory infrastructures, museums, and archives in the context of technoscience. She is a member of the *Ethnographic Terminalia* Collective, which curated exhibitions and projects at the intersection of anthropology and contemporary art from 2009 to 2019.

Douglas R. Holmes is SUNY Distinguished Professor of Anthropology at State University of New York at Binghamton. His collaborative work builds on an ethnographic trilogy: *Cultural Disenchantments: Worker Peasantries in Northeast Italy* (Princeton University Press, 1989); *Integral Europe: Fast-Capitalism, Multiculturalism, Neofascism* (Princeton University Press, 2000); and *Economy of Words: Communicative Imperative in Central Banks* (University of Chicago Press, 2014). He is currently working with a team at University College London investigating the nature of information and policymaking at the Bank of England and with Knut Christian Myhre in Oslo on a series of sustainability agendas orchestrated by the Norwegian Sovereign Wealth Fund.

Cymene Howe is professor of anthropology at Rice University. Her books include *Intimate Activism* (Duke University Press, 2013) and *Ecologics: Wind and Power in the Anthropocene* (Duke University Press, 2019), which follows the human and more-than-human lives intertwined with renewable energy futures. She is coeditor of the *The Johns Hopkins Guide to Critical and Cultural Theory* (Johns Hopkins University Press, forthcoming) and the *Anthropocene Unseen: A Lexicon* (Punctum Books, 2020) and has published widely in transdisciplinary journals and volumes. Her current research on cryohuman relations examines the changing dynamics between human populations and bodies of ice in the Arctic region and sea-level adaptation in lower latitude coastal cities around the world. From 2015 to 2019 she hosted the weekly *Cultures of Energy* podcast with Dominic Boyer—a series of conversations on environmental precarity and responses to it in the human sciences. She also produced with Boyer the documentary film *Not OK: A Little Movie about a Small Glacier at the End of the World* (2018) and, in August 2019, initiated the installation of the world's first memorial to a glacier fallen to climate change. The Okjökull memorial event in Iceland served as a global call to action and in memory of a world rapidly melting away.

Martin Høyem studied at NTNU (Norwegian University of Science and Technology) and at Katholieke Universiteit Leuven, and then—after doing field work among Mexican American lowriders in Los Angeles and other parts of the American Southwest—he received a Cand. Philol. degree in social anthropology from the University of Oslo. Høyem is also a visual artist and has been exhibited in Norway and Iceland with an interactive, electronic sculpture ("No title") and with a pornographic cross-stitch embroidery (". . . while the moments do somersaults into eternity"). He has worked professionally with various types of digital data distribution and with graphic design since 1995. Right now, heis sitting around trying to come up with something new to think about. Or he is thinking about the history of sitting around thinking. Or he is contemplating—in the light of cultural traditions and techniques of extraction—which shade and saturation of red is best. He has also taught himself relief printing.

Christopher Kelty is a professor at the University of California, Los Angeles, with a joint appointment in the Institute for Society and Genetics, the Department of Information Studies, and the Department of Anthropology. He is a cofounder of *Limn* magazine and author of *The Participant: A Century of Participation in Four Stories* (University of Chicago Press, 2019) and *Two Bits: The Cultural Significance of Free Software* (Duke University Press, 2008).

Andrew Lakoff is professor of sociology at the University of Southern California. He is the author of *Pharmaceutical Reason: Knowledge and Value in Global Psychiatry* (Cambridge University Press, 2006) and *Unprepared: Global Health in a Time of Emergency* (University of California Press, 2017). With Christopher Kelty and Stephen J. Collier, he is a founding editor of *Limn* magazine.

Rebecca Lemov is Professor of the History of Science at Harvard University. Her research focuses on key episodes and experiments in the history of the human and behavioral sciences. Her most recent book, *Database of Dreams: The Lost Quest to Catalog Humanity*, examines attempts between 1942 and 1963 to map the elusive and subjective parts of the human psyche via once-futuristic data-storage techniques. Looking at innovations in data-gathering methods, her research investigates the ongoing transformation of knowledge, technology, and subjectivity in the twentieth and twenty-first centuries. She is currently at work on a history of coercive interrogation in relation to brainwashing.

George E. Marcus is Distinguished Professor of Anthropology at the University of California, Irvine, and founding director of its Center for Ethnography since 2005. His history of collaborations is marked by coproduction of the following publications: *Writing Culture: The Poetics and Politics of Ethnography* (University of California Press, 1986), *Anthropology as Cultural Critique: An Experimental Moment in Human Sciences*, 2nd ed. (University of Chicago Press, 1986), the Late Editions annuals series (University of Chicago Press, 1992–2000), *Designs for an Anthropology of the Contemporary* (Duke University Press, 2008), *Fieldwork Is Not What It Used To Be: Learning Anthropology's Method in a Time of Transition* (Cornell University Press, 2009), *Theory Can Be More Than It Used To Be: Learning Anthropology's Method in a Time of Transition* (Cornell University Press, 2015), and *Ethnography by Design: Scenographic Experiments in Fieldwork* (Bloomsbury, 2019).

Fiona P. McDonald is assistant professor of visual anthropology at the University of British Columbia, Okanagan where she is director of the Collaborative & Experimental Ethnography Lab. Her research focuses on water rights, cold climate housing, sensory ethnography, the anthropology of art, and open access digital publishing. She is a founding member of the *Ethnographic Terminalia* Collective, which curated exhibitions and projects from 2009 to 2019.

Alli Morgan is a medical student at the Icahn School of Medicine at Mount Sinai. Her work examines the politics and practices of clinical diagnosis in the United States. She received a PhD in science and technology studies from Rensselaer Polytechnic Institute.

Keith M. Murphy is associate professor of anthropology at the University of California, Irvine. Most of his work explores design and designing from a sociocultural perspective, with a particular emphasis on language, material culture, and human experience. He has worked with architects in Los Angeles, furniture designers in Stockholm, and experts on graphic language, mostly in the United States. He is the author of *Swedish Design: An Ethnography* (Cornell University Press, 2015) and coeditor of *Toward an Anthropology of the Will* (Stanford University Press, 2010).

Coleman Nye is assistant professor in the Department of Gender, Sexuality, and Women's Studies at Simon Fraser University. She is the coauthor of *Lissa: A Story of Friendship, Medical Promise, and Revolution* (University of Toronto Press, 2017) and is completing a book entitled *Biological Property: Race, Gender, Genetics*. Nye's work has been published in such journals as *Social Text*, *TDR: The Drama Review*, *Women and Performance*, *Global Public Health*, and *ADA: A Journal of Gender, New Media, and Technology*.

Lindsay Poirier is assistant professor of science and technology studies at the University of California, Davis. Her research examines the history and culture of data infrastructure design work. She is the lead platform architect for the Platform for Experimental Collaborative Ethnography (PECE).

Lisa Rofel is professor emerita and research professor at the University of California, Santa Cruz. She is also codirector of the Center for Emerging Worlds at UCSC. Her ethnographic work addresses China's transition from socialism to capitalism, with an emphasis on the historical contingencies and affective desires of that process. Her most recent publications include a coauthored book with Sylvia Yanagisako, *Fabricating Transnational Capitalism: A Collaborative Ethnography of Italian-Chinese Global Fashion* (Duke University Press, 2019), which was based on their joint Morgan Lectures, and *Desiring China: Experiments in Neoliberalism, Sexuality, and Public Culture* (Duke University Press, 2007). She is currently working on a Ford Foundation–funded project on China's rising presence in the Global South.

Trudi Lynn Smith (PhD) is an anthropologist and artist interested in experimental ethnography, feminist collaborations, and social practice. Her research and art practices embrace expressions of impermanence and change in communities of art, archives, ecology, and collections. She is a member of the *Ethnographic Terminalia* Collective, which curated exhibitions and projects at the intersection of anthropology and contemporary art from 2009 to 2019.

Stephanie Takaragawa is associate professor of sociology and associate dean of the Wilkinson College of Arts, Humanities, and Social Sciences at Chapman University specializing in the anthropology of visual communication. Her research explores race in North America, with an emphasis on Asian American history, popular culture, and media representation. She is a member of the *Ethnographic Terminalia* Collective, which curated exhibitions and projects at the intersection of anthropology and contemporary art from 2009 to 2019.

Sylvia Yanagisako is Edward Clark Crossett Professor of Humanistic Studies and professor of anthropology at Stanford University, where she codirects the Center for Global Ethnography in the Stanford Institute for Research in the Social Sciences. She is also Eilert Sundt Professor of Social Anthropology at the University of Oslo. Her recent publications include the coauthored book with Lisa Rofel, *Fabricating Transnational Capitalism: A Collaborative Ethnography of Italian-Chinese Global Fashion* (Duke University Press, 2019) and *Producing Culture and Capital: Family Firms in Italy* (Princeton University Press, 2002).

Alexei Yurchak is associate professor of anthropology and core faculty member of the Department of Dance, Theater, and Performance Studies at the University of California, Berkeley. His theoretical interests include the analysis of human agency and its interplay with language and discourses of power especially in post-Soviet Russia and Eastern Europe. He is particularly interested in the analysis of how ideologies are projected on and work through language, and what methods of discourse analysis social scientists can use to unpack their discursive power. His book *Everything Was Forever, Until It Was No More: The Last Soviet Generation* (Princeton University Press, 2005) won the Wayne Vucinic Award from the American Association for Slavic, East European, and Eurasian Studies; the expanded Russian edition of the book won the Prosvetitel Award for Russia's best nonfiction book of the year in 2015. He is currently completing a book on the science and politics of Lenin's embalmed body.

Index